DELUGE BEFORE DAWN

DELUGE BEFORE DAWN

HEARTBREAK, SURVIVAL, AND RESILIENCE AFTER THE GUADALUPE RIVER RAGED

THOMAS R. FOX

Stoney Creek Publishing

Stoney Creek Publishing
A Member of the Texas Book Consortium

Published by

Stoney Creek Publishing Group

StoneyCreekPublishing.com

ISBN: 978-1-965766-75-0
ISBN (ebook): 978-1-965766-76-7
Library of Congress Control Number: 2026911539

Cover and interior photos courtesy of The Kerr County Lead. Used with permission.

Cover design by Rebecca Byrd Arthur

Printed in the United States

This book is dedicated to those who lost their lives in the July 4 flood, to the loved ones who carry their memory, and to all who were forever changed, held now in grace, prayer, and remembrance.

CONTENTS

PREFACE

I did not come to this book as an outside observer. I came to it as a member of the Kerrville community, as someone who loves this place, who has walked beside the Guadalupe River in its beauty and peace, and who, like so many others, watched in grief and disbelief as the flood of July 4, 2025, changed Kerr County forever.

I moved to Kerrville in 2021 because I attended a summer camp, Camp Stewart for Boys, in the late 1960s. As a youngster, I lived in Houston, and in my 60s, I moved here because of the physical beauty of the Hill Country that had moved me so much as an eight- and nine-year-old who had never seen a hill before. I can still remember the awe I felt looking at Joy Bluff, across the Guadalupe River as it flowed through Camp Stewart. There was a cross near the top of Joy Bluff that remains there today, looking out over the camp.

There are some events that divide time into before and after. The July 4 flood was such an event. For those who lived here, for those who lost loved ones and friends, for those who survived, for those who searched, prayed, helped, and mourned, life after that day could never be quite the same as life before it. The water receded. The debris was cleared. The work of recovery began. But the loss remained, and it remains still. This book is offered in the spirit of remembrance. It is also offered in humility.

The July 4 flood bothered and upset me even more than 9/11, which I did not think was possible. Immediately after July 4 and for several weeks, I struggled to find my role in the recovery. I donated. I volunteered. But it did not seem like it was enough. In the middle of one night, it came to me. My role was to write the book about the flood. Sheepishly, I asked Joe Herring what he might think of the idea, and he encouraged me to do so. I asked Kathy Ragsdale if I could write a chapter about her daughter Jane, who died in the flood, and she told me she thought it would make a great tribute to her daughter. Many others in our community similarly encouraged me.

No single book can fully capture an event of this magnitude. No one volume can hold all the sorrow, all the courage, all the confusion, all the hard questions, and all the acts of grace that followed in the wake of the flood. This is one attempt to honor an unfinished story. The story of the July 4 flood is not over. It lives on in grief that has not fully lifted, in families who continue to mourn, in communities still rebuilding, and in the enduring work of memory itself. I have been deeply conscious of that truth on every page.

I have also been conscious of the fact that many people shared their stories, memories, and reflections in the midst of grief. That is no small gift. There were lots of tears in my interviews, including many from me. There were tears in writing this book. To speak of loss is hard enough. To do so while still carrying the immediacy of loss requires courage, generosity, and faith. I have tried to receive those stories with care and to render them with the dignity they deserve. Where this book succeeds, the credit belongs in no small part to those who were willing to speak. Where it falls short, the shortcomings are mine alone.

Kerr County did not begin its story of resilience in 2025. That is an important truth, and one this book seeks to honor. The people who faced the July 4 flood drew upon something older. They drew upon the character of a place shaped over generations, by ranchers and river families, by churches and schools, by civic leaders and volunteers, by neighbors who understood long before this tragedy that life in the Hill Country requires faith, endurance, mutual help, and respect for the power of nature. In that sense, the response to the flood was not created in a moment. It was inherited. It was built over time by those who came before us and who left behind a culture sturdy enough to bear grief without surrendering to it.

That inheritance matters. Kerr County has long lived with the paradox of the river and the land. There is beauty here that feels almost sacred. There is also danger here that is not theoretical but recurrent, woven into the very nature of this place. As this book shows, each generation in Kerr County faces the need to remember what the land and water can do because forgetting invites tragedy anew. Yet memory alone is not enough. It must be joined to action, to preparedness, to stewardship, and to the kind of civic resolve that turns suffering into a determination to protect those who come after us. As the book also makes clear, resilience in Kerr County is not merely dramatic heroism in a single moment, but endurance sustained through faithful work over time.

That is one reason I felt compelled to write this book.

I wanted to honor those who were lost, those who survived, and those who responded. I wanted to preserve the voices of people who bore witness. I wanted to tell the story of what happened in a way that was honest about both suffering and strength. And I wanted, in some small way, to contribute to the work of communal memory because communities need memory if they are to endure. They need facts, yes. They need timelines, testimony, and records. But they also need narrative. They need a way to say: this happened here; these people lived, loved, struggled, and mattered; this loss was real; this courage was real; and this place, wounded though it is, still endures.

If there is a thread running through this book, it is that remembrance is itself a form of service. To remember the dead is to refuse to let them be reduced to numbers. To remember acts of courage is to preserve examples of grace under pressure. To remember failures, gaps, and hard lessons is to offer the living a chance to do better. And to remember together is to resist the erosion that time can bring, especially in a place where each new generation must be taught again what the river can mean.

I offer this book, then, not as the final word, but as one faithful word. I offer it to Kerr County, to those who mourn, to those who continue to rebuild, and to those who will inherit both the beauty and the burden of this place. Above all, I offer it in memory of those whose lives were taken in the July 4 flood, with prayer for those who loved them and with gratitude for a community that, even in heartbreak, has chosen grace, endurance, and remembrance.

ONE
CAMP MYSTIC: THE NIGHT OF THE FLOOD

The Guadalupe River did not reveal its intent on the evening of July 3, 2025. It rarely did. The waters that curled past Camp Mystic that night looked no different from the waters that had carried generations of girls in canoes, inner tubes, and memory. The river at dusk reflected the soft violet light that always settled in the bend below the cypress trees, giving the impression of a landscape that understood its own rhythms. The girls moved through their evening routines without anxiety. Taps played over the loudspeaker shortly after 10 p.m., the final ritual note of a place that had come to define childhood summers for nearly a century. Over 600 campers had settled into their bunks over two areas: The Flats and Senior Hill. The cabins were warm with the soft static of whispered conversations and the familiar creak of wooden frames.

Dick Eastland, the seventy-year-old patriarch of the family that had operated Camp Mystic for nearly 70 years, was in his creekside home on the property. His son, Edward Eastland, lived with his wife, Mary Liz, in a house even closer to the river. Both men had grown up on this landscape and believed they understood its moods. Heavy rain was in the forecast, but the Hill Country had issued such forecasts many times before. The family had taken their usual precautions: The large war canoes were pulled from the water around 10 p.m. and set higher on the bank. This was routine. Nothing about the evening suggested it would become the most catastrophic night in the camp's history.

But upstream, the storm had already begun to change shape. The atmosphere over the western Hill Country thickened with moisture, draping heavy bands of rainfall across the steep watershed that fed the Guadalupe River. Rainfall amounts upstream began to surpass ordinary thresholds by late evening, in some places exceeding intensities that the region's narrow canyons could safely absorb. Camp Mystic, downstream and partially sheltered by trees and terrain, did not experience the early violence of the storm. The rain reached it as a steady drumming on rooftops, a sound campers associated with comfort rather than danger.

At 1:14 a.m. on July 4, the National Weather Service (NWS) issued a warning that flooding could become life threatening. Inside the camp's administrative office, Dick monitored the weather with Glenn Juenke, the night watchman. Edward arrived soon after. A group of workers had returned to camp from a day off, describing a difficult drive in the pouring rain. The rain gauge at Dick's house had already accumulated several inches. Still, the river had not yet revealed the scale of the water racing toward the camp through the dark.

At approximately 1:45 a.m., Dick radioed his son. They had received roughly two inches of rain in the past hour, and they needed to move the remaining waterfront equipment to higher ground. Members of the grounds crew acted quickly. Smaller canoes were hauled up the hillside nearest the cabins. Even then, Edward later recalled, no one believed the water would reach that height.

At 2:14 a.m., Juenke filmed Bubble Gum Creek, a normally dry channel that now surged with fast-moving water. *The New York Times* reported that by this time the severe thunderstorm cell hovered almost directly above the camp, and radar views suggested persistent, intense rainfall that would not pass as quickly as early forecasts suggested. Edward texted Mary Liz to look at the radar.

She replied that it looked as if it would end soon. The couple, like so many others that night, were still interpreting the storm through historical experience rather than the unprecedented reality unfolding around them.

Minutes later, two counselors from Bug House, a cabin in the Flats located closest to the river, arrived at the office to report water running down the steep hill into their door. Edward and Dick drove them back to reassure them. Edward remembered thinking at that moment that this still resembled a normal flood. The ground was saturated, the creek was active, but the river had not yet signaled the danger that would soon engulf the entire camp.

That changed shortly before 3 a.m.

A call came over the radio from the Gatehouse Cabin at the camp entrance, which sat only a few yards from the river. A staff member reported that water was entering her cabin and that she could not get the door open. Then her radio emitted strange noises. She could not be reached again. The cabin was eventually swept away. The staff member survived only by clinging to a tree downstream.

Around this time, Dick radioed from Bug House that the river was rising. The sense of urgency sharpened into something else, a recognition that the situation was changing too quickly for normal protocols. Edward recalled that his father told him, "We need to get Bug House out." Thus began the hurried, improvised evacuation of the lowest cabins on the Flats that were closest to the Guadalupe River.

The camp's safety plan, as reported by *The Kerr County Lead*, was only a single page. It instructed counselors to shelter in place during floods. That guidance reflected the institutional belief that the cabins were on high enough ground to remain safe, a belief reinforced by the Federal Emergency Management Agency's (FEMA) map amendments from some 12 years earlier. But as water moved across the sloping grass between the cabins and the river, the plan unraveled in real time.

Edward, Dick, and Juenke began loading campers from Bug House into their vehicles in two trips, driving them to the office and directing them toward the recreation hall. Counselors in Nut Hut watched this unfolding evacuation. They were told initially to remain in place, according to allegations in later lawsuits, though Edward denied issuing such directions. Regardless of the exact phrasing, the counselors in Nut Hut made their own decision. They evacuated their campers up a steep hill behind their cabin. Juenke assisted another cabin in doing the same. More cabins followed.

At 3:26 a.m., a counselor photographed girls walking through ankle-deep water toward the recreation hall. At the same time, a video taken from above the commissary captured deepening water accelerating past the two Twins cabins (Twins I and Twins II). Edward said that on their second evacuation trip, the water was running over the road, up to the tops of his truck tires. Lightning illuminated canoes floating across the soccer field. The camp's landscape was transforming into a riverbed.

Edward and his father moved next toward the youngest campers in the Bubble Inn and Twins. These cabins housed girls as young as eight years old, and the Guadalupe River was rising toward them with astonishing speed. *The New York Times* report reconstructed these minutes with harrowing clarity, noting that the water outside Twins at 3:26 a.m. was moving fast enough to resemble rapids even before the deepest surge arrived. The suddenness of the escalation defied every prior experience the Eastlands had with the Guadalupe River. The Eastlands relied on earlier floods at Camp Mystic, including high-water events, during which none had placed water beyond the Guadalupe River's banks so violently or so quickly.

By the time Edward reached Bubble Inn, the water had reached two to three feet around the cabin, swirling in tight currents between the buildings. Dick parked his SUV by Bubble Inn's entrance. Edward remembered seeing the water rushing around his father's legs as he stood outside the vehicle, assessing how to extract the youngest girls from the cabin. That was the last moment Edward saw him alive.

From there, Edward waded toward Twins. Waist-high water surged past him as he felt for footing. Two counselors were calling from the porch of one of the cabins. Inside, eight-year-old girls were huddled on upper bunks, clustered together in the dark while the waterline crept upward along the walls. Edward moved between both Twins cabins, surveying the situation, calculating possibilities. At one point he asked if anyone had a screwdriver, thinking he might remove a ceiling vent and climb the children upward through the low roof space. But the water was rising too quickly.

The recollections he shared later are details of terror. He remembered the sound first, the roar of water against the walls. Then the cold weight of it against his chest. Then the realization that the river was not rising by inches, but by feet. A *New York Times* report noted that at approximately 3:50 a.m., water inside one Twins cabin nearly reached the ceiling and forced girls from the bunks into the current as the doors blew outward under pressure.

Meanwhile, inside Bubble Inn, Dick attempted to load the eight-year-olds into his SUV to move them to higher ground. It is unclear whether all thirteen campers and the two counselors made it inside. What is clear is that the water lifted the vehicle, carried it over the soccer field, and slammed it into a grove of cypress trees downstream. Vehicle crash data correlated precisely with the moment Dick's Apple Watch recorded that he went underwater. Three campers from Bubble Inn died with him in the vehicle.

Back at Twins, the water reached Edward's shoulders. Counselors shouted that water was rising over the windows. Then came the moment Edward would recount with a voice still shaking many months later. As he stood in the doorway between the two cabins, the pressure of the current burst the door of the first Twins cabin. Three girls were swept through the doorway. He caught two. A third disappeared into the dark. Another girl, swept from the second cabin, grabbed onto him from behind. He tried to hold onto her too, but the force of the water was overpowering.

According to a report from Texas Public Radio, at 3:56 a.m. the first 911 call came in from Camp Mystic. It came from a camp counselor or another nonmanagerial employee of the camp. It reported "the rising water up and a lot of the cabins are flooded."

At 4:09 a.m., Edward's Apple Watch recorded that he went underwater. The current tore him from the doorway and pulled him along a path he had walked only an hour earlier while moving campers to safety. Now the waterline had risen to the branches of the trees lining the road. Edward reached for them as he passed, but the branches broke under the pressure or slipped from his grasp. He felt the weight of the water holding him down, forcing him deeper. He described the sensation of reaching for the surface, believing he was close, only to find nothing but dark water above him.

Eventually, the current pushed him into the canopy of two large trees just below Bug House. In the tangle of branches, he found survivors. Several campers and counselors from the Twins cabins were already clinging to the limbs, half-submerged, shivering, and trying to hold on in the dark. Eight campers and three counselors survived by holding onto these trees. One counselor clung to a separate tree down the road, surviving alone. One camper was found alive nearby. Three more were found alive downstream once the waters receded.

But eleven campers from the two Twins cabins died. All thirteen campers and both counselors from Bubble Inn died. And one girl from Jumble House, who had evacuated successfully, was swept away trying to return for her blanket.

Juenke ended up inside Wiggle Inn, a cabin where floodwater reached levels high enough to force the campers and counselors onto floating mattresses. Juenke tried to reassure them, telling them repeatedly that they would be all right, even as the rising water pressed against the walls and windows. His calm presence in that moment became one of the small anchors of stability in a night defined by chaos.

Up at the recreation hall, some ninety-five campers and fifteen counselors made it to the second-floor balcony. The building, open on the first floor with a wraparound balcony above, allowed the floodwaters to fill the ground level completely. The children and staff watched the water surge beneath them, carrying debris, furniture, and sections of cabins downstream. Water rose to the first floor ceiling in some spots, pushing against beams and posts but never collapsing the building.

When dawn arrived, Camp Mystic was a landscape transformed.

The morning after was time suspended between silence and shock, with debris lodged in trees, waterlines painted on cabins, and the unmistakable absence of voices that should have filled the air. Survivors emerged from trees, from the recreation hall, from cabins on higher ground. Counselors searched for one another. Some called out names into the still morning, listening for any reply.

But the scale of the loss became clear only as the water retreated further. The waterlines in the Twins cabins reached seven to eight feet, in some places only inches from the ceiling. In Bubble Inn, the waterline measured six feet three inches off the floor. The concrete block base of one Twins wall had been pushed inward. The camp landscape that had felt unshakable—cabins shaded by mature cypress, footpaths stitched across the hillside, gathering spaces that had hosted generations of girls—now held physical evidence of a night that had exceeded imagination. Canoes rested in trees. Vehicles lodged in equally improbable places. Debris lay high on the riverbank where no one had ever seen water before.

Search teams and first responders arrived to scenes that felt closer to a riverine disaster zone than a camp. The magnitude of the event continued to unfold by the hour. Sorrow settled heavily over the grounds as families began to arrive and authorities continued their work.

Records show that at 4:19 a.m., less than thirty minutes after Dick Eastland was swept away, a resident who lives down river from Camp Mystic called emergency dispatchers. She reported, "We've gotten two little girls swept who've come down the river and we've gotten to them," but she doesn't know about any others. She said she lived about a mile down the road from Camp Mystic.

At 7:11 a.m. an unidentified caller from Camp Mystic said, "We are missing a whole cabin." She then tried to add up the girls missing from the Bubble Inn, Twins and another cabin whose name is not audible on the recording. She says it adds up to "about 30 girls." At 7:22 a.m., the first call from a member of the Eastland family, co-director Britt Eastland, was recorded. He says, "We need search and rescue" and that they are "missing as many as 20 to 40 people." He also says the camp is out of power and has "hardly any cell service."

The Guadalupe River, having spent the night behaving like an unbound force, now flowed past as if nothing had happened. Yet its presence was everywhere. Debris hung high in the limbs of cypress trees. The soccer field was buried under mud and fragments of cabins. Parts of the waterfront had vanished. Footpaths were gouged into raw channels. Several cabins stood intact but watermarked up to their ceilings. Others were filled with silt and debris. The gatehouse had been destroyed. Vehicles that once belonged to the grounds crew and to Dick Eastland now rested downstream in a grove of trees.

Search teams arrived as the water continued to drop. They moved carefully through the wreckage, working cabin to cabin, structure to structure. *The New York Times* noted that the scale of the loss became clear only as bodies were recovered from the cabins, vehicles, and river channel in the hours that followed. For the families of the missing, the waiting was unbearable. Some arrived early, standing in small groups near the camp entrance or inside the main office, while staff and responders tried to shield them from the unfolding grim details.

The Eastland family, central to Camp Mystic for nearly a century, faced an overwhelming collision of responsibility and grief. Edward had survived only through the narrowest margin. His father, Dick, was gone. The image of his father's SUV lodged against a tall cypress became one of the most painful and enduring symbols of the night. Edward returned repeatedly to that spot in the weeks that followed, standing beside the tree, the river now moving gently past. "Every morning is horrible," he would say later. "I want to help the families. I do not know what to do though." His wife, Mary Liz, echoed his devastation. "I feel like no one thinks that we are sorry."

In the days that followed, investigators gathered information, collected statements, reviewed phone data, vehicle crash records, and photos taken throughout the night. The *New York Times*'s reconstruction relied in part on Apple Watch timestamps and video footage, which allowed for a nearly minute-by-minute account of the water rise inside the lowest cabins. The precision of that evidence only deepened the tragedy, making clear how quickly the situation had shifted and how little time staff had to respond.

Families began to raise the inevitable questions. How could cabins that had flooded to their ceilings have been considered safe? Why had evacuation procedures relied on sheltering in place? Why had so many structures stood so close to the river's edge in the first place?

The answers led back to decisions made years earlier. Camp Mystic had sought multiple FEMA Letters of Map Amendments (LOMAs), using elevation surveys to argue that nearly two dozen cabins sat above the Base Flood Elevation and should therefore be removed from the Special Flood Hazard Area. FEMA granted the LOMAs. Once removed from the mapped floodplain, the cabins no longer required flood insurance or elevation improvements. For the camp, the LOMA decisions validated long-held beliefs that the upper cabins were on safe ground in the Flats. These official FEMA determinations were a powerful reassurance. But the river did not conform to the map.

Earlier warnings had indicated that the true floodplain was larger than the mapped boundaries suggested, a point hydrologists and regional flood experts echoed repeatedly after the event. There was a long history of floods along this stretch of the Guadalupe River, including events that reshaped channels, destroyed low-lying structures, and carved new paths through sediment and stone. The FEMA map, by contrast, remained anchored to older rainfall assumptions and outdated modeling. It did not incorporate newer hydrologic data, intense short-duration rainfall, or the speed at which water could move through the steep canyons upstream.

In interviews, Edward acknowledged that the family had believed for decades that the cabins were on high ground. The 2011 FEMA map had placed many of them inside the flood zone, but after the camp hired surveyors and contested the elevations, FEMA removed the cabins from the hazard area in 2013. The Eastlands felt vindicated. They had seen high water before, but never water that reached these cabins. "The July 4 flood changed what high ground was for the camp," Edward said later. They would never again house campers or counselors in those cabins. "No, never."

In the aftermath, lawsuits were filed on behalf of several families. One suit claimed that the camp chose not to evacuate until counselors demanded it, creating a situation in which a last-minute rescue effort became a "hopeless attempt" to reverse a disaster that had already formed. The suits alleged that the camp relied on faulty assumptions about the floodplain and had not implemented adequate emergency procedures. The Eastlands, devastated and defensive in equal measure, denied that they had ever instructed counselors to stay in place. They argued that their decisions were based on decades of lived experience and that the storm behaved in ways the camp had never seen before.

The questions extended beyond the camp. State officials, including the lieutenant governor, called for hearings to examine what had taken place and how the camp's structures had been permitted so close to the river. The Texas Legislature began preparing inquiries. Hydrologists weighed in publicly, offering detailed explanations for why FEMA's modeling had not aligned with the river's actual behavior. In the broader community of Kerr County, the tragedy became part of a larger conversation about how the Hill Country should understand and prepare for extreme rainfall, especially in Flash Flood Alley.

Camp Mystic itself faced the impossible task of balancing its legacy with its future. The Guadalupe River that had shaped the camp's culture and reputation had now shattered its central assumptions. The Eastlands announced that they would rebuild only Cypress Lake, the adjacent camp set higher on the hill, which had remained dry during the flood. Families of Mystic campers were divided. Some welcomed the reopening. Others expressed outrage that the camp would continue to operate before full accountability had been reached.

For the surviving girls, counselors, and families, the memory of that night became part of the landscape. The cabins that once symbolized childhood independence and joy now held waterlines near the ceilings. The trees where Edward and the Twins survivors had clung for their lives became markers of both tragedy and resilience. Each piece of debris, each broken branch, each shifted stone carried a story.

The Guadalupe River remained unchanged in its nature. It had always been capable of sudden violence. It had always carried the histories of storms, droughts, and floods. What changed was the community's understanding of it. The flood of July 4 did not rewrite the river's character. It only revealed it again, in a way that could not be ignored. The map had offered a simplified picture of danger. The river offered the truth.

In time, Camp Mystic will reshape itself. Families will continue to seek answers. Engineers, legislators, and hydrologists will debate the future of floodplain management in the Hill Country. But the memory of that night will remain braided into the stones and cedars of the Guadalupe River, carried forward the way all river stories are carried: quietly, insistently, and with the full weight of what happened.

The survivors will remember the roar of water against cabin walls, the cold of the current, the grip of a branch or a hand in the dark. The families of those lost will remember far more. And the river will continue to flow past the bend beneath the cypress trees, holding in its depths the traces of that night and the truths that no map could contain.

TWO
JANE RAGSDALE: A LIFE OF CAMP, SERVICE, AND STEWARDSHIP

Jane Ragsdale's story begins long before the July 4 flood, long before she became the steward of Heart O' the Hills Camp for Girls, and long before her life became inseparable from the river valleys of the Texas Hill Country. Her life was rooted in a childhood of laughter, songs in four-part harmony, long car trips, and the early wonder of camp that shaped her spirit. That spirit, equal parts gentleness, curiosity, grit, and service, would carry her from Denton to El Salvador, from Buenos Aires to Guatemala, and home again to Hunt, where she became one of the Hill Country's defining voices and caretakers.

It is impossible to tell the story of the western Kerr County camping community without telling the story of Jane. And it is impossible to tell the story of Jane without telling the story of camping and service in Kerr County.

Her mother, Kathy Ragsdale, remembered Jane as "cute as could be," a child whose thick blond hair was "always flying everywhere" and who carried a smile that radiated like sunlight through cypress branches. She was the middle of three children, the one who tried instinctively to keep the peace, the one "always striving to please and make sure everybody was happy." Even then, she read the room before anyone asked her to. She understood how people felt. She moved toward others rather than away.

Those early years were defined by movement, Kathy's work with Texas Woman's University, her father's work with the Denton Chamber of Commerce, and weekend trips where the family folded themselves into a car and traveled across Texas. They "explored, laughed, traded stories, played cards, and sang in four-part harmony" as they crisscrossed the state, usually going to visit summer camps. The road was their living room. Songs were their shared language. Stories were their inheritance. Eventually, that road carried them to the Hill Country, where a single decision would shape generations.

The Camp Years Begin

Jane still lived in Denton and was nine when she first arrived at Camp Mystic. She had long hair she refused to cut, a wide-open grin, and, as Kathy put it, the kind of optimism that made every difficulty feel like an adventure. Her grandmother worried she was homesick, but when her parents arrived for a surprise visit, a very different picture emerged. Jane spotted them, sprinted across the field, grabbed her beloved puppy, Funny Bunny, from the car, and shouted over her shoulder, "I cannot wait to introduce Funny Bunny to all my friends" before disappearing again into camp life. It was clear that camp had already taken hold of her.

Cindy Stacy Janke, a lifelong friend who had known Jane since childhood, traced Jane's roots to Camp Rio Vista and Camp Mystic, highlighting her early love of camp and lifelong devotion to it. She was one of the eulogists at Jane's celebration of life at First Presbyterian Church in Kerrville. There she read from a newspaper clipping from the *Denton Record-Chronicle* about a letter written by nine-year-old Jane declaring her dream of becoming a counselor, an aspiration Jane fulfilled beyond measure. Jane was described as someone who loved the Hill Country's natural beauty, her family, music, and, above all, camp. Kathy said that Jane viewed her role not as a job but as stewardship, saying Jane called herself a "trustee of this treasure." Janke emphasized Jane's attentiveness to individuals, her ability to make anyone feel fully seen, and her small daily acts of kindness: saving candy for delivery drivers, singing blessings, sharing puns, baking cakes, and celebrating life. Jane was remembered as joyful, generous, musically gifted, deeply faithful, and utterly present.

After that first year, she never looked back. Camp became the center of her summers, a place where friendships were sacred, songs were essential, and the land itself taught lessons she carried for the rest of her life, both Camp Mystic and Heart O' the Hills. When her parents bought Camp Stewart, the family moved to Hunt permanently in 1967. Jane mastered phones, tours, prospect calls, and every detail of camp operations long before she could drive a car. "At age 10 and 11," Kathy recalled, "she learned to answer the telephone professionally, how to take numbers, how to give a camp tour, how to talk to people about the value of camp." This was not a child dabbling in the family business. This was apprenticeship. This was a calling.

And as she grew older, her love of camp evolved into something richer: It became a love of service. Her mother later observed that Jane "had a servant's heart," a phrase she used only after long reflection following Jane's passing. That servant's heart guided her toward caring for individual campers, knowing each one, knowing their histories, knowing their families. It pushed her toward a leadership style defined not by authority but by presence.

She learned the full structure of camp by watching from the edges at first: listening to staff training at Camp Stewart, absorbing the counsel of the legendary Brice "Pinky" Quarles and "Perky" Perhamus, hearing her father, Si Ragsdale, talk about programming and character development. By the time she became director at Heart O' the Hills, she had lived every rung of camp life. She had been a camper, counselor, instructor, waterfront staffer, horsewoman, wrangler, and later the program director whose touch shaped an entire generation of girls. Heart O' the Hills became her life's work, her mission, and her joy.

The Land That Shaped Her

Camp is not only a place of buildings and bells. It is a landscape with its own voice. For Jane, the Hill Country was a living companion, a spiritual teacher. Kathy remembered how the children, during those first months after the family bought Camp Stewart, would leave in the mornings "to discover caves, natural springs, fossils, bird nests, and childish treasures," returning at dusk "dirty, exhausted, and beaming from ear to ear."

The river, the bluffs, the limestone shelves—they formed Jane's internal compass. They gave her a sense of scale. They taught her calm and resilience. They showed her beauty that required no ornament.

Kathy reflected on the spiritual dimension of the land. The river, she said, gave campers "a connection to something bigger," whether a child sat alone at the outdoor worship space known as Green Cathedral, hiked Joy Bluff, or found an arrowhead along the bank. Jane carried that same connection into adulthood. She prayed through the land. She listened through the land. She healed through the land. She found her calmness in the limestone and cedar country that defined her life.

The Scholar, the Traveler, the Journalist

Before she returned home to lead Heart O' the Hills, Jane stretched her wings far beyond the Guadalupe River. At Texas Woman's University, she double-majored in journalism and Spanish while continuing her lifelong devotion to music, graduating in 1979. Professors noted that she spoke "pure Castilian Spanish" despite never living abroad prior to college, evidence of the musical ear that shaped her life in harmonies and song.

She was ambitious, curious, and fearless. When assigned a feature article on midwifery for the *Denton Record-Chronicle*, she signed up for a midwife course so she could understand the story from the inside. She completed the training, became a certified midwife, filed the article, and, as Kathy noted, "never practiced, but she was prepared." That was Jane: If a job mattered, she learned it fully.

She traveled through Europe on almost no money, living from youth hostel to youth hostel with paper sheets for bedsheets she stretched as far as they would go. She worked in Guatemala City translating news stories and absorbing the complex politics of Central America. She earned a journalism fellowship in Buenos Aires during the early days of the Falklands conflict, filing stories for international outlets while navigating a foreign newsroom in turbulent times.

Her life was wide, but it always pointed home. The Hill Country waited for her like a river waits for its tributaries: open, constant, ready. When she came home, she committed to camp not as a summer tradition but as her life's purpose.

The Heart of the Heart

Jane's leadership at Heart O' the Hills was never confined to program design or administration. It was lived daily, carried in tone, attention, and expectation. Those who passed through her orbit as children would later recognize that she was building capability. One of those people was Bailey McEachern.

Bailey, a former camper and now program director at Heart O' the Hills, offers a living confirmation of what Kathy had already made clear: Jane's leadership was not abstract or positional. It was learned, practiced, and transmitted. It was one relationship at a time. Bailey first arrived at Heart O' the Hills as a ten-year-old camper. Like so many girls, she encountered Jane first as a figure of quiet authority. Jane was admired, watched carefully, and taken seriously. "She was not scary," Bailey recalled, "but she was intimidating in a way because you knew she cared, she wanted you to be your best, and you did not want to disappoint her."

That expectation was paired with uncommon attentiveness. Even after a year apart, Jane remembered names, places, and stories. "You just felt like you were home," Bailey said. What Kathy described as Jane's instinctive ability to read a room, Bailey experienced as being fully seen.

As a camper, Bailey encountered Jane most clearly through the culture Jane shaped rather than through instruction alone. Life-skills classes for older girls and the Heart LITe (Leader in Training) program for would-be counselors stood out. They were practical; thank-you notes, budgeting, empathy, even changing a tire but their purpose ran deeper. Jane wanted girls to leave camp confident in themselves, prepared for life beyond the gates.

Music was another constant. Jane's guitar, her singing in the dining hall and at Vespers, and her insistence on shared song created emotional memory as much as tradition. "When you think of camp songs and you think of the guitar," Bailey said, "that is Jane. She brought people together through her music."

Years later, when Bailey returned as a counselor and then on the year-round staff, her understanding of Jane's leadership deepened. What once felt like quiet authority revealed itself as deliberate restraint. Jane did not micromanage. She allowed room for mistakes and growth. "She believed camp was the place where you could fail," Bailey said, "and grow." Jane's expectations did not soften with familiarity. They sharpened but without fear. "She did not even have to say much," Bailey recalled. "You knew when you messed up. And she was there to say, 'Okay, how do you do better next time?'"

As Bailey's responsibilities increased, Jane's role shifted from supervisor to mentor, from decision maker to steward. Conversations turned toward the future of Heart O' the Hills, not in transactional terms but cultural ones. Jane spoke of care rather than control, of responsibility rather than ownership. Bailey came to understand that Jane did not see herself as the center of camp but as its caretaker.

That understanding shaped how Bailey later viewed the transition of stewardship following the flood. When John and Elisabeth Hay stepped forward, Bailey recognized familiar values: humility, continuity, and reverence for what had already been built. "Jane was the heart of the Heart," Bailey said. What Jane taught, Bailey carried forward: Stewardship is not possession but trust. And when the moment came for that trust to be held by others, it passed not as a rupture but as a continuation.

As director of Heart O' the Hills, Jane became far more than an administrator. She became an emotional anchor for the girls, a guide for young counselors, and a steward of tradition. She built a culture grounded in kindness, music, and the belief that every girl could rise to her fullest potential if she was given room to grow without fear of judgment. Kathy described her leadership this way: "Her interest was strictly on each individual. She knew each camper" and knew their families, often across generations. This was character work. This was soul work.

She meticulously shaped the program, but she shaped the community even more. She was nonjudgmental, sometimes, Kathy admitted, "much to my chagrin," because Jane struggled with the idea of sending a girl home, even when necessary. She believed in second chances. She believed in the possibility of growth. She believed in the goodness she could see in people even before they could see it in themselves.

Music was her tool of connection. She brought her guitar everywhere, into the dining hall, to campfires, to morning assemblies. Girls did not sing the way boys at Stewart did; they were not boisterous, not thunderous. Their voices rose together in gentler harmony, filled with intention more than volume. "Girls are more mannerly and orderly," Kathy recalled. "They do not let go the way boys do," but they sing with a beauty all their own. Jane nurtured it.

A Life Woven Into the Community

Jane's service to Kerrville extended far beyond camp. She served as a deacon and elder at First Presbyterian Church, rarely missing choir practice. She served on the board of the Riverside Nature Center and the Board of Trustees at Schreiner University. When Schreiner University President Charlie McCormick thinks about Jane, he does not begin with tragedy. He begins with a boardroom.

In 2021, Schreiner University was facing a decision that carried real risk: whether to commit more than twenty million dollars to new residence halls. Enrollment projections were uncertain. Construction costs were climbing. Trustees worried aloud about empty beds and long-term debt. At the end of a long day, the board chair voiced what everyone was feeling. He said he wished they had a crystal ball.

The next morning, before the meeting was even called to order, Jane walked to the podium with a crystal ball in her hand. Her message was simple. She believed the university should move forward. Waiting would only make the decision more expensive and more difficult. The humor of the crystal eased the tension, but it was her clarity that mattered. For President McCormick, that moment became emblematic of Jane's leadership. She did not speak often, but when she did, she changed the direction of the room. He said of her, "She could look five, ten, twenty years ahead and help us make decisions that positioned the university not just to survive but to thrive."

Jane never demanded attention. On a large board filled with strong personalities, she distinguished herself by listening. She was quiet, present, and deliberate. People trusted her judgment because they knew she had considered the consequences, not just the arguments. McCormick said, "Jane never demanded the floor. She was quiet, she listened, and over time that gave her extraordinary moral authority."

Her service exceeded strategy. McCormick believed that "Jane had real skin in the game. She showed up, she did the work, and she backed her values with time, talent, and treasure." She attended games, scholarship events, and campus gatherings not out of obligation but because she believed presence mattered. When she entered a room, people felt seen. McCormick recalls that she always sat in the same seat during board meetings, never distracted, always attentive. When he had to stand before the board to explain a setback or a failure, he knew where to look. Jane's expression said everything: This would be worked through, together.

She also put her resources behind her values. Jane and her

family established an endowed nursing scholarship, creating a permanent pathway for Hill Country students who aspired to serve in a profession both demanding and essential. For McCormick, the impact of that gift cannot be measured solely in dollars. It changes families. It strengthens local health care. It allows students who might never leave the region to build meaningful, stable careers within it.

Over eighteen years as a trustee, including as a board officer, she convened camp leaders, pushed the university to think creatively about serving the camping community, and brought people to the table who might never have come otherwise. When Jane asked, people showed up.

One of her final defining moments came during deliberations over whether Schreiner should add a football program. After a year of study, the board faced a vote. Jane spoke first, framing the issue not around prestige or revenue but opportunity. Football, she said, could offer young men a path to education they might never otherwise have. The vote passed unanimously. Schreiner would have a team.

Only later, at Jane's remembrance, did President McCormick realize how much of her life he had not fully seen. Beyond Schreiner and Heart O' the Hills, she had performed mission work in Guatemala and in countless quiet ways that never intersected with his world. Listening to others speak, he understood that Jane's influence transcended any single institution. On the breadth of Jane's life and impact, McCormick stated, "Only after her remembrance did I realize how much deeper and broader her life was than I ever knew. She touched far more worlds than just ours."

What he knew for certain was this: Jane practiced a kind of leadership that did not announce itself. It steadied rooms. It lifted people. It left institutions stronger than she found them. And long before the river tested her final resolve, she had already shown what it meant to stay present, to shoulder responsibility, and to lead without noise.

Guatemala: A Parallel Expression of Stewardship

For those who knew Jane only through Heart O' the Hills, her work in Guatemala can sound like a separate chapter in her life. It was not. Let Hope Begin Here Guatemala was founded by Scott Robertson and begun in 2007 in response to a food crisis following a hurricane that devastated the corn crop of subsistence farmers and their families. It serves the time-limited partnership between the citizens of Guayabales, Santa Rosa, and volunteers toward holistic community development in support of market competitive secondary education for their children. Jane was a crucial centerpiece of the operation, as Robertson said in an article for the *HCC Community Journal*. "Calling Jane an enormous asset," he said, "would be an understatement."

As Kristy Vandenberg saw it, Guatemala was simply Jane in a different place. Kristy had been traveling to Guatemala for five years, originally at Jane's invitation. It was Jane who approached her and suggested the Let Hope Begin Here Guatemala project, sensing, correctly, that it would speak to Kristy's faith and sense of service. Kristy had never been on a mission trip before. She went because Jane asked. Now it was different. For the villagers and for the volunteers, Jane's absence was immediate and unmistakable.

"They expected to see Jane's face there," Kristy recalled. "And it was very different for those of us who went down because she wasn't there. She was so much the heart of that operation." Jane did not arrive in Guatemala as an outsider bringing solutions. She arrived as a steward. She wore the same skirt, the same boots, the same small rotation of clothing, deliberately indistinguishable from the people she served. Over time, that consistency became its own language.

"If they saw that skirt and those cowboy boots coming around the corner, they knew it was her," Kristy said. "She didn't want anyone to think she was better than them." Jane prayed at every meal. She sang. She translated. She moved easily among villagers, medical teams, and volunteers, not as a manager issuing instructions but as a presence holding the work together. When children were frightened or upset, they ran to Jane. She knelt to their level, met their eyes, and spoke to them with the same attentiveness Kristy had seen her give campers back home. That attentiveness was not performative. It was operational.

Jane served as one of the primary translators in the medical clinics, bridging Spanish-speaking villagers and English-speaking medical professionals. She handled logistics, supplies, assignments, and communication. When something needed to be explained, Jane explained it. When someone needed reassurance, Jane provided it.

The first year without her, the strain became visible, not dramatically but unmistakably. "Jane was glue. She held all of that together," Kristy said. The clinics still ran. Roofs were replaced. Fences were installed. CPR and first aid training went on, training that Kristy herself had been leading for years, with the goal of equipping one first responder from each of the 23 villages scattered across the mountain. The work went on. But it required more effort, more coordination, more stepping in by others to cover what Jane had once done almost invisibly.

That invisibility was part of her leadership. She brought people with her, camp staff, volunteers, skilled tradespeople, not to showcase them but to empower communities. One year she brought a foreman from camp who spoke Spanish and could fix almost anything. Soon village men were working alongside him, installing gutters, repairing solar panels, improving water systems. Jane's instinct was always the same: Bring what is needed and bring it in a way that leaves others stronger. That instinct extended to the future.

In Guatemala, Jane had been deeply involved with a long-term vision for sustainable health care. Clinics were improved, roofs replaced, equipment installed. But she also understood the risk of building structures without stewardship. A clinic without staff was not a solution. It was a shell.

That is why the next phase of the work matters so much to those who knew her. Plans are underway to build a new clinic in Guatemala in Jane's memory, through a separate nonprofit created for that purpose. It will be called Jane's Heart. The name is not symbolic. It is descriptive. The clinic is intended to reflect how Jane worked: practically, humbly, and with continuity in mind. Kristy sees this not as a memorial but as stewardship transferred. "She would want it to flow," Kristy said. "That is who she was."

Jane's absence raised quiet questions among the volunteers. Who would take over coordination? Who would step into the connective role she had played so naturally? Those questions were not signs of fragility. They reflected how deeply Jane had been woven into the work. "She was glue," Kristy said again. "People ran to her. The villagers ran to her. The kids ran to her."

Kristy had seen that same response at Heart O' the Hills. She remembered a moment when a special needs camper spotted Jane across the grounds and ran full speed into her arms. Jane caught her without hesitation, as if nothing else existed in that moment. "That was who she was," Kristy said. "She made you feel like you were the most important person in the world."

In Guatemala, as at Heart O' the Hills, Jane did not seek ownership. She practiced stewardship. She served with love. She led with presence. And even in her absence, the work continues, changed, challenged, and strengthened by the quiet imprint she left behind.

The Final Day

On July 3, Jane spent the day reaching out to family, friends, her younger sister. She went to lunch. She made calls. She followed her rhythms of kindness. Those ordinary acts, seen in hindsight, feel like the soft closing gestures of someone who had spent her entire life in service.

In an interview with ABC News, her brother, Silas B. "Jeeper" Ragsdale III, said that Jane called him around 3:30 a.m. on July 4 because water was at the base of her bed. Jeeper urged her to break a window or do anything to vacate the house. It was the last time they spoke. She texted her brother. She continued to text him. He would later describe those messages as one of the last threads that tied her to the world beyond the river that morning.

"I couldn't do nothing," Jeeper told the outlet. "I was, like, 'Get out of the house.'" While he hoped she was able to escape the floodwaters, he was not sure what had happened. But the early morning call allowed him to alert others in danger in his own camp, saving at least five people, Jeeper told ABC.

He ended the interview saying the worst part about July 4 was "the hours that he didn't know where she was. Not knowing if she was OK," he said. It meant everything to him that she'd called him that morning," he said. And he said she'd texted him at some point that morning, as the floods ravaged the area. In one message she said she was worried about reopening the camp, Jeeper said, but he still hasn't looked back at her last texts to him. "I just haven't been able to go back there," he said, "but I know I talked to her."

What happened next is chronicled elsewhere in this book. It is enough here to say that Jane lived her final hours as she lived every hour before, with courage, steadiness, and with a heart that never stopped caring for others.

Legacies of and From the Heart

Jane understood something long before the river tested it. Camps do not endure because of buildings, and they do not survive because of programs alone. They endure because people understand stewardship. Jane often spoke of Heart O' the Hills as something she held in trust. She described herself as a caretaker of a living institution. In that sense, Jane was not merely the director of Heart O' the Hills. She was, in the words many would later use, the Heart of the Heart. That understanding shaped how she led, how she planned, and ultimately how succession at Heart O' the Hills would unfold.

Long before the flood, Jane and Kathy spoke quietly about continuity in the same deliberate, values-based way Jane approached everything else. Camp, in Jane's view, was generational work. It required foresight. It required humility. And it required preparing others to carry the work forward as stewards. That cultural preparation would matter more than anyone could have known.

When the flood came, it did not only damage land and structures. It threatened continuity itself. In those early days, grief and urgency coexisted. There was mourning, and there was the unspoken recognition that if Heart O' the Hills was to remain Heart O' the Hills, decisions would need to be made with both reverence and resolve. Into that moment stepped John and Elisabeth Hay.

They were already woven into the fabric of the Kerr County camp community. John's connection to camp reached back to his own childhood. He first attended Camp Stewart at six years old and spent decades returning as a camper, counselor, chapel speaker, consultant, and chief. Camp shaped his friendships, his faith, and his sense of belonging. Elisabeth came to camp culture later but with equal conviction, watching firsthand how camp became central to their children's lives.

Their twins, a boy and a girl, had just completed their third summer at camp when the flood struck. Camp was more than a seasonal experience for them. It was identity. They wore camp shirts year-round. They counted the days until summer. Camp had already begun shaping who they were becoming.

Years earlier, the Hays had purchased a property in Hunt on the North Fork of the Guadalupe River, nestled between Camp Stewart and Camp Waldemar. It was a place their children called the "River Ranch House," a gathering spot for holidays and weekends. John recognized the land immediately from canoe trips he had taken decades earlier as a camper. Only later would they learn that the property itself carried camp history, that Jane and Kathy had once stayed in its main building during the purchase of Camp Stewart. The land, like camp, remembered.

When the flood came, the Hays were close, both physically and emotionally. They arrived the next morning with equipment to help clear roads so electricity and infrastructure crews could reach Heart O' the Hills. They housed displaced families and first responders. They were neighbors doing what needed to be done.

What they saw, however, went beyond immediate damage. They saw the fragility of continuity. They saw that without swift, thoughtful action, Heart O' the Hills risked becoming memory rather than lived experience. Their first instinct was not ownership. It was assistance.

Drawing on their professional backgrounds in real estate and development, they approached the Ragsdales with an idea. The Hays would sell their property at cost, help facilitate acquisition of a neighboring tract, and enable Heart O' the Hills to rebuild and continue on land that already held deep camp meaning. John prepared conceptual layouts to show feasibility. The goal was preservation rather than reinvention.

The conversations that followed were restrained and deliberate, rooted in trust. Jane and Kathy had already been thinking about succession in cultural terms. The flood accelerated the moment. When the possibility emerged that stewardship might pass to the Hays, it did not arrive with ceremony. It arrived quietly, and it carried weight.

John later recalled calling Elisabeth after meeting with Kathy and telling her plainly that they had been asked to carry Heart O' the Hills forward. The timing was almost surreal. The family was about to leave on a cruise with their eight-year-old twins. For a week, the decision unfolded in fragments, in quiet corners between family activities, carefully shielded from young ears.

Elisabeth remembers those conversations as emotionally dense. The flood was still raw. The loss still near. By the middle of the week, they reached a shared conclusion. They did not know whether they could succeed. But they believed that choosing not to try would have been harder to live with than the risk of failure. They prayed simply that doors would open if the path was meant to unfold. And doors did open.

While they were still on the cruise, the contract to purchase the neighboring property was finalized, creating a site large enough to support a viable camp. Soon after, they listed their primary home in Fredericksburg, a complex, deeply loved property they had spent years restoring. In a difficult real estate market, it sold in ten days. Capital was freed. Momentum gathered.

From the beginning, they were clear about their role as Heart O' the Hills preservationists. Continuity and Jane's culture mattered more than any individual decision. Elisabeth spoke openly about seeing what camp gave her daughter and recognizing what it might have given her own younger self. She did not seek visibility. She sought to lift others. Her vision of stewardship centered on sustaining the values Jane embedded and creating a place where the community itself could bring the magic back.

John described their role more structurally. If camp is a living institution, then someone must build and maintain the foundation. He often said they were creating the slab upon which the Heart O' the Hills community could rebuild itself. Buildings, permits, safety protocols, infrastructure, staffing—these were necessary but not sufficient. Their task was to make space for something older and deeper to return.

Again and again, the Hays emphasized that this was a collective effort, powered by a community Jane had spent a lifetime nurturing. Women who had grown up at Heart O' the Hills returned with traditions and memory. Counselors came back with songs, rituals, and expectations. The culture Jane built proved resilient. That resilience was not accidental. Jane had prepared for it. She'd made others feel responsible for the place because she trusted them with it. Succession, in that sense, had already begun long before it was formalized.

Today, stewardship of Heart O' the Hills rests with people who understand that legacy is preserved through continuity of purpose. The Hays did not replace Jane Ragsdale. No one could. What they accepted was the responsibility of carrying forward what she built, honoring her belief that Heart O' the Hills was never about one person but about generations of girls finding their strength, voice, and community.

Jane remains the Heart of the Heart.

What has changed is who now holds the trust she prepared to pass. Heart O' the Hills endures as a living continuation of what Jane made possible. Kathy said it simply: "She was as lovely inside as [on] the outside. She had a constant zest for life. She loved her Lord. She loved life. She loved nature and beauty." Jane once told Kathy, "I am such a paradox. I am happy with dirt floors, but I want crystal chandeliers." Both were true because both reveal the span of her spirit. She could see beauty in rough edges and elegance in simplicity. She could live in the dust without complaint and appreciate art without pretense.

Jane's monument is the Hill Country itself. It is the generations of girls who found their strength at Heart. It is the river where she prayed. It is the chapel songs that still echo in the trees. It is the children of Guatemala who drink clean water because she showed up year after year. It is the land she loved and the people she served.

Her story, like the river, does not end. It goes on. It moves forward. It finds its way.

THREE
SURVIVAL AND LOSS

The Guadalupe River has always carried its own kind of serenity at the bend between Ingram and Hunt, where the Parsley family kept their river house. It perched fifty yards upslope from the waterline, set on concrete pillars built after the 1987 flood, a reminder carved into local memory by ten lost teenagers. The house sat above the one-hundred-year floodplain, high enough that it felt almost untouchable. Many summers passed with the river drifting green and slow beneath the cypress canopy, the yard falling away toward the swimming hole where children splashed in afternoons that seemed immune to danger. Aaron Parsley wrote his family's story in *Texas Monthly*.

On July 3, the river looked exactly as a holiday weekend should promise. Rosemary, four years old and full of motion, bounced from one family member to the next. Clay, only twenty months, toddled in his diaper, chasing after laughter. Dinner was pizza; the night closed with charades. By 9:30 p.m. the lights were off, and the cabin settled into the quiet breathing of sleeping people, seven in all: Clint, the grandfather; Alissa and her husband, Lance; Rosemary and Clay; Aaron and his husband, Patrick. Nothing in the air hinted at catastrophe.

Around three in the morning, rain woke Aaron. It sounded like an ordinary Hill Country storm, loud but familiar. He drifted back to sleep imagining he would still manage his early run. But near 4:30 a.m., Rosemary climbed down from the top bunk and told her father that something was on the roof. Lance got up, listened, and felt the first flicker of unease.

Aaron stirred again, this time to movement and voices. In the main room, his father, Clint, and Lance stood by the sliding-glass doors staring into the dark. Clint's flashlight beam cut across the yard and hit water, not below them where the slope normally led down to the river but even with the back deck. The Guadalupe River had risen twenty feet. The river they had floated in only hours earlier now stood against the porch railing. The realization came as a quiet sentence from Clint: "We are in trouble. Big trouble."

In seconds, the seven of them gathered in the living area, trying to understand the situation. No one had imagined being surrounded by dark, fast-moving water, cut off from any path to higher ground. The roof was unreachable—no ladder, no way to pull themselves up. The large live oak behind the house was too far from any window. Lance dialed 911. The dispatcher could not promise help or even estimate when help might come.

The river rose another foot and pressed hard against the glass. The air in the house changed; the smell of the river seeped in, a musty, woody scent mixed with the sharpness of fresh splintering timber. Vinyl flooring in the kitchen began to bubble. The carpet in Clint's bedroom lifted off the floor like a blanket. Rosemary and Clay were placed on the kitchen island, the highest, safest point they could reach.

Then the first structural failure arrived. The porch roof crashed down. A window blew out in Clint's room. Pendant lamps swung above the counter like the cabin had turned into a vessel at sea. The sliding-glass door gave way slightly under water pressure, water pushing in. Lance fought it back, leaning his weight into the frame. The house shuddered once, sideways, as if nudged by an unseen shoulder. Then it lurched sharply. "We are moving," Patrick said.

It made no sense. The house was built on concrete pillars

anchored deep in the slope. But the flood did not care about engineering or history. The house was afloat, lifted by a force that could not be countered. In the dark, they felt themselves drifting.

What happened next took only seconds. The house slammed into something, maybe a tree, maybe debris. A wall cracked. Windows shattered. The deck ripped free. The structure folded into itself. In less than fifteen seconds, the cabin that had held generations came apart and dissolved into the river. When the water swallowed them, no one had time to plan. No one had time to prepare. Alissa held both children when they went under. In the swirl of darkness, she heard Clay cough once and Rosemary call "Mama." That was the last moment all three were together.

Above the waterline, the storm and the river blurred into the same color, black-gray, indistinguishable. Aaron surfaced gasping, stripped of shoes and phone. He fought through debris, coolers, couch cushions, bottles and tree limbs, grabbing at branches that snapped in his hands. Finally, he reached a tree thick enough to hold him and climbed into its crook, trying to catch his breath against the cold pounding in his chest.

Patrick, swept into darkness, found refuge on a piece of metal roofing. Lance escaped the sliding-glass door he had tried to hold shut, pushing it open underwater before swimming free. Clint, seventy-three years old, was pinned beneath a massive object in the river, furniture, perhaps, or part of the frame. Aaron thought clearly, *This is how drowning feels*, and prepared for the end. He twisted once, pushed with all the force left in his arms, snapped free, and kicked upward until air hit his face. All along the river, separated by hundreds of yards, members of the family clung to trees, drifting debris, or anything that could keep them above the churning black water.

Aaron checked his watch when he reached a higher branch. It was 5:20 a.m. Sunrise was an hour away. Rain still fell in sheets—insult layered on top of injury. He watched in disbelief as water heaters, a trailer, even a car with its headlights pointing straight into the sky floated past. Then he heard screaming, raw and primal. It was Alissa. "I am with Rosemary," she shouted through the storm.

"Clay is gone." Those words carved a permanent mark into the night.

As dawn tried to push through the clouds, Patrick appeared on the riverbank below, running along debris-littered ground. His presence looked unreal against the storm, a human shape moving with intention. Lance appeared moments later. The two had landed in the same pecan tree and made their way to shore once the water slowed enough to pool instead of surge.

They searched the bank for survivors. When they spotted Rosemary up in a tree with Alissa clinging below her, both men moved into action. Patrick retrieved a blue kayak floating by. A couple watching from a nearby home brought an inflatable inner tube. They rigged the tube with a green garden hose and tied it to debris lodged in the slope. The rescue played out in frantic, precise movements.

Lance waded into the water with the tube. Alissa pried Rosemary's hands from the branch and dropped her, twenty feet, straight into the center of it. Rosemary landed perfectly, terrified at first, then calm as Lance pulled her toward shore. Alissa followed, and Aaron, having jumped from his own tree, met her with arms around her as she reached land.

On the riverbank, surrounded by neighbors offering towels, water, and clothes, the family began to gather. Patrick found Clint alive at another house, shaking under a towel but safe. Rosemary had survived without a single scratch. The adults were scraped and bruised but alive. Clay was still missing.

The fire department transported them to Ingram Elementary, now a reunification center. Through rain-blurred windows they saw the broader catastrophe for the first time: flattened trees, crushed cars, houses destroyed, water flowing over the Ingram Dam. The scale of destruction made survival feel both miraculous and devastating. Later, at the hospital in Fredericksburg, they held onto hope they feared to name. But the next day, officials notified Lance that a child matching Clay's description had been found along the Guadalupe near the Rio 10 Cinemas in Kerrville, twelve miles downstream.

Lance identified him. He touched his son's chest, smoothed his blond hair, and whispered, "That is my boy. We love you. Your ama tried to save you." In the quiet that followed, the family understood the full measure of what the river had taken and what it had spared.

The house was gone. The landscape was torn apart. But the love within that family, and the courage of each member in the moments when the river became a force too large to comprehend, remained intact. And for Rosemary—brave, determined, fearless Rosemary—Aaron began writing the story so that she would one day know not just that "the river house broke" but how her mother saved her, how her father reached her, how her family held on in the darkest hours the Guadalupe River had ever delivered.

The House That Floated Away—Cindy Collier and the River She Knew Too Well

For nearly half a century, Cindy Collier lived at the quiet seam where Hunt fades into Ingram, a corridor of riverbend and cedar breaks that had shaped the contours of her everyday life. Forty-five years in one place gives a person a sense of permanence. The trees become familiar neighbors. The bends in the Guadalupe River become background scenery. The soundscape of the river— crickets, cicadas, and the occasional thrum of weekenders towing kayaks —settles into the same category as breath: ever present, rarely examined. Maci Cottingham wrote their story for *The Kerrville Daily Times*.

In the early-morning hours of July 4, the river reminded her that permanence along its banks is always a shared fiction. She woke first to car horns, sharp, insistent blasts that she chalked up to holiday travelers arriving late. Hunt traffic does that sometimes, especially in summer when the camps are awake and the Hill Country takes on its seasonal pulse. But then came a cat's meow, thin but startled, the kind of sound that made her imagine a scuffle on the porch. She went to check.

When she cracked open the front door, the Guadalupe came inside. Not politely. Not slowly. It surged in, as if the river had been waiting for that small opening to reclaim what it had always assumed was its own. Her husband, Ken, ran toward her, already understanding the truth. "We are flooding."

The power had already blinked out. Darkness turned the familiar into the unknowable. Cindy reached instinctively for light but found only absence: Her flashlight was stranded on the porch, now lost to the current. She dug through drawers until her fingers found battery-operated candles, the little blinking kind that give off more hope than illumination. Their thin glow ricocheted off rising water as Ken steadied a flashlight above the growing chaos.

She tried desperately to gather the important things: her birth certificate, documents tucked into drawers, the unspoken inventory of a life built in one place. She tossed what she could onto the bed, telling herself she would come back for it in a moment. There would be no coming back.

Within seconds, the water rose to their waists. That is when the calculus changed. That is when the river stopped being an inconvenience and declared itself an authority. "We are going to have to ride this out," she said, the words suspended between resolve and disbelief. In the fog of rising panic, she called her son. There was no small talk. No time for careful phrasing. "I told him goodbye because I thought we were going to die." "No, you are not," he answered. "I know the fire department right there. I am calling them now. Hold on, Mom."

Ken tried calling 911 but could not break through the overloaded system. They did the only thing left: They retreated to the bathroom, the most structurally confined space they had, and shut the door. Cindy climbed onto the sink as Ken attacked the ceiling with a curtain rod, trying to gouge an escape hatch into the attic. Insulation drifted down like strange snowfall, layering over the bathroom tile as the river pressed upward from below.

Then, just as quickly as it had surged, the water dropped. A false mercy. The river often grants these momentary reprieves, a breath, a pause, a suggestion that its fury has passed, before returning with renewed force. Cindy and Ken did not yet know whether this was mercy or manipulation. They only knew they were still alive.

Using a blinking flashlight, they shone light through a frosted window, hoping someone on the outside would notice the stuttering pulse. And eventually, help came. Rescue crews pried them out of the bathroom, out of the house, and into a world that no longer resembled the one they knew. What they saw stopped them cold.

"We looked down, and we were in an empty field," Cindy recalled. Not just debris. Not just uprooted fences or scattered trash. An empty field. "All our neighbors ..." Ken began, before realizing the truth. It was not the neighbors who had been swept away. It was them.

Their home, forty-five years of accumulated life, had been ripped from its foundation and carried downstream. The only thing that prevented it from traveling farther was the sudden collision with a cement well on another property, a brutal and miraculous anchor. "We were floating down the river and did not even know it," Cindy said later, grateful not to have seen the journey because knowing it in the moment might have broken her.

When they returned to the place where their home had once stood, nothing remained recognizable. The river had redrawn the landscape with an indifference that bordered on artistry. Their house. Three storage sheds. A greenhouse. The garden. Two porches. Both vehicles. All gone.

Cindy's Mercedes, the one her father had left her, was found 15 feet up a tree, a quiet, absurd monument to water's violence. Ken's truck was wrapped around another tree like a crumpled piece of paper. The only object that remained exactly as it had been before the flood was his lawnmower, sitting obediently in its original spot. The juxtaposition bordered on cruel comedy: The river erases homes but leaves the mower.

A room addition filled with toys for grandchildren, family photos, keepsakes spanning decades—all of it disappeared without a trace. "When you live somewhere your whole life, you do not get rid of anything because you never move," Cindy said. The flood got rid of it all in an instant.

They salvaged a few items but nowhere near enough. The only piece of clothing Ken managed to recover was his father's leather riding jacket, a small, tactile connection to the past when everything else had dissolved. She spent days struggling to see because she had left her glasses on the nightstand, a detail that captured the surreal absurdity of disaster: catastrophic loss followed by the small frustrations of daily life, layered like sediment over the trauma.

What the river took from Cindy and Ken was not just property. It was continuity. It was the illusion that the river respected seniority, that living forty-five years beside its banks earned you some unspoken treaty. The Guadalupe River has no such diplomacy. It remembers only its own pathways, carved in ancient stone long before homes appeared along its edges.

And yet—and this is the rhythm of loss in the Hill Country—survival becomes its own kind of narrative. Cindy did not romanticize the river or the night it changed her life. But she understood something essential: She and Ken lived because the house collided with a well at precisely the right moment. They lived because rescue came. They lived because, in the dark, Ken kept punching at a ceiling he could not see, and because Cindy kept calling for help even when she believed none would come.

The river misread their home as just another vessel to carry. It misjudged their resolve. It miscalculated the exact geometry of a well placed in an otherwise open field. It misjudged the stubborn instinct of two people who had lived along its banks long enough to know when to fight and when to wait.

Their home floated away. But their story did not. It stayed anchored, like the house itself, by the narrowest margin, preserved through memory, resilience, and the sharp awareness that surviving a flood is not just a matter of the water's whim but of grace.

The Night the River Chose Its Own Time—Lorena Guillen and Blue Oak RV Park

On most summer evenings in the Hill Country, the July air settles into a familiar stillness. On July 3, that stillness looked almost cinematic across the property that stretched from Blue Oak RV Park to the back deck of Howdy's Restaurant, Bar & Chill. Lorena Guillen remembered the day with a kind of disbelief, as if recalling a scene filmed on another planet: sun shining, grass impossibly green, water so clear that you could see straight through to the limestone floor. There had been just enough rain the night before to tamp down the dust and give the Fourth of July fireworks a rare blessing. After years of droughts and burn bans, the staff had gone all in, about a thousand dollars' worth of fireworks sitting ready for the next night's celebration.

Howdy's had been alive that evening. Lorena moved through the restaurant as only an owner who had built the place with her own hands could, one moment delivering plates, the next greeting tourists from the deck, the next disappearing into the kitchen to check on a stove she knew by sound more than sight. The outside stage carried the music easily across the patio, and locals danced with the casual confidence that comes from knowing you will see these same people at the grocery store, at the feed store, at church.

The restaurant had not always been Howdy's. When she and her husband, Bob Canales, bought the property four years earlier, it was The Hay Barn. Another restaurant leased the space then, but when that tenant left, the couple looked at each other and figured they might as well take the chance. Lorena had always loved to cook. She loved the hum of people talking over food. It was a dream that did not require much analyzing. They opened the doors, the town walked in, and the place never really slowed down again.

That same purchase included Blue Oak RV Park, a small, tightly knit patch of riverfront spots, and it tied together everything about their life in the Hill Country. They had lived in Tierra Linda Ranch for years, at first part time, then full time, before selling their home to buy the restaurant and park outright. Her husband's company, Aggie Construction, had already spent forty years building across the region. In a sense, they had roots here long before they fully arrived.

By the time the last plates left the kitchen on July 3, the skies had begun to shift. Rain came down harder than the earlier drizzle, steady enough that Lorena decided to close a little early. She sent home her last employee, Julian, with the instruction every parent wants to hear: "Go home to your babies." She walked across the property to her house, showered, tried to unwind. But somewhere close to two in the morning, the unease settled in. It was still raining, harder now.

At 2:08 a.m., she called the Kerr County Sheriff's Office. How were things upriver? Were they seeing anything? Rumors of heavy rain had circulated earlier in the week, the same way they always did. Forecasts mentioned numbers that rarely materialized. But she had people sleeping feet from the river. She needed to know whether she should wake them. The dispatcher had nothing to offer. No alerts, no warnings.

So, Lorena did what river people do. She got dressed, stepped outside, and drove down to the edge of the water. She looped the property in the dark, taking account of the man-made creek that always gave her a reliable early read. If that creek rose, water was coming. But it sat quiet. No trouble. No urgency. She went back. Checked weather apps again. Watched the radar swirl. A flash-flood watch pinged through her phone. Nearby Goat Creek floods often, and the alert felt routine. Close to 3 a.m., she finally lay down again. Rain hammered on.

What woke her at a little after 4 a.m. was light, flashing, pulsing, unmistakably urgent. She looked outside. Fire-rescue trucks were on the property with their lights cutting through the dark. She shouted for her husband. They dressed and ran. According to *The Kerrville Daily Times*, Lorena said, "We had an evacuation plan. We tested it last year—it worked. This time, it helped us to get people out."

The moment she reached the responders, she yelled the information she had already catalogued in her mind: "There are five people on the island!" The island was the lowest plot in the RV park, a small wedge pinched between water channels that was always the first to flood. She knew exactly who was down there. She knew who was home, who was traveling, who had pets, who had mobility issues. That knowledge would become its own survival tool in the minutes ahead.

The weather had turned from rainstorm to battlefield. Lightning cracked with enough frequency to paint the landscape in jittery glimpses: the ramp, the line of RVs, the river already louder than it should be. Thunder rolled like something hitting steel. The water, invisible except for brief flashes, grew louder with each minute.

Her husband, Bob, ran toward the ramp leading to the island. Lorena turned toward the upper RV area, then the lower one, shouting to people who had already stepped outside in confusion. "Go to the restaurant! Go to higher ground!" The water on the lower level reached waist height fast, faster than anything she had seen in any previous flood, which had topped out near sixteen feet. This was different. This was not rising water. This was incoming force.

She ran between RVs she knew by name, by owner, by who had kids, who had pets. As reported, she told them, "No time for possessions. Just go!" She moved toward the last one she had not yet accounted for: the RV belonging to Michael Abner and Trish Isbell. She banged hard on the door, shouting. It took several tries to wake them. When they opened the door, half dressed and disoriented, she told them plainly: "You do not have time. Leave now." Fifteen minutes later, their RV floated downriver, but the family had escaped.

By then the second wave had hit. RVs on the upper level began to shift, then lift, then slide. Vehicles groaned as they scraped along gravel, then slipped into the current. The darkness made everything surreal; the lightning made it worse, illuminating scenes you wished you could unsee. A container that held Lorena's macaw and her chihuahuas lifted and drifted away, still locked, still unreachable.

Down below, the force of the water swept Bob thirty to forty-five feet downstream. He later told her the only reason he survived was that the lanyard of his flashlight snagged on rebar embedded in a retaining wall. He clawed his way back up before the wall collapsed.

When Lorena tried to move back toward the restaurant, she felt the water tingling, almost like electricity. Maybe imagination, maybe not. Electrical posts had fallen. Main service lines had been ripped apart. The water was freezing and alive with debris, roaring past in total darkness.

Inside Howdy's, evacuees gathered for what little shelter the building could offer. The fire-rescue team soon ordered everyone out, as it was no longer safe. The water rose to the base of the restaurant, and the structure shuddered against the impact of floating debris. Downstream, vehicles slammed into trees. People trapped in cars honked for help. In the lightning flashes, Lorena could see hands on windows.

The third wave came as the sky began to lighten toward dawn, somewhere around 5 a.m. This wave took the warehouse. Everything in it—the construction trailers, the Polaris, the welding rigs, the stack of restaurant overflow equipment—lifted and folded and broke apart as the water forced it downstream, smashing pieces against the deck of Howdy's.

Just after that, with the property fully evacuated, Lorena ran to her house, grabbed her passport, her dog, and essential documents. She and her husband drove their vehicles up to Citywest Church at Junction Highway and Goat Creek Road. Only then, after reporting to emergency response personnel on site and the sheriff's deputies, after handing over the one paper copy of her guest list that she salvaged, did she begin to understand the true scale of the loss. There were four people missing, the family who had been on the island. Everyone else had made it out.

Around nine in the morning, the water finally began to recede enough for Lorena to return to the house and restaurant. It would take until afternoon before the upper RV area could be reached. The lower area remained inaccessible for days.

Earlier, around six that morning, She and her husband had walked back down the road and stood at the arch, looking out over what had once been a neat grid of riverfront spaces. The water was still too high to see everything clearly, but the damage was plain. In the rising light, she tried to reconcile what she saw with the place she had walked through only hours earlier.

She never saw the water-rescue crew again, the team she had first seen only in red helmets, sprinting into the flood like figures from another world. They moved so fast she remembered them as "ninjas," launching boats straight into the current while everyone else was running away from it. In the end, the memory that stayed with her was not only the destruction. It was the coldness of the water. The screaming of neighbors. The flashes of lightning showing hands in windows. The way the river rose not like a tide but like a verdict, arriving in waves that ignored every map, every expectation, every familiar pattern of the creek she had watched for years. The day before had been beautiful. Perfect. The river had been clear enough to see the bottom. Then, in one night, it became something else entirely, something that decided its own time and took what stood in its way.

Lorena told *The Kerrville Daily Times* that she was "ever so grateful that she and her husband escaped." But the memories still haunt her. "Once you see, you can't unsee." In her *Kerrville Daily Times* story, reporter Nance Foster ended her piece on Lorena by simply stating, "And that will never change."

The Hill Above Panther Creek—Valerie Tucker's Escape into the Dark

In the upper reaches of the Guadalupe River, where the South Fork tightens into a corridor of limestone, cedar, and old ranch roads, night still holds its shape. On July 4, in the earliest hours of morning, that dark wrapped quietly around Valerie Tucker's house as she and her husband tried to comfort their storm-frightened dog, Oscar. The rain hammered down, but out there near the headwaters it was easy to believe the river could rise only so far. Flood watches were common. Flood disasters were not. They had groceries for the weekend and a familiar plan: Ride it out, keep an eye on the waterline, and let the storm wander off the way most storms do.

Their rental sat between Camp Mystic and River Inn Resort, on land owned by a family whose roots in the property stretched back to the 1940s. That kind of legacy creates confidence in a place, a sense that the land knows you, that it will warn you in time. But the warning that arrived was not subtle. At 3:06 a.m., fists pounded against their door. "We need to get out. We have to go." The owners themselves were already in their vehicles, engines running, headlights cutting frantic streaks into the rain-thick darkness.

Valerie grabbed shoes and the dog, her sense of orientation dissolving in the panic and noise. Her car sat in water, hood shining under the flattening rain. She doubted it would start. Her husband urged her on, "Try anyway. If it starts, do not sit in the water. Drive straight to the highway." It did start. She pulled out, but the highway offered no safety. Everywhere, water pressed upward in sheets, roads turning into corridors of moving black.

They made their way toward the gate of Panther Creek Ranch, where her husband forced the electric gate open by hand. He told her to drive up the hill. The hill was no hill anymore; it was a river disguised in land's clothing. Water streamed down it hard enough to push rocks and boulders loose, sending them tumbling under her tires. "Keep going," he told her. And she did. Everyone did. Elderly neighbors, disabled residents, babies wrapped tight against the rain, pets wide-eyed but calm. All of them climbing higher.

At the top they stopped the cars and turned to look back. Lightning split the horizon, laying bare a landscape they no longer recognized. The ranch owner had attempted to return to the house and was swept away, saved only when he caught a fence line. His sons pulled him out, their clothes torn away by the force of the water. Down below, what had been a neighborhood became a broken, churning plain. Under the flashes they could see only the tips of houses and the tops of vehicles, their headlights still glowing as they drifted downstream like lanterns for the dead.

They stayed on that road until sunrise, three long hours of wind, rain, and watching. When dawn finally lifted, it exposed a mosaic of wreckage: uprooted cypress trees stripped bare, debris fields lodged under carports, storage buildings from upriver carried to new, strange places. Pavement vanished. Cars lay scattered in impossible positions. It looked as though the river had unwound the valley and rearranged it out of spite.

Most of all, there was the news that stopped everyone cold: Two longtime residents, Jose Olvera and his wife, Alicia, people who had lived there for forty years, who seemed permanent fixtures of the land, were missing and soon confirmed gone. "We thought he would be the first one we'd see," Valerie said later. "He knew everyone." But the river had taken them before dawn.

By 5 a.m., county maintainers, bulldozers fitted with the authority of necessity, began carving rough escape paths, shoving trees and wreckage aside to open a route out. Helicopters moved nonstop from Camp Mystic to River Inn, the sound of rotor blades merging with the river's guttural roar. Valerie and her group remained in their cars all day, drenched and exhausted, watching rescue helicopters skim the valley like hawks searching for movement. The ranch owners returned, gave them the gate code, and led them higher up the hill where they could catch a bar of cell service, just enough to tell family they were alive.

Her husband's boss had already sent a helicopter to look for them. When it approached overhead, they waved it off. "Go help other people," they said. They still believed, in those first hours, that this was a flood they could repair: Soak up the carpet, replace a window, maybe repaint. The truth was waiting for them at the bottom of the hill.

Sunrise revealed what night had hidden: Their stairs were gone, the trampoline gone, basketball goal gone, barbecue pits gone, trees gone, almost everything recognizable ripped away. Debris was piled chest high under the carport. Inside the house, water had risen far higher than Valerie imagined. Her husband climbed up onto the balcony and retrieved a few things. The rest was lost.

Oscar, ever alert to storms, stayed strangely calm. So did every pet on the hill. Children, too, babies to nine-year-olds, weathered the night with a resilience that seemed impossible. One little girl, Lucy, the ranch owners' granddaughter, had her birthday that day. All her presents had washed away. What she wanted most, she said, was for everyone to get her new ones. A child's logic, simple, pure, and devastating.

When county crews finally allowed them out, Valerie's drive through Hunt was a gauntlet of heartbreak. Camp Mystic's entrance bristled with emergency vehicles. Game wardens launched airboats into places where roads had been. Cars hung from trees in quarter-mile intervals. At Heart O' the Hills, every structure was gone but one, and a bus was pinned against it like a matchbox toy in a giant's hand. Somewhere along the trip, she stopped filming. "Maybe I don't want to have to see this again," she said.

The farther they traveled, the more the valley revealed the true breadth of the disaster: slabs where homes used to be, entire neighborhoods peeled away to foundations. She kept thinking of the people who did not have a hill to climb. Where had they gone? Who had reached safety, and who had been caught in the dark? Questions without answers, suspended over miles of destruction.

In the days that followed, Valerie and her husband returned to salvage what they could—guns, documents, small personal items. Looters struck a nearby house. Volunteers arrived in steady waves: churches from Houston and Austin bringing snacks, drinks, gift cards; FEMA teams verifying claims within days; neighbors offering furniture, grooming for pets, hands to lift what could still be lifted. The smallest gestures mattered. The smallest gestures kept them upright.

Looking back, Valerie realized she did not feel the fear she should have felt. She told her father, "I should have been a lot more scared." He agreed. But fear often arrives late, in quieter hours, when the rain has stopped and the mind has time to replay what it lived through.

"It flooded," she said. "It flooded a lot. We had to leave the house. That's crazy." Only later did she understand what it meant to survive a flood where both the South Fork and North Fork rose together, an almost unheard-of confluence of fury at the literal headwaters.

Yet even amid the ruin, she felt something else: Kerr County showing up for its own. Churches, neighbors, volunteers, construction crews, real estate agents, strangers, everyone stepping forward in a way she described simply but powerfully: "For something like this to happen in a community, Kerrville was probably the place for it to happen."

In the end, the hill above Panther Creek became more than a refuge. It became the line between loss and survival, between what the river took and what it spared. In the dark, in the rain, among neighbors and pets and children who had no shoes, they found a way to endure the longest night of their lives.

Karen Taylor—Rising Above in a Fight for Survival

In the earliest hours of July 4, Karen Taylor was not thinking about river gauges, forecasts, or the language people would later use to describe the flood. She was thinking about the ordinary things that frame a normal morning at home: the quiet of the house, the familiar rhythms of a pet, the routine of checking on her mother. That is what makes her account so unsettling. It begins not with a siren but with a cat. Karen's story was reported by Cottingham in the *Kerrville Daily Times*.

Karen's cat, Opal, woke her around 4 a.m., an unusual interruption in a household routine where the animals typically slept later. The timing mattered. It gave Karen minutes she did not know she needed. She got up and heard a sound she said she had never heard before. It was not wind, not rain on a roof, not the distant rumble of thunder. It was the river, and it was close enough to be on the deck.

She walked to the front door. A flash of lightning lit the view just long enough for her to understand what her mind could not immediately accept: The Guadalupe River was in her driveway. But Karen was not alone in her home. Her 95-year-old mother was with her, having moved in two years earlier because of mobility issues. The moment Karen saw the water, she did not have the luxury of deliberation. She ran to her mother's room and told her they needed to evacuate. She helped her mother dress, grabbed a flashlight, and rushed to her own room to throw on shorts, a T-shirt, and tennis shoes. She picked up her purse, thinking in those first seconds that this might still be the kind of emergency where you drive somewhere safe and wait it out, maybe in a hotel, and then come home to a mess and an inconvenience.

"I was going back down the hall through the dining room," Karen recalled. The next moment did not unfold gradually. It arrived like impact. "The wall of water hit and blew out the French doors immediately," she said. "Glass shattered. The furniture shattered, and furniture was breaking."

It is hard to explain to someone who has not lived through it how quickly a house can stop being shelter and become current. Water surged through the home with enough force to transform familiar rooms into a rushing corridor of debris. Karen tried to get back to her mother's door, which was next to the kitchen, but the floodwater was already making it impossible. She could not reopen the door. She could not reach her.

She did what many people do when they realize they are in a situation too big for their own strength. She yelled through the barrier and asked if her mother was all right. Her mother answered from the other side: "I am fine, just laying here." Karen tried to break the door down with the flashlight. She could not. The door held. The water kept rising.

In those minutes, the mind grasps at one more tool, one more step, one more authority that can intervene. Karen climbed onto the kitchen counter and tried to call 911. She got through, but the call dropped as she began to give her address. She did not blame dispatch. She understood, even in the middle of panic, what the limits were. "I knew there was no help, but it was not their fault," she said. "They could not have gotten to us anyway."

She concluded that a helicopter would have been the only viable rescue option. Meanwhile, her home continued to fill. At the flood's peak, she estimated the house took on seven feet of water. Even in the most human emergencies, there are small moments that cut through like a needle. As Karen balanced on the counter, her chihuahua, Molly, swam up to her shoulder. It jolted her back into another layer of responsibility. She had been so focused on her mother's safety that she had not thought about the animals.

She lifted Molly and placed her on top of the cabinets. She called out for Opal and for her other dog, Gidget, but she feared they were trapped beneath shifting furniture and rising water. In a home turned into a violent container, even reaching down to look can be dangerous. She did not know where they were, only what the conditions suggested. Then came the decision that still sits in her voice.

Karen realized she would not survive if she stayed where she was. She also realized what it would mean to leave. In a flood, you can drown in inches or in feet, and you can drown trying to save someone you love. Karen had already lost the ability to reach her mother. The water was not slowing down. The house was becoming deeper, darker, more unstable by the minute. "I thought she would not want us both to die," Karen said.

She made the agonizing decision to leave her mother behind in order to get help, trying not to alarm her. She took Molly and swam to where the French doors had been, slipping through that broken opening beneath the frame. Outside, she climbed onto a pergola and used it to pull herself up to the roof. "I am on the roof now," she said.

Roofs are supposed to be above the danger. In floods like this, roofs become a thin line between life and loss. Karen and Molly stayed there for hours. Those hours were not dramatic in the way movies portray. They were a long stretch of exposure, uncertainty, and a kind of forced stillness where the mind keeps replaying what happened behind the closed door.

Karen remembered thinking, "I know that she is dead." She described "mixed emotions" and said the guilt over not being able to save her felt overwhelming. It was also about the pets she could not find. It was about the calculation she had to make between two lives, and the way survival can feel, in the moment, like an accusation.

Eventually, as floodwaters began to recede, the outdoor solar lights clicked on. That small detail matters because it marks a shift from chaos to visibility, from being isolated to being seen. Karen spotted people on the hill above her using a flashlight and called out. They told her to walk toward them, and she clarified that she was on the roof at eye level because of the slope of the hill.

A group returned with a ladder and helped her down. When she reached them, she told them she had not been able to save her mother. The group turned immediately to the next task: trying to enter her mother's room through the patio door. Debris blocked access. The house had become a jam of broken things pressed against openings, as if the flood had packed the rooms tight. Finally, someone broke through a window.

What they found was the outcome Karen had not allowed herself to hope for. Her mother was alive. Her room had a slightly vaulted ceiling, not a large vault, but enough. The mattress had floated up, and an air pocket formed. In that strange physics of disaster, the very elements that should have killed her mother had saved her. Karen was overjoyed.

Karen is clear-eyed about what might have happened if she had tried to get her mother out by herself. She does not romanticize it. She does not imagine a heroic carry through rushing water. She sees the constraints, the risks, the likely ending. "If I had tried to swim with her," Karen said, "one or both of us would have died."

She believed that at best she might have gotten her mother onto the kitchen counter, but even that was unlikely. The flood did not offer the kind of time and space those maneuvers require. The violence of the water turned ordinary caregiving into impossibility. More than 30 hours later, Karen returned to the house with her daughter and others. Returning after a flood is often its own ordeal because the mind expects finality and instead finds evidence that the story is still moving.

As they entered, they heard barking. They looked up and saw Gidget perched on top of the bookshelves, alive. Two days later, Opal was found alive as well. Those survivals did not erase what was lost, but they did what small survivals sometimes do in a landscape of devastation: They reintroduced the possibility that not everything ends in the worst way.

In the days after, Karen tried to sort what mattered from what could be replaced. She did not pretend it was easy. She did not dismiss the shock of walking through wreckage. But she drew a boundary line around what she would allow herself to mourn. "At the end, I am not going to cry over a table or chairs," she said. "Those can be replaced."

That statement carries the quiet ethic that threads through many survivor accounts: the refusal to confuse property with life, even when property is tied to memory and identity. And yet, like so many who made it out, Karen also carried the question that follows survival like a shadow. She struggled with survivor's guilt, knowing others were not as fortunate. "For a brief moment, I was like, why did I survive when they did not?" she said. She did not offer an easy answer. She reached for faith as a way to live with what cannot be solved. "I just have to go back and think God has got another plan for me."

Karen Taylor's story is not only about a flood that entered a driveway and then a home. It is about the split-second sequence when ordinary life becomes unimaginable, when a daughter becomes a rescuer, when the house becomes water, when a roof becomes refuge, and when a decision made for survival becomes a weight carried long after the water recedes.

In the survivors' stories, there are accounts of people being pulled from trees, carried across currents, and found in places no one expected. Karen's story belongs among them because it shows another truth of that morning: Sometimes the most searing acts are not the ones people choose freely but the ones forced on them by physics, time, and love.

Kyle Ames—Rapid Chaos and the Choice To Move

Kyle Ames was jolted awake in the early morning hours of July 4 by something that did not fit any normal definition of "weather." He lived in Ingram, roughly 40 feet above the river, the kind of elevation that can make a person feel insulated from the Guadalupe's moods. Yet that morning water was already pouring into his home. In the first seconds, he was half asleep and in shock, trying to understand how the unthinkable had arrived so quickly and so high. Cottingham wrote Kyle's story for the *Kerrville Daily Times*.

It took him a moment to register the sounds around him. His two sons, seven and nine, were screaming in fear. They were asking the question that cuts through every disaster story: Water was in the house, and they wanted to know whether they were going to die. Darkness cloaked the rooms as the water rose rapidly and the flood pressed in from outside.

Others were in the home as well: his girlfriend, Hannah, and his mother, Cindy. In those frantic minutes, the two women told him the same thing, again and again, because repetition is sometimes the only way a plan forms inside a mind overwhelmed by adrenaline: They needed to get everyone on the roof. Kyle tried to gauge his options, searching for any alternative that might be safer, calmer, more controllable. Then he looked outside and saw his girlfriend's car floating away. It was not merely a detail. It was a signal. The flood was not creeping in. It was taking things.

"I really did not know what was going on at first," Kyle said, "but after a few moments I had to decide what to do." In floods like this, the decision point is rarely dramatic. It is often brutally practical. The water is rising. The exits are shrinking. The seconds are counting down. Kyle opened the front door and began lifting his loved ones up to the roof. He hoisted Hannah first. Then he lifted each of his sons. The work was physical, immediate, and dangerous, but the sequence mattered: Get them up, get them stable, keep moving.

By the time he went back to help his mother, the water in the front yard had reached his neck. The flood had not merely entered the home; it had erased the normal boundaries of inside and outside. Kyle struggled to get his 70-year-old mother up safely, knowing that every second counted. He was trying to do two impossible things at once: remain calm enough to lift and steady her while also feeling the water's force and the urgency in his sons' voices behind him.

And just as he was preparing to climb up himself, his mind snapped to what was still inside. His dog, Remy. His cat, Clover. People who survive disasters will tell you that the mind does not always run in a straight line. It runs in circles: child, parent, exit, phone, keys, pet, back to child, back to parent. In a house filling with water, those circles can kill. Yet Kyle did not hesitate. He turned back inside.

It was pitch black. Furniture hit him as he moved through the rushing water, the house now a violent channel of floating objects. Somewhere inside, Remy was stranded, crying. When Kyle found him, the dog was on a floating mattress, a small and surreal island in a room that had become current. Kyle fought his way to him anyway. "I had furniture hitting me," he said, "but that did not stop him," the newspaper account noted, capturing that split-second posture of refusal that shows up in so many survivor stories: The body says danger, but the heart says keep going.

Clover, the cat, could not be found. In the chaos, there are losses that happen quietly, without ceremony, and then land later with full weight. Kyle got Remy out. Clover was gone. The family huddled together on the roof in the darkness for about an hour, waiting and watching. They listened to the water below and tried to guess what it would do next. During a flood, time on a roof is the long stretch when fear can finally catch up because the immediate tasks are done and there is nothing left but to endure.

Then, as quickly as it had come, the water began to recede. They climbed down and began to assess the damage. Kyle would later describe what others across Kerr County described in different words: The speed was part of the trauma. "It came up so fast and went down so fast," he said. The home was marked physically by the flood, but it was also marked emotionally, by the memory of darkness, screaming children, and the moment he stepped back inside for his dog.

In the aftermath, what surprised Kyle was not only the devastation. It was the community response. In a disaster that scrambled roads, communication, and normal services, support still found its way in. He said he was overwhelmed by the support of the community, an observation that echoes through so many accounts: In Kerr County, people show up. They show up with hands, with trucks, with ladders, with food, with patience, with time. And then, long after the worst night, came the kind of ending that does not erase the story but softens one corner of it.

Nearly two months after the flooding, Clover was found. Kerrville Pets Alive captured the cat, who was in shock, injured, and hesitant to approach. The nonprofit paid for Clover's medical care, including removal of an injured eye. Over time, the cat made a full recovery. In a flood defined by sudden loss, Clover's return was a reminder that survival sometimes unfolds on a different clock and that recovery is rarely a straight line.

The emergency did not announce itself with a gradual escalation. It arrived in darkness, it climbed fast, and it forced ordinary people into decisive action. Kyle did not have time to be brave in any cinematic way. He had time only to move, to lift, to choose, and to go back once more into danger for a living thing depending on him. In the space of minutes, a home became water, a roof became refuge, and a father's first job became keeping his children alive while the river rewrote the rules outside their door.

Coda—the Burgess Family at Blue Oak

Most of what you have read in this section has a common spine: Someone gets out. Someone finds higher ground. Someone is pulled from a current, a window, a roofline, a treetop. Even when the water takes everything else, there is a human being left to tell you what it sounded like, what it smelled like, what it felt like to watch the river turn from a neighbor into a force.

This final story does not fit that spine. It is still part of the same night. It happened in the same corridor of the Guadalupe River, in the same darkness, under the same rain, with the same rising panic and the same hurried decisions. But it ends differently. It ends with what the flood also did, again and again, even when good people ran toward danger and tried to change the outcome.

It ends with a family being taken.

The danger in the Hill Country is how quickly "heavy rain" becomes "flash flood," and how quickly "flash flood" becomes a wall of water that outruns any intention to evacuate. The river does not negotiate. It does not pause so someone can gather a child, find keys, or grab a phone. It moves on its own schedule, and when it comes in force, it collapses the time a family believes it has.

In that chaos was the Burgess family. They were in Kerrville for a simple reason that would be recognizable to any parent: to pick up their daughter from a nearby camp. John Burgess and his wife, Julia, had traveled from their home in Liberty, Texas, with their sons, five-year-old Jack and 21-month-old James, and their family dog. They checked in and settled into what was supposed to be a brief stopover, an ordinary night before an ordinary pickup. There was nothing about their purpose that suggested risk. There was nothing about their plan that suggested they were stepping into the path of a disaster. They were on the island at Blue Oak RV Park.

In normal conditions, the island is the kind of place people choose intentionally. Surrounded by water, it is a small private world. In flood conditions, that same feature becomes a trap, because the river does not simply rise around you. It accelerates. It pulls. It makes distance greater than it looks. It turns a short span into something you cannot cross with a child in your arms.

Bob Canales went toward the island with a flashlight. He was not doing it for credit or cameras or a story to tell later. He was doing it because he could see people in immediate danger and because, in a moment like that, you either move toward the danger, or you live with the knowledge that you did not. He waded into water that was already rising. He could see the family. He could see John holding onto Jack and James as the current surged around them. He could see them close enough to recognize faces and far enough away that the river was already dictating what was possible. Bob yelled the line that has become inseparable from this loss: "Throw me the baby."

It is difficult to read those words and not feel the desperation that sits behind them. There was no elegant plan. There was no equipment and no rope team and no slow, careful sequence of steps. There was only a man in floodwater, reaching toward another man on an island, and a child who might be saved if the laws of motion and grip and chance aligned for a single second.

Bob later said he understood why John did not do it. In that moment, John was not weighing pros and cons the way a calm mind does. He was being asked to let go of his child in a storm, over moving water, to a man fighting the current. If he throws the child and the child slips past the catch, the outcome is immediate and irreversible. If he does not throw the child, that outcome is still possible, still horrifying, but not yet written in ink. That is the kind of decision a disaster forces on a parent: two terrible options, neither of them chosen freely.

Before Bob could get close enough to try again, the current took him. It swept him downstream. He later estimated it carried him nearly a hundred feet until he grabbed a retaining wall at the edge of the campground and held on. That detail matters because it shows the strength of the water even against a grown man who is fighting it with his full will. He pulled himself up, regained footing, and fought his way back. By the time he did, the family was gone.

In his last glimpse, the Burgess family were near a tree in the river. "I remember seeing them standing by that tree," Bob told KERA News, pointing to a large cypress near the middle of the river. "That was the last time I saw that fine young man with his family." That image has the shape of a memory that does not leave. In disasters, people do not remember only what happened. They remember what they last saw. They remember a hand on a branch. They remember a light in the dark. They remember a voice yelling over the roar. Those final images become a private replay, running at the edges of normal life long after the cleanup crews leave.

As the flood moved through Blue Oak, it turned the park into a river of debris. Bob described transformers popping in the darkness. He described cabins on neighboring property slamming together and falling "like dominoes." He described cars floating by with headlights still on, and people inside waving and screaming for help, and then, as he put it, "within a flash, they are gone." There is no heroism in that sentence, only a witness describing the speed at which life disappears when water becomes a moving wall. And then morning came.

Morning after a flood is never what people imagine when they think of daylight. It does not bring relief. It brings inventory. It shows you what was there and what is no longer there. It reveals the spaces where families slept and the emptiness where they should be. It makes the loss visible.

In the days that followed, the fate of the Burgesses became

known. All members of the family were confirmed dead. There is no softer way to write it. There is no sentence structure that makes it less brutal. A mother, a father, and their children, gone. The dog, gone. The flood did not simply interrupt their plan to pick up their daughter. It erased the family that was supposed to arrive.

For Lorena and Bob, and for the people who ran that night, the aftermath did not allow time for grief to unfold in the way it does in quieter tragedies. People needed food. Searchers needed shelter. Volunteers arrived. Donations came in. Power was out. The work of recovery started before the shock had even settled.

At Blue Oak, people ran. They banged on doors. They waded into moving water. Bob yelled "Throw me the baby" because doing nothing was not morally available to him. Lorena moved through the park because she understood that the window for escape was closing. They did what human beings do in the face of imminent harm: They tried to make one more person safe. The flood took the Burgess family anyway.

If this chapter has shown anything, it is that Kerr County is filled with ordinary people doing heroic things. This final story adds the other half of the ledger: Sometimes the heroic thing is attempted and still does not change the outcome. The effort remains real. The intention remains honorable. The loss remains.

And that is why this story is here, at the end, as a coda. It serves as a reminder that the river made no promises that night, and it kept none.

FOUR
THE SYSTEM ACTIVATED

The flood did not begin with sirens. It began with weather radar, red and orange blooms west of Hunt. It began with warnings issued into the night by the NWS. It began with radio broadcasters repeating alerts into largely sleeping communities. And then, at 3:34 a.m., it began with phones ringing.

By the time survivors along the river were clinging to trees, and long before Kerrville's Emergency Operations Center (EOC) was formally established, the county's professional emergency system had already activated. It initiated inside a room filled with headsets, keyboards, and people trained to respond before the scale of a disaster is fully understood.

The Warnings Before the Calls

At 1:14 a.m., the NWS issued its first flash-flood warning for central Kerr County. The language escalated quickly: "life-threatening flash flood." The warning carried the "considerable" damage tag, a designation that automatically triggers FEMA's Integrated Public Alert and Warning System (IPAWS), which in turn pushes Wireless Emergency Alerts (WEAs) to mobile phones.

But the Hill Country is not a technical map. Hunt and the Guadalupe River's North and South Forks corridors sit inside a terrain defined by limestone ridges and deep draws. Cell service is limited even on clear days. Hunt has one primary cell tower covering roughly seventy-nine square miles. When heavy storms degrade already marginal connections, alerts do not move with certainty. Phones must be connected to a participating carrier tower at the moment of broadcast. In a rural valley, during a severe thunderstorm, in the middle of the night, that requirement becomes fragile. Some residents later showed messages proving they received every alert. Others received none.

This gap would become central to public perception. In legislative hearings, critics pointed to a three-hour-and-forty-seven-minute window between the 1:14 a.m. NWS warning and the county's eventual CodeRED alert at 5:01 a.m. The narrative that emerged was simple: Officials were asleep while residents drowned.

The dispatch logs tell a more complicated story.

Before Dawn, Before Scale

At 3:30 a.m. Kerrville Police Sgt. Ben Ledesma was already checking low-water crossings within the city limits. This was standard protocol during heavy rain events. Kerrville's law enforcement monitored known trouble points early, placing barricades when water rose. At nearly the same moment, Dalton Rice was finishing his early-morning run along the Kerrville River Trail. The river, within city limits, still appeared calm. The catastrophic surge was still upstream.

At 3:33 a.m. inside the Kerrville Police Department's 911 center, the Public Safety Answering Point for all of Kerr County, dispatcher Riley Gordon logged the first emergency positioning for water rescue teams in the Ingram and Hunt areas. One minute later, the flood announced itself through human voices. At 3:34 a.m., a caller reported four people on a roof. Three seconds later, another caller reported cars gone and houses flooded. Another call: five people. The entries came in fragments—abbreviations, clipped phrases, incomplete addresses as dispatchers typed as fast as phones rang. The river had reached crisis level west of Hunt.

The First Decision That No One Saw

At 3:40 a.m., Gordon made a decision that would not make headlines. He contacted the Southwest Texas Regional Advisory Council (STRAC), activating a regional mass casualty protocol. This decision did not require direction from an elected official. It did not wait for a disaster declaration. It was based on training and on the volume and tone of calls coming in through his headset. STRAC activation alerts trauma centers across twenty-two counties. It prepares hospitals from San Antonio to the Gulf Coast to receive patients from a mass casualty event. It ensures blood supplies, emergency rooms, and trauma surgeons are mobilized before ambulances arrive.

This occurred before sunrise, before public officials were fully briefed, before Kerrville's unified command structure was established. It was professional instinct under pressure. The log reads: "STRAC contacted." Seconds later: "Task force team in area." In public discourse that followed, few people mentioned that the hospital network was mobilizing before dawn because a dispatcher recognized the pattern of catastrophe.

That one action by Gordon put Peterson Hospital on notice and ready to act. It also put other hospitals ready to act on one of the busiest holidays of the year. That was professionalism, but equally important, it was one person, doing their job, in the middle of an unfolding crisis. That type of action would occur over and over again on July 4 and in the coming days.

While the Phones Rang

Between 1:14 a.m. and 5:01 a.m., the system was besieged. Kerrville's 911 center handled all emergency calls for the county. When River Inn Resort guests dialed, when homes in Hunt called, when drivers on State Highway 39 were trapped, those calls routed first to the same center Kerrville City Manager Rice would soon rely on for situational awareness.

At Camp Mystic, the timeline remains contested. Information laid out in the various lawsuits filed against Camp Mystic suggest that around 2:10 to 2:20 a.m., counselors reported water entering cabins. At 2:57 a.m., night watchman Juenke called the Hunt Volunteer Fire Department (HVFD) chief directly, bypassing 911. That call suggests local recognition that something extraordinary was unfolding upstream. The first documented Camp Mystic call to the county's 911 system appears at approximately 3:53 a.m. (*The Kerrville Daily Times* reported it to have been at 3:57 a.m.); discrepancies remain between Kerrville Police Department logs and Kerr County Sheriff's Office (KCSO) records.

According to The *Kerrville Daily Times*, at 2:08 a.m., 911 had its first call inquiring about road conditions. At 2:53 a.m., 911 received a call from the River Inn Resort in western Kerr County reporting that "water is coming over the riverbanks; dispatch advises the inn visitors of flooding; no evacuation is ordered." At 3:35 a.m., dispatch alerted HVFD for swift water rescue. Eight minutes later the KCSO alerted Kerr County Special Operations for swift water rescue. At 3:41 a.m., a deputy confirmed Schumacher Crossing is "not passable."

By 3:50 a.m. calls were coming in from the community of Casa Bonita that "the community is flooding; dispatch advises callers to seek higher ground." At 4:08 a.m., the KCSO alerted the unincorporated community of Mountain Home for swift water rescue at Casa Bonita.

In one of the most chilling sequences reported by *The Daily Times*, at 4:22 a.m., HVFD requested a CodeRED alert for Hunt. Dispatch acknowledged the request and advised a supervisor would have to approve the request. At 4:23 a.m., a KSCO sergeant approved the CodeRED. Not until 5:01 a.m. did the KCSO issue a CodeRED alert.

Meanwhile, on Highway 39, vehicles were being swept off the highway and into the raging torrent. Mollie Schaffer became one of the first confirmed victims when her SUV was overtaken near River

Inn. The geography between Camp Mystic and River Inn had no escape routes left. Highway 39 was flooded, and the only escape was to get to higher ground. Dispatchers did not yet know the amount of rain or the force and speed of the water roaring down the South Fork. They knew only the pattern: roofs, vehicles, rising water, multiple victims.

Parallel Timelines

At 4:09 a.m. Edward Eastland's Apple Watch registered as submerged. At roughly the same time, in Kerrville, Rice received his official call and began moving toward Louise Hays Park. Inside the 911 center, between 4 a.m. and 5 a.m., call volume spiked dramatically. Reports of people on rooftops, people trapped in vehicles, entire structures gone. At 4:20 a.m., Sheriff Larry Leitha was notified.

The public perception would later focus on who was physically present and who was not. But inside the dispatch center, the apparatus was operating without pause. The distinction between "county" and "city" did not matter to the ringing phones. Calls were answered. Units were dispatched. Rescue teams were positioned where roads still allowed passage. This is the part of disasters that is rarely visible: the early minutes when the system activates before the full narrative is formed.

The Warning Gap—Infrastructure and Assumptions

The most contentious issue after the flood was warning. Or, rather, the lack of a warning. Why did so many residents say they never received alerts? Why did the county not manually issue additional IPAWS notifications? W. B. "Dub" Thomas, Kerr County's emergency management coordinator, testified in a state legislative hearing that more than a dozen automatic IPAWS alerts were triggered by the NWS's warnings. But technology does not override terrain.

WEAs depend on active cell connectivity. Hunt's infrastructure is sparse. Storm conditions degrade signal strength further. In the Hill Country, it is entirely possible for two neighbors to have different outcomes: one phone buzzing repeatedly, another staying silent. The NWS warnings predicted one to three inches of rain, possibly up to seven inches. What forecasters could not determine precisely was where the storm would park and how quickly runoff from upstream ridges would converge. Meteorologist Alan Gerard later explained the core misunderstanding: Flash floods in this terrain are not about rainfall where you stand, but rainfall miles upriver.

The Kerr County Lead reported that Camp Mystic leadership looked at rain gauges and radar apps, trying to predict whether the rain would stop. The river was not responding to the rain at their feet. It was responding to water already descending from beyond their sightline. Warnings were technically correct. Infrastructure was technically functioning. The water's distribution outpaced comprehension.

Quiet Heroism Under Fluorescent Lights

Inside the 911 center, there were no crystal balls. There were only voices and screens. Dispatchers typed fragments: "4 on roof." "Cars gone." "Houses flooded." They dispatched units into areas where roads were already failing. They coordinated with volunteer fire departments. They escalated to regional trauma networks. They did this without knowing the death toll at this point or even if there were fatalities.

They did this without knowing that 135 people would die in a span of hours. Their heroism was procedural. It was calm speech under pressure. It was recognizing patterns and activating protocols early. It was not dramatic. It was disciplined. When Gordon contacted STRAC at 3:40 a.m., he could not know how many victims there would be. He knew only that the call volume and content justified escalation. That decision meant trauma centers were ready before the first full daylight rescue operations were underway.

The River Was Faster

The Guadalupe River moved between Camp Mystic and River Inn faster than rescue boats could launch. It moved homes off piers that were thirty-six feet above normal river levels. It severed escape routes within minutes. Emergency systems are designed to respond. They are not designed to outrun water moving at highway speed.

And yet what the 911 operators did accomplish was contain chaos into process. Between 3:30 and 5 a.m., it turned screams into dispatch codes. It turned fragments into coordinates. It activated layers of response before sunlight revealed the scale. The flood did not begin with sirens. It began with phones ringing and with people trained to answer them.

Emergency systems are built to respond. They are not built to outrun water moving at highway speed. Between 3:30 and 5:30 that morning, the 911 center did what it was trained to do. Phones were answered. Units were dispatched. Volunteer fire departments were alerted. Regional trauma networks were activated. STRAC moved before dawn. Hospitals prepared for patients they had not yet seen. But the river was faster.

It tore down the South and North Forks and Camp Mystic before formal structures could fully align. It severed Highway 39. It lifted homes from foundations that had held for decades. It overwhelmed the difference between rainfall at one address and runoff from miles away. But the record inside the dispatch logs is clear. The system did not sleep. It did not wait for elected officials to assemble. It did not pause for daylight. It activated.

When calls began to stack in fragments; phrases like "four on roof," "cars gone," "houses flooded". Dispatchers translated panic into process. They converted fear into coordinates. They escalated early, not because they knew the final toll, but because training told them the pattern was wrong.

This is the kind of response that rarely becomes narrative. It has no dramatic soundtrack. It unfolds under fluorescent lights, inside a room where the only visible measure of catastrophe is the speed at which keyboards move and phones return to ringing. By the time the sky began to lighten over Kerrville, the emergency apparatus had already been operating for more than two hours.

Dalton Rice—Inside the First Hours

Rice did not wake up on the morning of July 4 expecting to manage the most consequential disaster in Kerrville's modern history.

Years in the military, time in special operations, work as a firefighter and paramedic, and later in hospital and public administration had shaped a rhythm that did not include sleeping late. Between three and five in the morning was his normal window to run, think, and quietly check on the city before the day officially began. On July 4, with a major holiday event scheduled at Louise Hays Park and more than twenty thousand visitors expected, that habit took on added purpose. The river trail along the Guadalupe was one of his favorite routes, a six-mile stretch that demonstrated Kerrville's relationship with the water. He wanted to see how the setup was progressing.

It was raining lightly to moderately when he ran that morning. Nothing unusual. The river was within its banks. At that moment, it looked like it always did, calm enough to host fireworks and families in a few hours. Less than an hour later, that reality would no longer exist.

By the time Rice's phone rang at 4:59 a.m., the river had already torn through the North and South Forks. the system had already been awake for more than an hour. Phones had been ringing inside the Kerrville Police Department's 911 center since 3:34 am Dispatchers had logged reports of people on rooftops, vehicles swept away, houses flooding. STRAC had been activated. Rescue units were moving toward Ingram and Hunt in darkness. The emergency apparatus was no longer theoretical. It was engaged.

Rice did not yet know the scale. Less than an hour earlier, he had been running along the Kerrville River Trail, passing through Louise Hays Park as he often did before sunrise. The rain was steady but not alarming. The Guadalupe River, inside the city limits, appeared contained. The river he saw was not the river that had already torn through the North and South Forks.

When the call came, the message was brief: flooding at the park. Equipment being washed away. However, the situation was unclear. He dressed and moved. By 5:43 a.m., he was meeting Fire Chief Eric Maloney near Louise Hays Park. In the span of that hour, the river had transformed. A pavilion that had stood dry during his run was now submerged to its roofline. Water moved with force across ground that had been stable minutes earlier. The speed of the change mattered. It would define everything that followed.

There is a moment in any disaster when leadership shifts from observation to commitment. For Rice, that moment arrived not with spectacle, but with recognition. This was different. He had seen hurricanes. He had worked disasters. He understood what rapid escalation felt like. But he recognized the pattern unfolding that morning did not resemble a slow, predictable rise. It resembled acceleration.

He and the fire chief barely cleared the park before water cut off access. From there, Rice moved directly to the police department to establish a command post. At 5:56 a.m., Kerrville formally stood up its initial command center. By then, the phones had been ringing for more than two hours. A unified command would follow. Disaster declarations would be signed. Elected officials would arrive.

Public hearings later focused on absence, who was at a lake house, who was home sick, who was notified when the dispatch logs reveal presence. Presence in a room where phones rang continuously. Presence in decisions made in seconds. Presence in the quiet understanding that something unprecedented was unfolding.

Rice stepped into what he later called mission mode, not as the first actor in the system but as the one responsible for aligning it. The dispatchers had translated panic into process. Field units were already navigating flooded corridors. Hospitals were preparing for patients. What remained was coordination: policy, authority, resource allocation, and the long arc of response.

What Rice did not yet know, and what would only later be fully reconstructed, was that a wall of water had already torn through the upper reaches of the South Fork watershed. Between Camp Mystic and River Inn, heavy flooding was underway by approximately 3:06 a.m. Video later confirmed that damage was already significant on the west side of town while Kerrville itself still appeared relatively untouched. That upstream surge, moving at extraordinary speed, would reach the city with little warning and almost no margin for reaction.

Kerrville law enforcement had begun monitoring low-water crossings at 2:42 a.m., following established inclement weather protocols. Those crossings never triggered alarms. That was not a failure of vigilance. It was a reflection of how this flood behaved differently from every model to which the city was accustomed.

By 4:54 a.m., a patrol supervisor drove west to the bridge over Bear Creek Road on his own initiative. There, he saw vehicles already in moving water, eastbound. He immediately ordered evacuation of the area and notified dispatch to contact the city manager. That decision, made without waiting for instructions, marked the first confirmed sighting of the advancing wall of water. Individual judgment, exercised early, would become one of the quiet through lines of the response.

From that point forward, events accelerated at a pace that overwhelmed conventional timelines. Between midnight and 3 a.m., Kerrville's Public Safety Answering Point (PSAP) received fourteen calls. Between 3 and 4 a.m., thirty-five. From 4 to 5 a.m., two hundred eighteen. From 5 to 6 a.m., two hundred thirty. The spike told its own story. Whatever was happening was happening everywhere at once.

Later modeling would estimate flow rates between nine hundred thousand and 1.6 million gallons per second. The *Kerrville Daily Times* reported that more than 100 billion gallons of water fell on Kerr County on July 4. By comparison, Niagara Falls sees an average of 75 billion gallons across three falls. In some stretches, the water moved at up to twenty miles per hour. The river gauge nearest to Camp Mystic registered a water height of 37.52 feet. In bends and constrictions, projections suggested walls of water reaching thirty feet and, in extreme cases, far higher. This was not a river rising. It was a system overwhelming itself.

Rice did not need to see it to understand it. He had been in disasters before. He had grown up in hurricane country. The sensory cues were familiar. The sound alone told him enough. Something in him narrowed and steadied, the emotional register dropping back as his mind moved forward into the work of decisions. There would be time later to take in what had been lost. For now, his attention fixed on a single, practical question: how to manage what was still unfolding.

By early morning, Rice had notified the mayor, Joe Herring Jr., and the city council. A disaster declaration was prepared and signed at 8:35 a.m., delayed only by a mundane but revealing obstacle, a printer that would not cooperate in the middle of chaos. The declaration formalized what was already happening operationally. Kerrville was in a disaster, and it needed help.

Within hours, communication was underway with the Texas Division of Emergency Management. State officials, including the lieutenant governor, arrived quickly. By 6 p.m. July 4, a unified EOC had been established at the Hill Country Youth Event Center, bringing together city, county, and state partners under the Incident Command System. What began as a small command post had become a coordinated response structure in less than a day.

Under unified command, no single individual ran the response. Instead, executive leaders from law enforcement, fire, emergency management, and state agencies established shared objectives and operational periods. Policy decisions were separated from operations. Rice and the sheriff focused on governance, communication, and strategic direction, while operational teams executed search, rescue, and recovery tasks. This division allowed the system to function under pressure without collapsing into confusion.

Rice spent much of those first forty-eight hours in the policy space, issuing regular updates to elected officials, setting management objectives, and ensuring that operations were resourced without political interference. He was acutely aware of the balance required when senior state officials arrived. Their presence could bring resources and authority, but it could also disrupt operations if not carefully managed. Rice's job was to make sure the former occurred without the latter.

Search and recovery dominated the early days. Texas Department of Public Safety and Texas Task Force One led ground operations, supported by National Guard aviation assets. Debris management emerged almost immediately as a parallel crisis. In Rice's formulation, every disaster produces multiple disasters layered on top of one another. In Kerrville, debris was not merely an environmental problem. It was a human one.

The force of the water had destroyed vehicles and structures. Debris fields became potential grave sites. Removal could not proceed until systematic searches were completed using human remains detection dogs. Complicating matters further, much of the debris lay on private property. Entry permits had to be secured. Property rights had to be respected even as urgency pressed in from all sides. Early debris management focused less on removal than on control, cataloging, and clearance for search.

At the same time, the city faced an influx of volunteers. More than 18,000 people would ultimately contribute over 130,000 hours of service. Their generosity was essential. It was also a risk. Uncoordinated volunteers working near a volatile river created the potential for secondary rescues. Incident-within-incident planning became necessary as rain returned and water levels fluctuated. Preventing additional loss became as important as responding to what had already occurred.

As the immediate rescue phase gave way to recovery, Rice began organizing the response in his own mind into three tracks: search and recovery, economic impact, and rebuilding. That mental framework shaped his next decisions. By the afternoon of Saturday, July 5, economic recovery was already underway. The city's Economic Development staff, led by Kelly Hagemeier, working with Todd Bock of the Kerr County Economic Development Corporation, was sent into the field identify struggling businesses and immediate needs. This work was essential: Small businesses would not survive prolonged uncertainty.

That effort evolved into a Long Term Recovery Group, deliberately housed outside direct government control. Rice believed strongly that long-term recovery should be community led, supported by government but not dominated by it. Case management, housing, mental health services, and unmet needs were organized through partnerships among nonprofits, faith-based organizations, and business leaders.

Throughout the response, Rice emphasized transparency. He viewed public trust as an operational asset, not a communications slogan. Regular updates, early notification to families before press briefings, and consistent information flow were treated as integral to the response itself. Faith-based organizations became central partners, providing shelter, food, counseling, reunification spaces, and quiet support for families of the missing. Rice described them as "quiet heroes," present day and night, absorbing trauma they had not signed up to carry.

Only later, when the river receded and the scale of destruction became visible, did Rice allow himself to fully see what had happened. He returned to Louise Hays Park before dawn the following morning. The river was lower. The damage was unmistakable. That was when the weight of the event finally settled in, after the system had stabilized enough to allow reflection.

By then, Kerrville was no longer simply responding to a flood. It was navigating grief, recovery, and beginning the long work of rebuilding. Rice understood that the institutional response would be scrutinized, debated, and second-guessed. He accepted that as part of leadership. What mattered to him was that decisions were made in good faith, grounded in available information, and executed with discipline.

What happened in those first hours was not dramatic in the way history often prefers. It was procedural, disciplined, and sustained under pressure that would have broken less prepared systems. Inside the 911 center, at the command table with Rice, and behind the wheel of school buses moving children toward safety, decisions were made that carried risk and consequence. No one paused to claim valor. Yet taken together, those actions formed a pattern of response that can only be described as quietly heroic, a reminder that in moments of crisis, people show up for their community not because they are asked to be heroes but because showing up is the work itself.

There is a temptation to call such people heroes and leave it at that. The word is easy, clean, and comforting. But to do so risks placing them at a distance, as if what they did required something rare or unreachable. The truth is both more ordinary and more profound. They were trained professionals, public servants, neighbors, people doing the jobs they had chosen and prepared for. What made the night extraordinary was not that heroes appeared, but that ordinary people stepped fully into extraordinary roles when the river demanded it. Perhaps the better description is this: they were not heroes by title, but they did heroic things.

The flood exposed the limits of prediction and the necessity of judgment. It demonstrated how quickly upstream events at Camp Mystic and the South and North Forks could cascade into a city with almost no warning. It also revealed the strength of systems built on trust, initiative, and collaboration. In those first hours, Kerrville did not wait to be told what to do. People acted, reported, adjusted, and adapted.

Rice did not frame his role as heroic. He framed it as responsibility. When the Guadalupe River changed, so did his day, his city, and his understanding of what being a leader requires when the plan no longer fits the problem. That lesson, forged in the dark hours before dawn, would shape Kerrville's recovery long after the water was gone.

FIVE
SCHOOL BUS DRIVERS ANSWERED THE CALL

The Call

When the call came, it was from Camp La Junta co-owner Katie Fineske to Dr. Brent Ringo, superintendent of Kerrville Independent School District (KISD), at 5:25 p.m. on July 4. It was not a formal alert. There was no siren, no emergency broadcast, no scripted instruction. Fineske said the boys camp's buildings were destroyed, but all 400 campers were safe and needed evacuation before sundown. The message moved the way messages often move in Kerrville, through people who knew one another, through phones already filled with familiar names. Camps upriver needed help as well. Children needed to be moved. Buses were needed and they were needed now.

Ringo immediately coordinated the district's emergency response, sending a text message asking anyone who was qualified to drive a bus to respond to this urgent request. Within 15 minutes, drivers, coaches, principals, and administrators responded. More than a dozen volunteers showed up in minutes to the KISD Bus Barn, with the district's transportation team mobilizing within 30 minutes of the initial call for help.

For the drivers, the request was simple and their responses direct. But while the request, *Come to the bus barn. Be ready to drive*, was direct, it was also incomplete. No specific word on the assignment. No one described road conditions. No one explained what the camps looked like. No one could say how many children were waiting or how long the drive would take. There was no guarantee of safety, only the assumption that if the call was being made, the situation was already serious.

One by one, the drivers made the same decision. They stopped what they were doing. They grabbed keys. They left their houses and drove toward the bus barn. Not because they were told they had to. Because they understood they were needed. Don Randall, a KISD bus driver, looked to his wife and said, "I am going." She responded, "Yes, you have to."

Even employees who did not have commercial driver's licenses (CDLs) jumped into their cars to help shuttle people safely to the buses. "Our superintendent, Dr. Ringo, hopped in his truck," Ken Noles, KISD's director of transportation, told KHOU-TV (Channel 11). Amanda Nicholson, a teacher and volleyball coach, said, "It didn't matter what we were being called in for, we just knew we needed to help."

Tivy High School Principal Rick Sralla did not start July 4 thinking he would be back behind the wheel. He certainly did not when he helped set up the high school campus as a working hub for first responders and swift water rescue teams arriving from across Texas. He was there handling the unglamorous necessities that make response possible, arranging warm showers, sleeping space, and a place to stage. For these rescue and recovery teams. Then the call came in that drivers with CDLs were needed. Sralla had kept his bus license from his earlier coaching years, and he did what Kerrville educators have done for generations when the moment demands it: He stepped into the operational lane and went.

The Coordinator

Shelby Balser, then assistant superintendent of human resources and administration and former principal at Tivy High School, learned early that morning that the day was not unfolding normally. As part of KISD's emergency operations structure, she had already been moving through campuses, preparing facilities in case first responders needed staging areas. That was familiar territory. That was part of the plan. The buses were not.

The request came indirectly, as so many things did that day, through relationships rather than protocols. Camp owners reached out. Roads were compromised. FEMA buses were not going to arrive before dark. Someone asked a question that had not been asked before: Could the school district do this?

Balser did not have a playbook for evacuating summer camps by school bus during an unfolding flood. What she had was a transportation system, a group of drivers, and a narrow window of daylight. She reached out to the transportation coordinator. Messages went out. Coaches with CDLs were contacted. The ask was modest in language and enormous in implication: If you can come, come. As the responses came back, Balser began to understand what was happening, not through reports or dashboards but by watching people arrive.

Another who answered the call was Aubrey Pruitt, a KISD teacher and coach who only that week had qualified for her CDL. She described the morning of July 4 as long and uncertain. "It was kind of a long morning of not really knowing what to do," she said, as news of the flood unfolded across Kerrville and the surrounding Hill Country. Like others in the district, she watched events escalate without clarity about where she would be needed. By evening, the call had come. Faculty and staff were being asked to drive buses to evacuate stranded campers. As a coach, a CDL was required, but she had not yet transported students. When she arrived at the bus barn, she believed she would ride with another driver. Instead, she was asked if she could drive. "It was no time to be nervous," she recalled.

The Convergence

At the bus barn, distinctions that mattered on ordinary days dissolved quickly. Veteran drivers parked next to those with only limited experience. Coaches arrived alongside full-time transportation staff. Titles and tenure did not matter once engines were running.

There was no roll call. No speeches. No motivational framing. Drivers checked buses, climbed into seats, and waited. Some asked quiet questions. Others said very little. Everyone understood that once the buses rolled out, turning back would not be simple.

Balser moved among them, answering what she could and acknowledging what she could not. She did not pretend to know more than she did. No one that afternoon truly understood what lay ahead. What they did understand was this: Children were waiting upriver, and darkness was coming. When the keys turned and the engines started, something shifted. The decision was no longer abstract. Whatever doubts existed were now behind them. They were committed.

The Road West

Sralla, driving Bus No. 6, was the first one out of the KISD Bus Barn. He was driving as the lead bus. The road from Ingram Dam toward Shoemaker Crossing was familiar to him in the way the Guadalupe River is familiar to so many families here: a place of summer routine and Hill Country beauty. That familiarity made the drive harder, not easier. Sralla said, "It hurts your heart, to see a stretch of river you have reveled in as beautiful, now absolutely decimated." It was the debris of cars up in trees, pieces of houses along the Guadalupe River, torn ground, and the visible "carnage of what the river did." The distance was not long, but the effort of taking it in was hard.

The drive toward Hunt did not feel dramatic at first. Traffic slowed. Law enforcement checkpoints appeared. Drivers rolled down windows, explained why they were there, and waited for permission to pass. As the traffic coordinator, Balser had to get off her bus and explain what they were doing and where they were going to multiple law enforcement personnel, who had set up roadblocks on Highway 39, the road into Hunt. But the farther west they went, the more the landscape changed.

By the time they reached Ingram Dam, the scene became one of utter destruction. Randall described it as "surreal," adding, "I've never seen anything like it in my life." Balser said, "It was awful. For two reasons: One, you had a lot of people just kind of walking around dazed. They were trying to move things because they knew something needed to be done. These are clearly people whose homes were there, people they knew were there."

"[Then] you had another group of people who had come out to take pictures and record the events," she continued. "I remember being on the bus thinking how devastated I was by that. You do not understand, we cannot find people, and you are out here videoing with your phone."

The convoy moved west toward Hunt under difficult conditions. Roads were damaged, debris scattered, and the scale of destruction grew increasingly apparent the farther they traveled. Pruitt did not frame herself as a rescuer or first responder. She simply stepped into a role that needed to be filled. Later, reflecting on the experience, district leaders acknowledged how raw the memory remained for many of them. "No one really knew what we were going to see," Balser said. Pruitt was among those who went forward without that knowledge.

It looked like a war zone. No electricity. Houses wiped through. Things so high up in trees you could not imagine how they got there. And the water was gone. That was the part that was hard to process: The water was gone, and you were standing there looking at what was left of people's lives.

You could see they were spray-painting, counting numbers, putting X's and orange marks. At the time, the drivers did not fully understand what all that meant. Later, they realized what they had driven past and recovery workers were marking sites of the deceased.

Debris lined the roads. Guardrails were bent or missing. In places, the shoulder had simply disappeared, washed away by water that had already receded. The Guadalupe River, normally a presence people admired or ignored, had become something else entirely, an absence that left damage in its wake.

Drivers began to realize that the roads themselves could not be trusted. Pavement dipped unexpectedly. Mud covered sections that should have been dry. At times, buses slowed to a crawl, not because anyone told them to but because instinct demanded it.

Inside the buses, the drivers' focus narrowed. Hands tightened on steering wheels. Eyes stayed fixed on the road ahead. Radios crackled intermittently, but there was little conversation. Each driver was managing the same calculation in real time, how to keep moving without putting the bus and the people it would soon carry at risk. The buses communicated with each other about obstacles along the route as they made their way through the flood-damaged terrain.

The drivers were about to reach one of the most dangerous and terrifying parts of the road. Schumacher Crossing is one of the most famous swimming holes on the Guadalupe River. It was surrounded by beautiful thirty-foot-high, hundred-year-old Cypress trees that provided a canopy of shade over the river. But on this day the trees were gone, the bridge was destroyed, and the placid swimming hole was still a raging torrent. "It was worse than the video shows" Balser said. "The road had been washed out in places. We were down to one lane. You could tell it might not be stable. There were deputies and first responders everywhere. We were going slow."

As the lead bus, Sralla had to attempt to pass Schumacher Crossing first. He said that the landscape at the Crossing there did not "match his memory." The asphalt was patchy and torn, the road forced detours, and gravel was piled where it had never been. Because he was the first bus, he also took the first risk, relying on the people working the crossing and trusting the route would hold. He described it plainly: "You puckered up a little bit." The crossing was a decision point, one the drivers had to make in real time so the rescue could move forward.

When Randall reached Schumacher Crossing, the pavement was no longer pavement in the way a driver expects it to be. "It was the roughest road I've ever driven on a bus," he said. Randall had driven all over Kerr County and far beyond. He had handled back roads, weathered highways, hurricane corridors. None of that compared to this stretch.

The surface was broken into ruts and patches three to six inches deep in places. The bus did not glide across the bridge. It undulated, literally rolling, rocking side to side over shattered pavement, dipping into holes, climbing back out again. Randall eased it forward slowly, creeping rather than driving. "We were just going, 'Wow. This is crazy.'"

Authorities had deemed the bridge stable at that point, and the buses followed one another carefully across. There was no rush. No attempt to power through. The damage required patience. Even so, nothing about it felt normal. Randall later said he had seen hurricanes, huge wildfires and tornado damage, but the force of what the water had done there—lifting vehicles, stripping trees, tearing pavement apart—was unlike anything in his experience.

Schumacher Crossing was not dramatic in the way headlines make something dramatic. It was worse than that. It was methodical. It was unstable. It required discipline. And the only way through it was slow, deliberate movement toward children waiting beyond it. "It took us a long time. Traffic. Checkpoints. The terrain itself. It was slow and deliberate. And by the time we got there, it was getting dark."

From one bus, it looked manageable. From another, it looked like a mistake. Drivers watched one another carefully. They saw how far a bus drifted before correcting. They noted where tires slipped and where they held. No one rushed. No one panicked. But everyone understood that a misjudgment here would not be minor. At least one bus moved farther than intended, its front end edging into a space that felt unstable. For a moment, there was no room for error, no place to turn, no way to accelerate out of trouble. Then the bus corrected, and it held. No one cheered. No one spoke. The crossing was behind them, but the lesson remained: This road was not forgiving.

Then came Hunt. Randall looked for the familiar landmarks of the Hunt Store and the post office. Both were gone. The post office was completely gone, wiped off its foundation. The Hunt Store was devastated. His heart sank as he thought about what that loss would mean for the community that depended on those buildings. "When you think about it," he reflected, "those things are built stout, and it was gone." The sheer power of the water, capable of erasing structures that solid, was what struck him most.

As the buses continued toward Camp La Junta, the scene remained the same: homes along the river torn apart, trees bent and debarked, debris piled in unnatural patterns. Randall knew that once the boys were loaded onto the bus, they would see all of it for the first time on the drive back. The devastation was not hidden behind fences or tree lines; it lay exposed along Highway 39. He realized he would need to prepare them for what they were about to witness because there was no way to soften what the river had done to Hunt. When they arrived at the camps, the urgency of the situation became clear.

Having previously visited Camp La Junta, Sralla was familiar with the area but was struck by the extent of the damage he encountered. As quoted by KHOU 11, he said, "We didn't know what we were in for. I can remember bus drivers calling, and it was hard for them to contain what they were seeing, and they picked up the microphone to the other buses and said, 'God be with us. This is bad.' The sheer devastation—it was very sobering. We had seen floods before. Not to this magnitude."

"Some of the boys were in their pajamas. They were holding teddy bears. They had what they could grab with them in the middle of the night to get on the bus." Sralla noted it was a day he will never forget, especially watching many children get their first look at the devastation while on the school buses. He told us every single time a mother came to pick up her child was an emotional experience.

The Weight of What They Were Driving Toward

As the buses pushed farther into Hunt, the evidence of loss

became unavoidable. Homes stood open where walls had once been. Objects that did not belong together lay tangled in trees. Spray-painted markings began to appear, the quiet language of search and rescue already at work. Some drivers later said it felt like passing through a place where life had been interrupted mid-sentence. Others struggled to find words at all.

What they shared was a growing awareness that whatever they had expected when they left Kerrville, this was not it. And still they drove on. Because ahead of them were children who had been waiting all day. Children who had been moved in the dark. Children who would soon step onto those buses and trust the adults inside to get them somewhere safer. The drivers did not yet know what that would feel like. They only knew they were close.

THE CAMPS
La Junta

Camp La Junta was the first pickup stop. The turn into the camp comes before the road carries on from Schumacher Crossing into Hunt. By the time the buses reached the camps, daylight was thinning. The drivers had already passed through neighborhoods that no longer looked like neighborhoods, crossed roads that could not be trusted, and seen enough devastation to understand that it was not temporary or isolated. At Camp La Junta, the waiting was visible before anyone stepped off a bus.

In Sralla's coaching years, he had been in and out of the camp for athletic end-of-year functions, and he knew the entrances and exits. And yet as he turned in, the empty bus already sliding in mud, the first sight was not buildings or cabins but lines of boys waiting. They were wet and muddy, some without shoes, carrying what they could hold: blankets and small personal items. "Some of the boys were in their pajamas. They were holding teddy bears. They had what they could grab with them in the middle of the night to get on the bus," Sralla recalled. They stood with counselors, organized in lines, confused about the full extent of what they had just lived through, and waiting for an adult to tell them where to go next.

Kids were still arriving from higher ground in the backs of trucks and trailers feeding into the rendezvous point. Sralla and another bus driver relayed conditions by radio, giving the drivers behind them a better picture of the road and the scene in camp.

By the time the buses reached the entrance, the drivers had already absorbed miles of devastation; uprooted trees, broken pavement, waterlines etched high into the hillsides. But inside the camp, the destruction was less visible than the disruption. The boys were accounted for, but they had no power, no running water, and no way out before dark. Ringo later described the scene as "very heart-wrenching," recalling children "in T-shirts and shorts, the clothes they slept in, and no shoes." The drivers did not linger on the image. They opened the bus doors and began the work.

The boys boarded in small groups, counselors guiding them forward. There were no loud conversations, no horseplay, no bus chatter that usually fills the aisle. The atmosphere was controlled, almost subdued. Shock and resilience existed side by side. A few boys quietly said "thank you" as they stepped up the stairs. Others climbed aboard without speaking at all. Drivers counted heads, checked seats, and moved deliberately. Nicholson would later say of that day, "That's all you needed ... is to be able to drive a bus." The task at La Junta was straightforward: load, account, move. Yet the vulnerability of the moment—bare feet on metal steps, boys waiting without knowing how long the ride would be—was unmistakable.

Before rolling back toward Kerrville, Sralla spoke to the boys in the tone of an educator who knows that order can be a form of comfort. He told them to "act right on the bus," but he also told them the truth: They were going to see something, and they were going to remember it. He asked them to sit down, look out the windows, and reach out if they had questions or felt overwhelmed. The ride back carried an even-keel quiet that sounded like shock, with pockets of reaction when the boys saw what the river had moved, mangled, and deposited. In that hush, Sralla heard fragments of what some of them had endured, including stories of kids sheltering in rafters. They were tired, wet, scared, and ready to get out.

The final mile was not geography, it was reunification. The

buses rendezvoused at First Presbyterian Church in Kerrville, guided by Colton Tucker, a school employee with longtime experience at La Junta. Parents were already gathering, and when Sralla pulled in as the first bus, the emotion came fast. He watched parents running up sidewalks, peering through the bus door, scanning faces, panicking because they did not yet know. Once the bus emptied, the hardest part was not the chaos, it was seeing the parents who still had not found their child. Sralla said it was "quite possibly one of the most difficult things" the bus drivers were involved in.

No one needed to tell the drivers to speak gently. Many did not say much at all. Others repeated a single sentence over and over, *You are safe now,* as if repetition itself could make it true faster.

Camp Mystic

At the staging area for Camp Mystic, the girls were arriving at Hunt United Methodist Church by whatever transport remained available. Pruitt described picking them up at the church where they were being brought in by military vehicles, "covered in mud, holding hands." Many were still in the clothes they had slept in. The scene was not chaotic but heavy. Counselors kept the girls together. Drivers opened doors and guided them on board. Pruitt moved from seat to seat as needed, focused on the same mission as the others: getting them to the reunification centers.

By the time Nicolson reached the girls from Camp Mystic, the devastation along the road had already left its mark. But like Sralla, what Nicholson remembers most clearly is not the broken pavement or the debris in trees. It is the line of girls waiting to board. "All we knew is that we had a bunch of young girls holding each other's hands, waiting to get on our buses." Many were still in pajamas. Some were barefoot. Some clutched what little they had been able to grab in the middle of the night. They boarded quietly, staying close to one another, counselors guiding them forward.

Inside the bus, something shifted. The space, though enclosed and rattling over damaged roads, became steadier than the world outside. At first, the ride was somber. Through the windows the girls watched the devastation along the riverbanks as they passed by. Then, softly at first, they began to sing. Camp songs. Christian songs. The kind of songs they had sung days earlier around campfires and at Vespers. The singing was not loud or triumphant. It was a way to hold themselves together. Nicholson drove and listened, aware that the bus had become more than transportation. It had morphed into a small moving place of reassurance.

The return to Kerrville did not end the weight of the night. At reunification, the girls stepped down one by one into waiting arms. Nicholson watched relief break across faces as children ran to parents. But not every parent found what they were searching for. "It was extremely difficult to have some of those parents ask you when everybody, everybody got off your bus, 'Is that it?' Because they didn't see their child." The question lingered even after the buses emptied. It was not something a driver could answer.

The drivers did not always have answers. What they had was motion. Forward motion, away from the river.

The Return

If the drive out to Hunt required concentration, the drive back required endurance. The buses were heavier now, not just with passengers but with responsibility. Drivers watched the road and the children at the same time, glancing in mirrors, listening for changes in tone, trying to anticipate fear before it turned into panic. Outside, the devastation became more visible. This was the first time many of the children saw what had happened beyond their camps. Drivers noticed faces pressed to windows, hands tightening in laps.

Some chose to narrate the road ahead, pointing out what could be seen and what should be avoided. Others let silence do the work. When the buses reached the reunification sites, the work became still harder. Children were processed carefully. Medical checks. Photographs. Wristbands. Movement from one location to another. Each step was necessary. None of it was quick. Parents waited. The question came again and again, sometimes quietly, sometimes not. *Is that it?* For the drivers, this was the moment that stayed.

Several said later that they could manage the roads, the debris, even the fear of crossing unstable bridges. What they struggled with was standing still while a bus emptied and knowing that for some parents, the child they were looking for would not step down.

The Witness, Again

Balser rode the first bus in and the last bus out that day. In between, she coordinated drivers, cleared checkpoints, and helped move the operation forward without ever pretending it was under control. Later, when she reflected on it, her words were not about success or failure. They were about responsibility.

She spoke about not knowing, about asking people to go without fully understanding what they would see or carry afterward. She did not distance herself from that reality. She accepted it. And when she searched for meaning in what followed, she returned to something simple, something that had surfaced again and again in the days after the flood. When things are hard, she said, you look for the helpers. They were there. They came in buses.

The KISD bus drivers recognized for driving campers out of Hunt in July 2025 were Vince Clark, Micky Pelletier, Don Randall, Geri White, Hal Poorman, Thomas Gough, Monica Umfress, Jeff Kubacek, Chris Ramirez, Aubrey Pruitt, Amanda Nicholson, Rick Sralla, and Shelby Balser. These individuals are credited with rescuing hundreds of campers from various camps, including Camp La Junta and Camp Mystic.

Nicholson said the community would never be the same after this tragedy, but they would get through it. "The saying we use for our school district is TFND: *Tivy Fight Never Dies*." After July 4, she revised it to *Tivy Faith Never Dies*. "It's just something we've all learned and grown to live our life on. We leaned on each other, and nobody hesitated" she said. "It didn't matter if they were from the school district, if they lived in this area, it didn't matter how old they were, how capable, what they had; everybody jumped in. And it was really amazing to see this community just pick each other up.

"... We were just fortunate to be a tool that was able to help get these kids out. I've never seen destruction like that in my lifetime, so just driving through was, there's just no words," Nicholson said.

Sralla said the trauma was clear on the faces of many of the children. "You could tell some of the younger kids, they were still thinking about what had happened the night before. They had been reliving the stories of the water in their cabins," he said. Bus driver Poorman added, "I stuck my hand out, and I said, 'Come on, on board, you're safe. I got you. Go back and find you a place to sit.' And I did that with every child that got on board my bus."

"We were humbled to be asked to help," Ringo had said of the call that set the buses in motion. By the time the convoy reached the reunification sites in Kerrville, the first phase of rescue had been completed not by sirens or flashing lights, but by steady hands on steering wheels and a line of children delivered safely home. Several drivers later said the same thing, in different words: This was the moment when the bus stopped being a vehicle and became something else.

On July 5, Sralla went back to his duties at Tivy High School and went back to his other response role, helping host incoming rescue resources, including water rescue boats and cadaver dogs. He did not frame his part as exceptional. He framed it as community. In tragedy, people rose to the occasion, and not only the bus drivers: educators, students, parents, neighbors. He called it "the silver lining," a glimpse of kindness that "restores your faith in humanity," even as he anticipated the later season of "finger pointing" that so often follows. And he closed with the one point he wanted on the record: He was glad the bus drivers were getting their names out there because "they deserve it."

"I picked up girls from a church from Camp Mystic. They were coming in on Army trucks covered in mud, holding hands," Pruitt said. Poorman said the hardest moments came when some parents realized their children were missing. "When that last child, when that last child got off that bus and those parents were standing out there and their child wasn't one of them, and the anguish … and those parents, the wives that buried their head in the husband's chest because their daughter wasn't there."

Noles, who was out of town on July 4th, said, “I’ve had the opportunity to review some of the footage and what you see is girls coming out hand in hand linked all the way onto this bus. You watch them get on to the buses. As they’re heading back into town they’re singing their Christian camp songs.” The emotional impact of the rescue mission has stayed with the transportation team. Noles noted that district leaders helped quickly mobilize the buses for the emergency response.

“We’ll never look at Bus 6 the same again,” Noles, the district’s transportation director, said, referring to the lead bus used in the rescue, driven by Sralla. He praised his team’s performance during the crisis, emphasizing how the bus drivers went beyond their normal duties to help those in need. “You can no longer say ‘I’m just a bus driver.’ Because that day, on July 4, and the next day, on July 5, you were a comforter; you were a rescuer. In my mind they’re all heroes,” Noles said. When asked about his pride in the team’s response, Noles was emphatic: “I’ve never been so proud of a team.”

In the days that followed, the buses returned to the barn. The drivers returned to their routines. The community began the long work of naming loss and absorbing what had happened. For the drivers, the experience did not end when the engines shut off. Some avoided certain roads for a while. Others found themselves replaying moments they had not fully registered at the time. Many said little at all.

What they shared was not pride so much as certainty. If the call came again, they would answer it. Not because they wanted recognition. Not because they believed themselves heroic.

But because that is what people in Kerrville and Kerr County do when the moment demands it.

The KISD bus drivers rescued 900 summer campers from western Kerr County and brought them safely back to Kerrville.

PHOTO GALLERY

A flood-ravaged home in Ingram, up river from Kerrville

Photo: Kerr County Lead / Courtesy of Louis Amestoy

Flood waters washing over the Francisco Lemos Bridge in downtown Kerrville on July 4

Photo: Kerr County Lead / Courtesy of Louis Amestoy

Louise Hays Park in Kerrville, July 4

Photo: Kerr County Lead / Courtesy of Louis Amestoy

The floodwaters uprooted large trees along the riverbanks and carried them downstream

Photo: Kerr County Lead / Courtesy of Louis Amestoy

The flood affected pets as well. Hundreds of cats, dogs, and other animals were rescued.

Photo: Kerr County Lead / Courtesy of Louis Amestoy

Search and Resuce Teams at Guadalupe Park in Kerrville

Photo: Kerr County Lead / Courtesy of Louis Amestoy

Water continue to pour over the dam at Nimitz Lake the day after the flood

Photo: Kerr County Lead / Courtesy of Louis Amestoy

Search and resuce Teams at Flat Rock Dam, south of Kerrville

Photo: Kerr County Lead / Courtesy of Louis Amestoy

Kerr County residents showed support for victims, their families, and displaced surivors

Photo: Kerr County Lead / Courtesy of Louis Amestoy

Flood damage Kerr County

Photo: Kerr County Lead / Courtesy of Louis Amestoy

Food and water donations pour in for victims.

Photo: Kerr County Lead / Courtesy of Louis Amestoy

A first responder amid flood debris on the still swollen Guadalupe days after the flood

Photo: Kerr County Lead / Courtesy of Louis Amestoy

Crosses for victims were erected at Nimitz Lake dam

Photo: Kerr County Lead / Courtesy of Louis Amestoy

A damaged home near Hunt, up river from Kerrville

Photo: Kerr County Lead / Courtesy of Louis Amestoy

The flood inundated cars and houses across the Kerrville area.

Photo: Tayiba8258 via Shutterstock

A trained search dog inspects a flooded area at Camp Mystic.

Photo: Tayiba8258 via Shutterstock

John Taylor, volunteer Crisis Response Operator, holds up a label for properly identifying evidence, July 11, 2025.

Photo: U.S. AirForce / Public domain

SIX
THE COMMUNITY FOUNDATION AND THE WORK OF RECOVERY

At 9:48 a.m. on July 4, 2025, the Kerr County Flood Relief Fund was created.

That time stamp has become something of a quiet marker in the recovery story. It captures how recovery often begins, not with full information but with recognition that waiting carries risks. At that moment, Austin Dickson and his team did not know the death toll. They did not know the scale of destruction. What they knew, from experience, was that in disasters, *speed without structure creates chaos, but structure without speed fails people*.

Long before the Guadalupe River rose and the rain fell in sheets across Kerr County, the Community Foundation of the Texas Hill Country (Community Foundation) already existed for this moment. Not in the sense that anyone predicted the precise contours of that flood, the rainfall totals, or the lives it would claim. But in a deeper, more structural sense, the Community Foundation had been built for disruption. Founded by a gift in 1982, it was designed to function when systems fracture, when normal channels clog, and when urgency collides with uncertainty. Like many of the most important institutions in the Texas Hill Country, it did not announce itself loudly. It did not seek attention. It simply stood ready.

By the time the Guadalupe River crested and began to fall, Kerr County already understood that the flood would not be defined solely by the moment the water arrived. Rather it was an event measured in minutes, feet, and decisions made under extreme pressure. What followed would be measured differently, in weeks without housing, in months of uncertainty, and in years of rebuilding lives that no longer fit where they once had.

Floods end when the water recedes. Recovery begins when people realize they are not going back to the same place. Not the rescues. Not the warnings. Not the infrastructure failures or emergency successes already explored. This chapter is about how Kerrville and Kerr County organized themselves after the crisis phase ended, how they translated shock into structure, generosity into governance, and compassion into a system capable of sustaining recovery long after national attention moved on.

At the center of that effort stood an institution that did not arrive with flashing lights or formal authority, but with something quieter and ultimately more durable: trust.

This chapter is about that moment.

Origins Rooted in Place

The Community Foundation was born out of a recognition that this region required its own philanthropic backbone. It was founded by a $5,000 gift from Mrs. Alma Dietert in 1982. The Texas Hill Country is not an abstract concept or a marketing label. It is a geographic, cultural, and economic reality. Communities here are small, dispersed, and deeply interconnected. County lines matter less than rivers, roads, churches, schools, and volunteer fire departments.

By the late twentieth century, civic leaders, nonprofit organizers, and donors recognized a recurring problem. Generosity was abundant, but coordination was not. Donors wanted to help their communities, particularly after floods, fires, and economic shocks, but there was no neutral, trusted institution dedicated to stewarding those resources over time. Money often arrived late, was misdirected, or disappeared after the immediate crisis passed.

The Community Foundation emerged to fill that gap. It was established to strengthen local charities. Its purpose was simple in concept and complex in execution: to connect people who wanted to give with the organizations that knew how to serve. From its earliest days, the Community Foundation positioned itself as a convener and steward rather than an operator. It would not run shelters, rebuild homes, or provide counseling directly. Instead, it would ensure that those who did could do so effectively and sustainably.

Trust as Infrastructure

Community foundations occupy an unusual space in American civic life. They are neither government agencies nor direct service providers. They do not command authority. What they steward is confidence, confidence that money will be handled responsibly, that local knowledge will guide decisions, and that urgency will not overwhelm governance. Before the flood, the Community Foundation had spent decades doing unglamorous work: grant reviews, board governance, donor stewardship, and relationship-building with local nonprofits. In 2024, it granted approximately $7 million. None of that work was designed for national attention.

But it built something essential. When the flood arrived, that accumulated credibility became infrastructure. As Dickson, chief executive officer of the Community Foundation, described it, donors were not asking for speeches. They were simply asking for assurance. "I had hundreds of calls," he said. "Three-minute calls. A colleague called them 'are you a knucklehead?' calls. People were listening for governance. For established processes and systems. For whether we could handle this."

The questions were basic but decisive. Did the foundation have a board? Policies? Financial controls? Experience managing large sums? A plan for distribution? Because those answers already existed, money moved. This echoes a theme: Systems that function under stress are almost never invented during the crisis. They are activated.

Purpose Over Personality

One of the defining characteristics of the Community Foundation is the absence of personality-driven leadership. This is not accidental. Boards came and went. Executive directors changed. Staff evolved. What remained constant was mission discipline. The body's core purpose was to manage charitable assets responsibly for the long term. Donor-advised funds, endowments, scholarships, and designated funds formed the backbone of its work. These were not quick transactions. They were relationships built on trust, governance, and transparency.

This long-term orientation shaped the Community Foundation's culture. Decisions were cautious but not timid. Governance was deliberate. Financial controls were rigorous. The Community Foundation understood that credibility is not declared; it is accumulated, one decision at a time. In a region where everyone knows everyone, reputational capital matters. The Community Foundation became known not for grand gestures but for quiet reliability. When it said funds would go where they were needed, they did. When it promised accountability, it delivered.

Learning From Crises

Long before 2025, the Community Foundation had observed how disasters unfolded in the Hill Country. The pattern was consistent. The first wave was always heroic. Rescues, shelters, volunteers, donations. The second wave was harder. Insurance disputes, housing shortages, mental health crises, nonprofit burnout. The third wave, often invisible, was long-term recovery.

The Community Foundation learned that its most important role was not in the spotlight of the first wave but in the quieter months and years that followed. It learned that money deployed too quickly without local input could do harm. It learned that outside organizations, while well intentioned, often misunderstood local dynamics. It learned that recovery is uneven and that equity requires attention long after headlines fade. It was there after the school shooting in Uvalde in May 2022. It was there after the Crabapple Fire near Fredericksburg in March 2025. These lessons shaped how the Community Foundation approached every subsequent crisis. By the time July 2025 arrived, the playbook was not theoretical. It was lived experience.

A Regional Anchor

By the early 2020s, the Community Foundation had become a regional anchor. It served multiple counties, each with its own needs, politics, and nonprofit ecosystems. It maintained relationships with food banks, housing organizations, health clinics, faith-based charities, and local governments. According to Benevity, by 2022 it ranked No. 578 in the World's Top Supported Nonprofits. In 2025, it was No. 5.

Importantly, it did so without becoming political. The Community Foundation understood that its legitimacy depended on neutrality. It was trusted across ideological lines because it focused on outcomes, not advocacy. This neutrality made it uniquely positioned to act during emergencies. When donors from outside the region wanted to help but did not know where to send money, the Community Foundation became the default answer. When local nonprofits were overwhelmed and needed coordination, the Community Foundation provided structure without control.

Governance as Preparedness

In disaster response literature, preparedness is often discussed in terms of physical infrastructure. Levees. Roads. Emergency management systems. Less attention is paid to financial governance. Yet without disciplined financial systems, recovery stalls. The Community Foundation invested heavily in governance long before it was tested. Board oversight was active. Grantmaking processes were well documented. Conflicts of interest were disclosed and managed. Audits were baked into its process so that they were routine.

These practices do not slow the Community Foundation down during a crisis. They speed it up. Because systems were already in place when the flood struck, funds could be deployed quickly without improvisation. Decisions could be made confidently because authority was clear. This is an often-overlooked truth: Strong governance is not bureaucracy. It is resilience.

The Human Element

While systems mattered, the Community Foundation never lost sight of the human dimension of its work. Staff members were not abstract administrators. They were also residents. They shopped at the same grocery stores, drove the same roads, and knew the same flood-prone crossings.

This proximity shaped how decisions were made. Grantmaking was informed by lived knowledge. The staff understood which organizations could scale under pressure and which were already stretched thin. They understood where aid would duplicate efforts and where it would fill gaps. Trust flowed both ways. Nonprofits trusted the Community Foundation because it respected their autonomy. Donors trusted it because it honored their intent while prioritizing community need.

In the months leading up to July 2025, nothing about the Community Foundation's operations suggested that a defining moment was approaching. It continued its regular work. Scholarships were awarded. Grants were made. Endowments were managed. This normalcy is important. It did not pivot into emergency mode prematurely. It did not overextend itself chasing hypothetical risks. It stayed focused on its mission, confident that when the time came, it would respond. That confidence was not bravado. It was earned.

When the flood hit, the Community Foundation did not rush to the front lines. It did not issue dramatic statements. It did what it had always done, only faster and at greater scale. Disaster relief funds were established with clarity of purpose. Criteria were defined. Local nonprofits were contacted. Needs were assessed in real time. Donors were given a trusted channel through which to act. The Community Foundation understood that its role was not to replace emergency responders but to support the ecosystem that would carry the community forward once rescues ended.

What distinguished the Community Foundation in the aftermath of July 4 was not speed alone. It was endurance. As national attention shifted elsewhere, the Community Foundation remained. It continues to allocate resources to housing, counseling, and community rebuilding. It monitors nonprofit capacity to prevent burnout. It adapts as needs evolve. This persistence reflects its original purpose. The Community Foundation was never meant to solve problems quickly. It was meant to ensure that help did not disappear when and where it was still needed.

A Quiet Beginning

Dickson did not wake up on July 4 expecting to become the chief architect of disaster recovery for Kerr County. Like many residents, he knew rain was coming. Like many families, his household had holiday plans. He had relatives visiting from out of town. The night of July 3 was stormy, but storms are familiar in the Hill Country. Nothing yet suggested that the next morning would reorder his professional life, his institution, or the trajectory of the community he served.

"I sleep with my cell phone in the kitchen for my own mental health and peace," Dickson said later. There were no emergency alerts ringing beside the bed. No immediate sense of urgency. The realization came slowly. A text from a friend out of state asking if he was okay. Another message. Someone checking Facebook for early reports. Floodwaters high. People missing. Then a call from the CEO of the San Antonio Area Foundation. "When I got that call," Dickson said, "I knew this was a disaster we needed to respond to."

At 9:48 a.m. on July 4, the Kerr County Flood Relief Fund was created.

Experience Without Illusion

The Community Foundation had responded to disasters before. Fires. Shootings. Local emergencies. In those cases, the pattern was familiar: create a fund, raise a few million dollars, make targeted grants, help stabilize the community, then return to normal operations. Dickson expected this would be similar. "We thought this would be the same. Some homes damaged. People in the hospital. Businesses out of commission," he said. "We create a fund, raise some dollars, help where the need is." But within hours, it became clear that the scale was different.

Donations began arriving almost immediately. Then they accelerated. Within days, phone donations were arriving every half a second. Think about that for a minute. Every half a second, someone locally, nationally or even across the world was logging on the Community Foundation's website and donating to help the recovery of Kerr County and its residents. By the end of the first week, $30 million had been raised. By the end of the first month, more than $100 million. Within six months, $150 million. This was not simply generosity. It was momentum. And momentum changes roles. The numbers tell a stunning story of generous support and giving literally from across the globe.

	AMOUNT RAISED	GRANTS MADE
JULY 4, 2025	$386	
JULY 5	$7,425	
JULY 7	$26,398	
JULY 11	$30MM	$5MM
JULY 18	$60MM	$4.3MM
JULY 31	$100MM	$11.2MM
AUGUST 15		$15MM
DECENBER 31	$150MM	
FEBRUARY 2026		$56.58MM

Source: RebuildKerr

The Community Foundation did not set out to lead recovery. It did not claim authority. But as donors, corporations, media outlets, and elected officials all searched for a trusted focal point, the Community Foundation found itself becoming the center of gravity. This is where recovery began to shift from reaction to architecture.

Supporting First-Phase Recovery Without Duplicating Response

While emergency responders focused on rescues and shelters, the Community Foundation focused on the organizations supporting those efforts. Rather than deploying money directly to individuals in the first days, it prioritized grants to nonprofits providing food, shelter, medical support, debris-removal coordination, and emergency housing assistance.

This approach avoided duplication and ensured speed. Local nonprofits already had trust, volunteers, and operational experience. What they lacked was liquidity and logistical support. The Community Foundation filled those gaps. Grants were issued quickly but not recklessly. Even under pressure, basic governance controls remained intact. This balance between urgency and discipline would define the Community Foundation's work through December 2025.

Mid-July: Reality Sets In

By the second week of July, the scale of the disaster became unavoidable. Fatalities were confirmed. Entire neighborhoods remained uninhabitable. Camps, homes, and businesses along the Guadalupe River were destroyed. The Community Foundation adjusted its posture accordingly. Messaging shifted from immediate relief to a dual focus: ongoing emergency support and the beginning of long-term recovery planning.

This was a critical inflection point. Historically, many disaster funds exhaust themselves in the first weeks. The Community Foundation made an intentional choice to preserve capital for later phases when needs would be less visible but no less severe.

Throughout July and August, the Community Foundation maintained close coordination with local governments, emergency management officials, school districts, faith leaders, and nonprofit directors. Importantly, it did so without attempting to lead them. The Community Foundation did not issue directives. It listened. It convened when helpful. It aligned funding with locally identified priorities. This posture mattered. In small communities, perceived overreach can erode trust quickly. The Community Foundation's credibility allowed it to act as a neutral intermediary rather than a competing authority. Indeed, in August and September, the Community Foundation funded emergency mental health responses for adults and children.

Deployment

The first major decision after the fund was launched was not about fundraising. It was about deployment. Within the first week, the Community Foundation committed to granting $5 million immediately. This was not because all needs were known—they were not—but because delay would compound harm. "We knew people were stressed," Dickson said. "We knew people were hurting. We knew waiting for perfect information would fail them." This number quickly expanded to $15 million, which included $5 million in cash assistance for businesses. At the same time, governance adapted.

Board members were engaged early. External philanthropic partners were enlisted to assist with due diligence. Volunteer experts synthesized information into decision-ready formats so that large volumes of funding decisions could be made responsibly and quickly. This was not improvisation. It was *scaling*. At this point, the Community Foundation crossed a line it did not intend but could not avoid. It became more than a steward of funds. It became the architect of recovery.

From Distribution to Design

Early disaster philanthropy is necessarily blunt. Cash assistance. Emergency support. Rapid relief. But blunt tools cannot rebuild communities. By late July, the Community Foundation recognized that the next phase required something different: a system that could move from emergency response to long-term recovery without stripping dignity or agency from those affected.

That realization produced the most important structural decision of the recovery effort. On August 1, RebuildKerr.org launched. This moment marked a fundamental shift. Until then, assistance flowed largely from the Community Foundation through intermediary organizations. Necessary, but limited. RebuildKerr.org created a digital front door where flood victims could document their own needs, losses, and circumstances.

Dickson described it as a turning point. "This was where we moved from emergency to dignity-based recovery." Instead of people fitting into preexisting aid categories, the system was designed to adapt to households. Case management replaced one-time distributions. Choice replaced uniformity. This mirrors the transition in Kerr County, from immediate lifesaving action to sustained coordination. The tempo changes. The goals change. The responsibility deepens.

A key decision was to invert the usual model of fund distribution. Dickson explained to the Kerrville Economic Summit that "Nationally, only twelve percent of disaster philanthropy goes to long-term recovery. Eighty percent of all donated funds were spent in the first sixty days. We decided early that we would invert that model, spending fifteen percent on emergency needs and investing the rest for the long rebuild." Dickson estimates that the total cost to complete the rebuilding and recovery process will be in the range of "$1 billion."

Housing as the Unit of Recovery

One of the most consequential design decisions was to treat the household as the fundamental unit of recovery. Housing was not simply shelter. It was stability. It was mental health. It was the ability to work, attend school, and make decisions without constant crisis pressure. The Community Foundation's Temporary Housing Program was designed as breathing room. Families were given time, sometimes up to a year, to decide what came next. This was intentional. In the first weeks after the July 4 flood, the Community Foundation allocated $1.6 million to cover short-term housing for flood victims through Airbnb Inc.'s nonprofit, Airbnb.org, so families have a place to stay while their homes get rebuilt.

"Temporary housing is not just a first step," Dickson explained. "It's an intermediate step. It lets people make planful decisions instead of chaotic ones." The Community Foundation has funded local case managers. They numbered 31 by February 2026, and they are fully funded through March 2027. These case managers are embedded in the community, walking alongside families. They do not dictate outcomes. They facilitate them. This architecture matters. It reflects an understanding that recovery is not linear. People move back and forth between stages. Needs evolve. Systems must accommodate that reality. By late February, *The Kerrville Daily Times* reported, "The Temporary Housing Program remains the backbone of stabilization, with 145 households currently housed as of Monday morning—that's 315 individuals who woke up in temporary housing." Dickson has publicly noted, with no small amount of pride, that there is "not one FEMA trailer in Kerr County."

By August, the Community Foundation had pledged over $40 million to meet housing needs. *The Texas Tribune* reported, "Austin Dickson said the organization is starting with housing efforts 'because rebuilding a safe, stable place to call home is at the heart of recovery ... . This is more than bricks and lumber.'" The Community Foundation partnered with such groups as Hunt Preservation Society, Habitat for Humanity Kerr County and All Hands & Hearts to repair and rebuild homes for the most vulnerable households. Additionally, it partnered with Global Empowerment Mission to obtain materials for use in home and building reconstruction. By late February, *The Kerrville Daily Times* reported, via the Home Repair and Reconstruction Program, the Community Foundation had "decisively shifted from assessment to visible rebuilding. There are forty-four homes under active construction and eighteen homes complete, representing meaningful momentum and tangible progress in neighborhoods across the county. There are [an] additional fifty-four homes in the current pipeline."

Initiatives included the Complex Repair Fund, which is

designed to provide a safety net for unexpected construction challenges. It covers unforeseen site conditions and closes repair gaps for the most vulnerable. The Down Payment Assistance Fund allows qualified flood survivors to receive help purchasing a new home through a partnership with the Texas State Affordable Housing Corporation (TSAHC) and local lenders. The RV and Mobile Home Replacement Fund, a partnership with Episcopal Relief and Development, provides replacement RVs and mobile homes. Collectively, these ensure all types of primary housing are considered in the recovery. The *Kerrville Daily Times* reported, "The RV Program now includes manufactured housing, increasing its ability to deliver durable, long-term replacement units. Thus far, 14 RV or modular homes have been delivered to qualified flood survivors."

The bottom line came from Dickson, who said, "Whether it's a rebuilt house, a repaired RV, or a safe temporary apartment, this fund will help families get home."

Mental Health as Core Infrastructure

If housing was the external foundation of recovery, mental health was the internal one. The Community Foundation treated mental health not as an adjunct service but as a core pillar. This was informed both by experience and by data. "We were told mental health symptoms would peak later," Dickson said, "and that the tail would be long." That message was driven home in a study conducted by the Meadows Mental Health Policy Institute (MMHPI), which was presented in Kerrville in early January 2026.

Dr. Andrew Keller, MMHPI's chief executive officer, said, in a talk reported by the *Hill Country Community Journal*, that the "county will see approximately 8,000 adults suffering from PTSD, compared to the typical 1,500 to 2,000 cases. The number of children experiencing severe mental health needs will increase from about 500 to 2,500." Regarding the timing of the need for mental health services for all these, Keller said, "The needs begin to unfold around month five for adults, and month six is where they really ramp up."

Grants were made early to stabilize local providers. As the scope of the disaster became clear, particularly the geographic spread of those who lost loved ones, the Community Foundation expanded its view of community beyond county lines. This was a notable decision. While the Kerr County Flood Relief Fund was rooted locally, the Community Foundation recognized that grief did not respect jurisdictional boundaries. Family members across Texas were carrying the weight of loss tied directly to Kerr County. The same *Hill Country Community Journal* article reported that the Community Foundation made "$1 million in immediate grants aligned with the assessments' priorities."

Mental health became a statewide concern because the disaster had statewide impact. This decision reinforces a recurring theme: Disasters create invisible geographies. Recovery systems must account for them. Here the Community Foundation worked with the MMHPI to create a statewide fund to "reimburse mental health costs for any family member who lost someone in the flood, regardless of where they live." Grants went across the state of Texas to support other nonprofits to provide mental health counseling and assistance.

Supporting Camps and Institutions

Summer camps along the Guadalupe River are not simply recreational facilities. They are cultural and economic institutions tied to multigenerational identity, seasonal employment, and regional reputation. The Community Foundation worked with camp-supporting nonprofits and community partners to address both immediate damage and longer-term viability. This included funding assessments, cleanup coordination, and planning support. The goal was not to preserve nostalgia but to sustain institutions that anchor the Hill Country's social fabric.

In January 2026, the Community Foundation announced a small-business recovery initiative of $10 million. When announcing the funding, Dickson said the foundation had partnered with Lift-

Fund, a community-based lender, to administer the $10 million in small-business disaster relief. As reported by the *Kerrville Daily Times*, when announcing the funding, Amy Hereford, LiftFund president and chief executive officer, said, "the $10 million initiative is designed to deliver fast, flexible financial assistance to small businesses impacted by the floods."

In his Kerrville Economic Forum speech, Dickson discussed efforts for other small businesses in Kerr County. He said the Community Foundation has granted $15 million to support six hundred businesses to date." In addition to these grants, the Community Foundation has been "buying down the interest rate to zero percent on loans of up to $500,000."

Governance That Breathes

As the recovery effort matured, the Community Foundation formalized advisory councils for housing, mental health, and community and culture. Not merely symbolic, these bodies were working systems, meeting monthly, reviewing data, and making recommendations grounded in local expertise. The composition of these councils mattered. Bankers. Builders. Clinicians. Educators. Business owners. People whose professional lives intersected daily with the realities recovery would face.

Governance was about legitimacy. This governance model allowed the Community Foundation to do something rare in disaster recovery: move quickly *and* remain accountable. Oversight does not slow response when it is embedded in the system before crisis arrives.

Progress, Not Perfection

As the Community Foundation became the architect of recovery, it also became a focal point for expectations, frustrations, and criticism. This was inevitable. When other systems such as FEMA or the Small Business Administration moved slowly or failed to meet individual needs, the institution absorbed the emotional overflow. Dickson acknowledged this openly.

"We became a lightning rod," he said. "Some of that was justified. Some of it was misplaced frustration. But it came with the role." This tension is not the defining feature of the Community Foundation's work, but it is part of its cost. Leadership in recovery is not only technical. It is emotional. What sustained the effort was clarity of values, sequencing, and communication. The Community Foundation did not promise perfection. It promised process.

One of the least visible consequences of disasters is nonprofit burnout. Staff leave. Volunteers disappear. Administrative systems break under prolonged stress. The Community Foundation recognized this risk and responded by funding organizational sustainability. Grants supported staff retention, technology upgrades, and operational recovery. This was not glamorous work. It was necessary work.

September: Shifting to Recovery

By September 2025, national attention had largely moved on. Media coverage waned. Outside donations slowed. This is when the Community Foundation's role became most consequential. Because it had resisted the urge to spend everything early, the body retained the ability to fund second- and third-phase needs. It continued issuing grants for housing stabilization, legal assistance, insurance navigation, and nonprofit capacity rebuilding. The Community Foundation also began evaluating gaps. Where were needs not being met? Which populations were falling through the cracks? Which nonprofits needed support simply to survive after months of crisis operations?

October: Accountability and Transparency

As months passed, donors rightly asked questions. How were funds being used? What impact had been achieved? The Community Foundation responded with transparency. It communicated clearly about grant allocations, remaining balances, and ongoing priorities. This communication reinforced trust and encouraged continued support even as urgency faded. Governance did not relax simply because time passed. Oversight remained active. Decisions were documented. Lessons were captured.

November: Weight of the Holidays

By November 2025, conversations shifted toward long-term recovery and resilience. Infrastructure, land use, floodplain management, and future preparedness entered the discussion. While the Community Foundation did not advocate policy positions, it supported convenings and planning efforts by funding facilitation, research support, and community engagement initiatives. Its role was to enable dialogue.

As the holidays approached, the emotional weight of the flood returned sharply for many families. Empty homes. Lost loved ones. Disrupted traditions. The Community Foundation supported holiday assistance programs, grief counseling, and community gatherings designed to restore a sense of connection. These efforts acknowledged that recovery is not linear and that emotional needs resurface in cycles.

December: Sustaining the Work

By December 2025, the Community Foundation was still fully engaged. Funds remained active. Grants continued. Monitoring and evaluation were ongoing. Importantly, the Community Foundation resisted the narrative that recovery had ended. It did not declare victory. It did not close the book prematurely. By December 31, 2025, the foundation publicly reported it had received $150 million in donations. Not content to rest, it positioned itself for continued involvement into 2026 and beyond, recognizing that some impacts of July 4 would unfold over years.

A Model of Endurance

From July through December 2025, the Community Foundation of the Texas Hill Country did not seek attention. It sought effectiveness. It did not try to solve every problem. It ensured that those who could solve problems had the resources to do so. In disaster response, heroism saves lives. Institutions like the Community Foundation make survival sustainable.

Its work after July 4 was not defined by a single act but by thousands of disciplined decisions made under pressure, guided by mission, governance, and local trust. When history looks back on the flood, the Community Foundation's contribution may not be easily summarized. That is precisely the point. Its success lies in what did not happen: unchecked chaos, wasted generosity, abandoned survivors. It held the center when the Hill Country needed it most.

Ordinary People, Extraordinary Pressure

Dickson voiced hopes that by the end of the July 4 flood's first anniversary, the majority of funds would have been allocated or pledged. Not scattered. Not frozen. Directed. The work is not finished. It will not be finished for years. But the architecture exists. Looking back, what stands out is how ordinary this institution was before July 4. A community foundation. A board. Grant processes. Local relationships. Nothing designed for national attention.

And yet, when extraordinary pressure arrived, it held. This is perhaps the quiet lesson of Kerr County's recovery: Resilience is not found only in dramatic moments. It is found in institutions that do their work faithfully long before they are tested. This architecture, the families rebuilding, the businesses reopening, the landscape reshaping itself—none of that happens without the systems that made recovery possible.

Sometimes, the most important response is not the loudest one. It is the one that endures.

SEVEN

ART AND HEALING AFTER THE FLOOD

In the days after the Guadalupe River rose and then tore its way through Kerr County, there was a silence that felt heavier than noise. Helicopters no longer thudded overhead. The chainsaws that once buzzed endlessly along the riverbanks slowed, then stopped. What remained was a community standing still, trying to comprehend what had happened and, just as important, what it meant.

Later chapters of this book will trace the physical realities of the flood: the hydrology, the speed of the water, the failures and heroics, the geography that shaped devastation. Earlier chapters captured the human cost through stories of survival and loss, of people pulled from windows, swept downstream, or clinging to trees until dawn. This chapter turns to something less tangible but no less essential. It asks how a community begins to live with what it now knows.

For Kerr County, part of that answer emerged through art. Not art as ornament. Not art as diversion. But art as witness, as memory, and as a bridge between grief and endurance. In the months after July 4, artists of many kinds responded to the flood in ways that were deeply personal yet unmistakably communal. Their work did not rebuild homes or repair bridges, but it addressed something equally fragile: the inner architecture of a wounded community.

Art first provided an answer in an unlikely time and place: on September 15, 2025, at the football season opener of Kerrville Tivy High School.

There is nothing more sacred in small-town Texas than high school football. *Friday Night Lights* (the book and television show) made that clear. But art brought all of Kerrville together at one point, at one time for an incredible moment of healing. On this season-opening night, after the tributes were made to the first responders, thirteen-year-old Skyler Derrington stepped to the microphone on the track surrounding the football field to being her version of Leonard Cohen's *Hallelujah*.

I was one of those in attendance for the opening night. With the exception of the very few moments before the prayer that starts every Texas high school football game, there is never a time when a stadium is completely bathed in silence. But on this night, it was as Skyler stepped to the microphone in front of the press-box side of the stadium, it was thorough, total and utter silence.

After the Water Receded

In the immediate aftermath of the flood, the community's focus was necessarily practical. Search and rescue operations dominated the first hours and days. Shelters filled. Donations poured in. Roads were cleared. Earlier chapters described this phase as one of adrenaline and motion, when there was little time to think and even less time to feel. But recovery has a second phase, one that arrives quietly. It comes when the pace slows and the questions change. What do we do with what we have seen? How do we remember without being consumed? How do we mark loss without freezing time at its worst moment?

For Darrell Beauchamp, executive director of The Museum of Western Art in Kerrville, those questions arrived almost immediately, carried in the voices of artists calling from near and far. They were not calling with proposals or polished ideas. They were calling with instinct. "How can I help?" was the question Beauchamp heard again and again.

Artists, he observed, are wired to respond to emotion. When feelings run high, they feel compelled to translate that intensity into form. After July 4, Kerrville was saturated with emotion: grief, shock, fear, gratitude, anger, disbelief. Artists recognized it as something they could not ignore. Some wanted to paint. Others wanted to photograph. A muralist asked if there was a blank wall where she could work. Musicians offered to play. Sculptors began thinking about memorials, even as they acknowledged that their medium required time.

Beauchamp understood both the impulse and the constraint. Unlike music, which can respond almost immediately, visual art often unfolds slowly. A painting takes weeks or months. A sculpture can take a year or more. Museums, too, plan far in advance. Exhibitions are scheduled years out. Space, funding, and logistics impose limits. This tension between urgency and deliberation shaped how art entered Kerr County's recovery.

Timing, Trauma, and Responsibility

One of the most difficult decisions facing cultural institutions after a disaster is timing. There is a natural impulse to document and display what has happened, to make sense of it collectively. But there is also the risk of reopening wounds before they have had time to close. Beauchamp and the museum's board wrestled with this balance. An art exhibition focused on the flood was an obvious idea. Artists were willing. The community was interested. Yet the museum's leadership hesitated.

Too soon and such an exhibition could feel invasive. Families who had lost loved ones might encounter images they were not ready to see. A place intended for reflection could become a site of renewed pain. Again and again, people spoke of how raw the early weeks felt, how even well-meaning gestures could overwhelm. Healing required space. Rather than forcing a single, large response, the museum chose a series of smaller, sustained actions. This approach allowed art to be present without being intrusive, to accompany recovery rather than define it.

The Tribute Garden: Art in Place

The most visible expression of this philosophy was the creation of a tribute garden on the museum grounds. Designed by architects and landscape artists, the garden was conceived not as an exhibition but as an environment. Where there had once been a relatively ordinary outdoor space, there would now be a winding path, subtly shaped like a river. Native plants would line the way. Benches would invite people to sit. At the end, a waterfall would provide movement and sound.

Names of those who did not survive the flood are incorporated into the design, along with acknowledgments of those who supported recovery efforts. The garden would be permanent but not static. Plants would grow. Seasons would change. The space would evolve. Beauchamp emphasized that the garden was not intended to be a place of perpetual mourning. This distinction mattered. Several residents spoke about the danger of being trapped by tragedy, of allowing July 4 to eclipse everything that came before and everything that might still come.

The garden, instead, is meant to be a place of reflection and continuity. It would remember, but it would also invite forward movement. By the following Independence Day, the hope was that the community could gather there not only to grieve but to mark resilience. In this way, the garden echoed the broader arc of recovery for Kerrville and Kerr County. The Guadalupe River had changed, but it remained central. The community had been wounded, but it endured.

Art as Community Infrastructure

What Beauchamp also witnessed in the months after the flood was an extraordinary outpouring of support within the arts community itself. Museums, galleries, and artists from Houston, Austin, Dallas, and San Antonio reached out almost immediately. Some asked if the museum staff was safe. Others offered to send people, equipment, or funds. Longtime competitors for grants and donors set aside rivalry in favor of solidarity.

This response mirrored the mutual aid among first responders, volunteers, and local businesses. The same instinct that sent neighbors into floodwaters to rescue strangers sent arts professionals from across Texas to help one another protect collections, move artwork, and stabilize damaged spaces. For Beauchamp, this reinforced the idea that art institutions are an integral part of the fabric of their communities. They are part of the same fabric. When that fabric tears, everyone feels it.

The Painter and the Image That Would Not Let Go

If Beauchamp's story reveals how art operates in public space, Elaine Capers's story shows how it works in private. Capers woke on the morning of July 4 to images on social media that did not make sense at first. The rain had not seemed extraordinary the night before. Yet the video streaming from the Sidney Baker Bridge told a different story.

Within minutes, she was driving toward the river, drawn by a need to see for herself. What she encountered stunned her: flooded streets, exploded garage doors, debris strewn across familiar ground, a dead horse in the road. The dam was unrecognizable. Trees were gone. The Guadalupe River had erased landmarks she had known for years.

Capers had lived through earlier floods, including the 2002 flood. She understood water's power. But this was different. This was faster, more violent, and more indiscriminate. In the days that followed, Capers did what she always did when confronted with beauty or devastation: She took photographs. Later, sitting in her living room, she scrolled through them, trying to reconcile what she had seen with what she felt.

One image refused to let go.

Lean On Me

The photograph showed two cypress trees along the riverbank. One stood upright, its bark intact. The other was uprooted, stripped, its root ball exposed. Instead of being carried away, the damaged tree leaned against the standing one, held in place. To Capers, the image was unmistakably symbolic. It spoke of strength and vulnerability, of endurance and dependence. It reminded her of earlier grief, particularly the death of her daughter in 2018, when painting had helped her process pain that felt otherwise unbearable. Capers began painting the image. She titled the work *Lean On Me*.

The act of painting became an act of healing. Each brushstroke allowed her to release emotion, to tell a story that words could not fully capture. She did not want to paint morbidity. There was already enough of that. Instead, she focused on resilience. As she worked, the painting lightened her emotional burden. It did not erase grief, but it gave it form. In doing so, it made grief shareable. When others saw the painting, they found their own meanings in it. Some saw the community supporting its most damaged members. Others saw faith, endurance, or hope. The image became a mirror, reflecting different truths back to those who looked at it.

Memory, Loss, and Preservation

Capers also recognized another role art plays after disaster: preservation. In the weeks following the flood, she encountered paintings of Guadalupe River scenes that no longer existed. Trees had been swept away. Riverbanks had shifted. Familiar vistas were gone. These paintings became records of what had been—not just visually but emotionally. They preserved how the Guadalupe River had been loved, how it had been experienced before it revealed its destructive force.

Many Kerrville and Kerr County residents were and are still grappling with the changed Guadalupe River. Art provided a way to hold both versions of the river at once: the source of beauty and the agent of destruction. Several members of Capers's cohorts in the Magnificent 7 artists group made paintings of how the Guadalupe River had changed: what was lost but what was gained. In this sense, paintings became living memorials. They did not deny what had happened. They contextualized it.

Music as Immediate Response

While painters worked through weeks and months, musicians responded almost immediately. Music, unlike visual art, unfolds in real time. It gathers people together in the present moment. For Gene Dowdy, a violinist and conductor of Symphony of the Hills, who is deeply embedded in the Kerrville community, this immediacy carried responsibility. When asked to play at memorial services for flood victims, including the service for a young child who died at Camp Mystic, Dowdy felt both honored and burdened.

He wanted the music to serve the family. He chose to improvise on familiar melodies associated with childhood and faith, allowing the music to emerge organically in response to the space and the people gathered. Dowdy described the experience as almost otherworldly. He was fully present yet focused entirely on giving others what they needed in that moment. Only later did he realize how deeply the act of playing had affected him.

"A Time To Remember"

Months later, the Kerrville symphony prepared for its opening concert of the season, on October 4, 2025. Coincidentally, that opening concert was titled "A Time To Remember." The program had been planned years earlier as part of the orchestra's twenty-fifth anniversary. After July 4, the title took on new meaning. Dowdy made a deliberate choice to alter the program. He selected the "Adagietto" from Gustav Mahler's *Symphony No. 5*, a piece capable of holding sorrow and hope simultaneously. He asked that there be no applause after the movement, allowing silence to do its work.

When the final notes faded, the silence in the hall was profound. Audience members sat together, breathing, remembering. Dowdy himself was overcome with emotion, experiencing a release unlike anything he had known onstage. This shared silence became a communal act of healing. It required no explanation. It simply allowed people to be together with what they felt.

A Child's Voice and a Borrowed Song

In every disaster, there is a moment when the story passes from institutions and adults into the hands of those who experienced it most vulnerably. In Kerr County, that moment came when Skyler, a young Camp Mystic survivor, stepped into the light—a witness speaking in her own voice. She was neither curator nor professional artist. She was a child who survived the flood and found language for it through music.

In the weeks after July 4, Skyler struggled to articulate what she had lived through. Like many survivors, especially young ones, she carried memories that were vivid but difficult to organize into words. Camp Mystic was meant to be a place of safety, ritual, and summer joy. The flood shattered that assumption. What remained was fear, gratitude, confusion, and an acute awareness of loss. Skyler did not begin by trying to tell a public story. She began by trying to make sense of her own.

Choosing *Hallelujah*

The song Skyler chose, Leonard Cohen's *Hallelujah*, is one of the most interpreted and reinterpreted (even by Cohen himself) songs in modern music, used in moments of sorrow, reverence, and reflection. It carries biblical language, emotional restraint, and a structure that allows lament and hope to coexist. That duality mattered. For Skyler, the word "hallelujah" did not feel like celebration. It felt like survival. It held grief and gratitude in the same breath. The original song's verses speak of brokenness, doubt, and faith that persists despite disappointment. That made it a fitting vessel for a story that could not be neatly resolved.

Skyler rewrote the lyrics as an act of translation. She took experiences that lived in her body—the rushing water, the darkness, the fears, the prayers whispered rather than spoken—and placed them into words that could be sung. She wrote about the Guadalupe River rising, about fear in the night, about holding on. She wrote about the people who helped, the counselors, the rescuers, the community that refused to turn away. And she wrote about survival not as triumph but as responsibility. In doing so, she transformed a familiar song into a personal testimony.

Writing as Survival

What distinguishes Skyler's rewriting of *Hallelujah* from countless other reinterpretations is intent. She was not trying to improve the song. She was not trying to showcase talent. She was trying to tell the truth. Children who survive disasters often lack the vocabulary to explain what they have experienced. Art becomes a bridge. Capers described painting as a way to put grief somewhere outside the body. Skyler's songwriting served the same function.

By rewriting the lyrics, she gained control over a narrative that had once overwhelmed her. She decided what to include. She decided what to emphasize. She decided where the story paused and where it moved forward. That agency matters. In trauma recovery, especially for young people, the ability to shape one's own story is a critical step toward healing.

From Private Expression to Public Offering

Skyler did not initially write the song for an audience. But as her family and community heard it, they recognized something rare. The song articulated what many adults still struggled to say. It honored loss without sensationalizing it. It acknowledged fear without surrendering to it. And it offered gratitude without pretending that gratitude erased pain.

When the opportunity arose for Skyler to perform the song publicly, the decision was not taken lightly. Adults around her understood the weight such a moment could carry. They also understood that the community needed a way to hear the story of the flood through a voice that was both honest and unguarded. The setting in Kerrville was significant: the opening home football game for the Kerrville Tivy Antlers.

The Performance

When Skyler began to sing, the noise of the stadium faded. Conversations stopped. The usual rhythms of a football night—announcements, shuffling feet, distant cheers—gave way to an eerie stillness. Her voice was not polished in any professional sense. It did not need to be. It was steady, clear, and unforced. The rewritten lyrics unfolded slowly, each line carrying weight.

Listeners recognized familiar phrases reshaped by new meaning. The word "hallelujah" no longer sounded abstract. It sounded earned. As Skyler sang about the flood, the Guadalupe River, and survival, many in the stands heard their own stories echoed back to them. Parents thought of children they had pulled from danger. First responders thought of nights without sleep. Survivors thought of moments they had not yet fully processed. There were very few dry eyes in the stadium. Mine certainly were not. Others wept openly. Some bowed their heads. But no one looked away from this girl who had taken a very personal tragedy and given us all a way to both grieve and be resilient.

How the Community Received It

Importantly, the silence that followed Skyler's performance was like that after the Mahler movement played by Symphony of the Hills. This pause mattered. When applause came, it was sustained, not celebratory but affirming. It was recognition. Skyler was not being praised for performance. She was being praised and thanked for courage. In that moment, the community accepted the song as a shared artifact. It no longer belonged only to Skyler. It became part of the collective memory of the flood.

People spoke afterward about how the song gave them permission to feel. Others said it helped them explain the flood to their own children. Some said it was the first time they felt the community exhale together since July 4.

A New Kind of Memorial

Skyler Derrington did not build a garden or conduct an orchestra. She did something quieter and, in many ways, more fragile. She offered her voice. Her rewritten *Hallelujah* is a living memorial. Unlike stone or sculpture, it exists in memory and repetition. Each time it is sung or remembered, it carries the story forward.

Skyler's contribution reinforces a central truth: Art after disaster does not belong only to professionals. It belongs to those who lived the story. Beauchamp spoke of timing and care. Capers spoke of resilience rendered in paint. Dowdy spoke of shared silence shaped by music. Skyler's song brought all of those elements together. It respected timing. It honored resilience. It created a communal moment.

And it reminded Kerr County that healing does not always arrive through institutions or plans. Sometimes it arrives through a child who survived, borrowed a familiar melody, and found the courage to tell the truth. In a community still learning how to live with what it knows, that voice mattered.

Art Does Not Fix, But It Holds

None of these artists claimed that art could fix what the flood had broken. Homes were gone. Lives were lost. Trauma remained. What art offered instead was presence. It provided spaces, images, and sounds that could hold grief without overwhelming it. It allowed memory to exist alongside movement. In earlier chapters, survivors spoke of moments when they realized they could not return to who they were before the flood. Art helped mark that transition. It offered continuity and resilience.

As Kerr County continues to rebuild, art will remain part of that process. Murals may appear on blank walls. Exhibitions may gather images of what was and what is. Music will continue to bring people together. The Guadalupe River will never be seen the same way again. Neither will the community. Art helps translate that change into meaning. It reminds people that while disaster reshapes a place, it does not erase its capacity for beauty, connection, or hope. In the long story of the flood, art is not an epilogue. It is a thread woven through remembrance and recovery, carrying the community forward one image, one note, one quiet space at a time.

EIGHT
FLASH FLOOD ALLEY: THE SCIENCE BEHIND THE DISASTER

A Land of Beauty and Peril

The Texas Hill Country has always been a land of contradictions. Its limestone hills roll gently toward the horizon, dotted with oak and cedar, and its spring-fed rivers have carved deep valleys that draw both visitors and settlers alike. To the casual eye, it looks like a paradise, a place of rugged beauty, endless skies, and waters that promise life. But beneath this postcard image lies another truth: The Hill Country is one of the most flood-prone landscapes in the United States. Meteorologists and hydrologists have long called it "Flash Flood Alley," and for good reason.

Here, the elements conspire against complacency. Soils are thin, slopes are steep, and rain, when it falls, can come in sudden torrents. Moisture sweeps north from the Gulf of Mexico, collides with frontal systems, and rises over the Balcones Escarpment. The result is a dangerous recipe: intense storms that can dump more than a foot of water in a day and rivers that rise from calm to catastrophic in hours.

For generations, people have learned this the hard way. Families built homes along rivers that promised shade and water, only to see them washed away in a single night. Communities rebuilt again and again, often with stronger bridges and better warnings, but still vulnerable to the forces of nature. The floods of 1932 and 1972 scarred memories. Yet in 1987, 1998, and 2002, the Guadalupe River reminded everyone that history was not behind them, it was repeating itself.

This happened again in July 2025, worse and with more fury and with devastating consequences. To understand its significance, we can look at it through three lenses: the historian's account of the disaster itself, the hydrologists and geologist's effort to model and reconstruct the flood with science and computers, and the meteorologist's attempt to untangle the statistical relationship between rainfall and flood peaks in the Hill Country. Together, these perspectives do more than recount a tragedy, they show us how nature, science, and society intertwine in Flash Flood Alley.

The Ground Beneath the Storm

Every flood in the Texas Hill Country leaves behind two stories. The first is human, loss of life and destruction of property. These tales, filled with heartbreak and survival, are the ones most retold after each disaster. But beneath them lies another story. It is the story of science. A story of limestone ridges and thin soils, of tropical air colliding with escarpments, of rivers whose channels are carved larger than their usual flow would suggest. Science is what explains why Kerr County floods so often and so violently.

To understand why, three scientific perspectives are essential. First, Charlie Flatten's *The Upper Guadalupe River: Stewarding a Hill Country Icon* (2017), written for the natural resources nonprofit Hill Country Alliance, which paints the Guadalupe River not only as a beloved river but as a system inherently prone to disaster. Second, the *Actuarial Weather Extremes Series Texas Floods–July 2025*, a report that dissects the Independence Day flood with actuarial precision, showing that these so-called "hundred-year events" occur every decade or two. And third, John Nielsen-Gammon et al's *Extreme Rainfall in Texas: Patterns and Predictability*, which catalogues the meteorology of Texas deluges and reveals why the Hill Country is ground zero for the fiercest downpours in the United States.

Taken together, these works show that the 2025 flood was not an accident. It was the intersection of geology, hydrology and groundwater, and climate. It was science unfolding in real time. And it forces us to ask whether Kerr County can ever truly learn from the river and creeks it loves.

A Landscape Designed to Flood

Stand on a bluff above the Guadalupe River in any part of Kerr County, and the view is beguiling. The river meanders beneath a canopy of bald cypress, its waters clear and green. To the west, limestone hills rise in a patchwork of cedar, oak, and pasture. It looks like a place built for beauty, for ranching, for summer camps, for Sunday picnics. But the land itself is engineered by geology to create flash floods.

Flatten, in his 2017 report, calls this landscape a "natural design for flash flooding." It is not a metaphor. It is the literal outcome of millions of years of geologic forces that shaped the Edwards Plateau and carved the canyons of the Hill Country. The same features that make Kerr County scenic—the steep slopes, the limestone bluffs, the thin soils—also make it vulnerable. To understand why the July 4, 2025, flood happened, one must first understand the ground beneath our feet.

The Edwards Plateau: A Geologic Stage for Disaster

The Texas Hill Country sits atop the Edwards Plateau, a massive uplift of limestone that dominates Central Texas. To the east, the plateau ends abruptly in the Balcones Escarpment, a dramatic fault-line cliff that separates the rocky highlands from the flatter coastal plains. Kerr County lies just inside this transition zone, where the plateau begins to break apart into hills and canyons.

The geology is distinctive:

- Limestone and dolomite formations (Edwards, Glen Rose, and Trinity Group) dominate. These rocks dissolve in water, creating caves, sinkholes, and underground channels.
- Karst topography allows water to vanish underground in one place and reemerge in springs miles away. This makes the land hydrologically unpredictable.
- Faulting and uplift have fractured the rock, creating steep valleys and sharp gradients that rivers eagerly exploit.

This is a landscape with almost no patience for rainfall. Where other regions might absorb water slowly into deep soils, the Hill Country shrugs it off. The combination of shallow soils and fractured limestone means that infiltration is limited during heavy storms. Once soils are saturated, water runs off as if poured onto pavement.

Thin Soils, Fast Water

If you scoop a handful of soil from land anywhere near Ingram, you will notice how shallow it is before limestone interrupts your shoveling. In many places, Hill Country soils are less than a foot deep. They are stony, thin, and easily saturated. Beneath them often lies a layer of clay that acts like a barrier, preventing further infiltration.

What does this mean in practice? During a summer shower, some rain will soak in. Springs and aquifers recharge. But during a deluge, ten inches in a night, the soil's limited storage capacity is quickly overwhelmed. Once that threshold is reached, every additional raindrop becomes runoff.

Hydrologists describe the Hill Country watershed as "hydraulically efficient." That is not a compliment. It means rainfall is converted into streamflow with remarkable speed. Flatten notes that creeks like Johnson Creek or Turtle Creek, which both flow into the Guadalupe River, can transform from calm trickles into roaring torrents in under an hour. This speed is why floods here catch residents and visitors alike off guard.

Valleys That Stack Water

The Guadalupe River and its tributaries carve through narrow valleys. Unlike broad rivers such as the Brazos or Colorado, which can spread floodwaters across wide floodplains, the Guadalupe River is confined by canyon walls. When floods come, the water has only one direction to go: up.

This vertical rise explains the terrifying numbers that appear in flood reports. On July 4, the Guadalupe River in Hunt rose thirty-five feet in just a few hours. During the 2015 Blanco River flood east of Kerr County, gauges recorded rises of five feet every fifteen minutes. These are not gradual inundations but walls of water.

Residents often compare the experience to a dam break. And in a way, that is accurate. The steep gradients and confined valleys funnel water downstream with such efficiency that creeks and rivers rise as though a gate had been opened. This is why so many deaths occur at low-water crossings: What looks like a shallow trickle can become an impassable torrent in minutes.

Human Choices, Amplified Risk

If geology and weather guarantee floods, human choices guarantee that damage will be worse. Flatten emphasizes how settlement patterns magnify risk. Houses built in floodplains, subdivisions on hillsides, and roads at low-water crossings place people directly in harm's way. Kerrville's growth means more impervious cover—roofs, roads, parking lots that accelerate runoff.

Recreation also plays a role. Summer camps, riverside cabins, RV parks and other camping areas place large numbers of people, often unfamiliar with flood danger, directly beside the water. The tragedies of 1987, of campers leaving a summer camp in a bus, and 2025, where the Camp Mystic campers drowned in or near their cabins, illustrate the consequences. The paradox is stark. The same qualities that make the Guadalupe River attractive—the cool water, the shady banks—are the ones that make it dangerous. People come for beauty and find themselves in the path of science.

Reflection: Land as Destiny

When Flatten writes that the Guadalupe's landscape is "designed for flash flooding," he means it literally. The land guarantees floods. The only question is when.

For Kerr County, this reality has profound implications. It means floods are not mistakes or flukes. They are expressions of the land itself. Every storm reveals what the soil, rock, and valley already dictate. To live here is to accept that truth. Some choose to forget, rebuilding in the same places, hoping the river will spare them. Others remember, moving to higher ground or advocating for stronger zoning. But the land remains unchanged. It will always flood.

In this sense, the science of Kerr County's landscape is less about prediction than about inevitability. The Guadalupe River is a river of beauty, yes. But it is also a river of floods. The hills and soils and valleys make it so. And until that truth is respected, the cycle of disaster will continue.

Meteorology

When it rains in the Texas Hill Country, it can fall with astonishing fury. In the space of a night, rivers rise like ruptured dams, creeks roar through valleys, and campers awaken to walls of water. The land guarantees floods, but it is the sky that supplies the rain. Understanding the meteorology of the Hill Country means seeing the atmosphere not as a backdrop but as a cook at work, assembling a recipe that has produced disaster again and again.

Nielsen-Gammon, Texas State University climatologist, calls these deluges "extreme rainfall events." His 2025 study catalogues them, showing that they are not flukes but recurring features of the state's climate. He and others have found that almost all the great floods of the Hill Country share the same recipe. The ingredients vary in strength, but the dish that results is always the same: too much water, too fast, over land that cannot hold it.

Recipe for Catastrophe

The Hill Country's floods can be explained as the combination of four atmospheric ingredients. Each alone may be harmless; together, they create disaster.

- **Tropical moisture surging north:** The Gulf of Mexico is the Hill Country's inexhaustible reservoir. Warm waters evaporate into humid air, which rides north on southerly winds. Sometimes this moisture is enhanced by remnants of Pacific storms that drift across Mexico. Whatever its source, the result is the same: skies heavy with water vapor, ready to be wrung dry.
- **Stalled weather systems:** In most places, storms move along, delivering rain and then passing on. But in Texas, quirks of upper-level winds sometimes cause systems to stall. When that happens, storms redevelop over the same counties for hours or even days. Meteorologists call it "training," like boxcars on a railroad passing along the same track.
- **Orographic lift at the Balcones Escarpment:** The Hill Country's terrain amplifies rainfall. Moist air moving north collides with the Balcones Escarpment, a dramatic rise in land where the Edwards Plateau meets the plains. With nowhere else to go, the air rises. As it ascends, it cools, and water vapor condenses into rain. This "orographic lift" is why storms intensify as they reach Kerr County.

- **Storm repetition and local focus:** When storms stall and redevelop, rainfall totals mount rapidly. Ten, twenty, even forty inches may fall in days. The precise county depends on subtle shifts in wind and temperature, but the pattern is consistent: Once the setup is in place, somewhere in the Hill Country will drown.

Nielsen-Gammon's study shows that these ingredients explain events as varied as the 1932 Guadalupe River flood, the 1978 deluge of Tropical Storm Amelia's remnants, and the July 2025 catastrophe. Each storm had its quirks, but the recipe was always the same.

Tropical Moisture: The Gulf's Endless Supply

The Gulf of Mexico is the engine behind most Texas rainfall. Warm, shallow, and vast, it produces humidity year-round. In summer, southerly winds pull this moisture north, filling the atmosphere with water vapor. Climatologists measure this with "precipitable water," the amount of rain that would fall if the entire column of air condensed. In extreme events, precipitable water values over Central Texas can rival those of coastal Louisiana during hurricanes. It means the air is holding as much water as a tropical rainforest.

Add in a dying Pacific storm, as in July 2025 when Tropical Storm Barry's remnants drifted across Mexico, and the effect multiplies. Suddenly, the Hill Country sky holds more water than the rivers below. When lifted, it will pour out in torrents.

Stalled Systems: When the Sky Refuses to Move

Why do so many Texas floods involve stationary storms? The answer lies in upper-level winds. Normally, the jet stream sweeps weather eastward. But sometimes it weakens, meanders, or splits. When that happens, storms lose their steering currents.

The result is "blocking" patterns: an upper-level low parked over

Central Texas, a high-pressure ridge boxing it in. Thunderstorms form, dump rain, dissipate, and then reform over the same spot. This is what happened in July 2002, when a low-pressure system stalled for days, producing catastrophic floods across the Hill Country. The July 2025 storm also stalled, pinned by larger atmospheric patterns. This refusal to move is what turned a rainstorm into a disaster.

Orographic Lift: The Hills as Rainmakers

When moist air reaches the Hill Country, the land itself forces it higher. The Balcones Escarpment acts like a wall, lifting air thousands of feet. As it rises, the air cools. Cool air holds less water vapor. The excess condenses into clouds and rain. This is why storms often intensify as they reach Kerr County. A system that drops a few inches in San Antonio may unload ten or more in the hills. In July 2025, orographic lift was decisive. The Escarpment wrung Gulf moisture like a sponge, concentrating it over Kerr and Kendall counties.

Storm Repetition: The Freight Train Effect

Meteorologists describe Hill Country thunderstorms as "training." One cell follows another along the same path, like cars on a track. The effect is cumulative. A single thunderstorm may drop two inches. Ten in a row over the same watershed may drop twenty. This pattern is why events like Amelia in 1978 produced four feet of rain. Storms redeveloped endlessly, each adding to totals until valleys could hold no more.

The Forecasting Dilemma

Here lies the meteorologist's torment. The setup can be recognized days in advance: Gulf moisture, stalled patterns, orographic lift. But the precise location is unpredictable. A shift of twenty miles may mean one county receives ten inches while its neighbor receives two.

This sensitivity explains why warnings often sound generic "flash flood watch for Central Texas" and why locals sometimes ignore them. After all, most of the time, the worst rains fall elsewhere. But when the dice roll against Kerr County, the results are catastrophic.

Forecasting tools are improving, with radar, satellites, and probabilistic models. Yet the challenge remains: The Hill Country is too small a target, and the storms too fickle, for precise predictions.

Why the Hill Country is Unique

Other regions face heavy rain. Louisiana endures hurricanes. The Midwest sees long-duration floods. But the Hill Country is different. Here, storms produce coastal-level rainfall over mountainous-style terrain. The result is the most dangerous flash flooding in the United States. Flatten notes that no other Texas river valley rivals the Guadalupe's frequency of catastrophic floods. The Mississippi River rises slowly. The Rio Grande floods rarely. Only the Hill Country combines intense rainfall with terrain that funnels it instantly downstream.

Why We Are Still Surprised

Science knows the recipe. History repeats it. Yet people remain surprised. Why? Partly, it is the deceptive climate. Much of the time, the Hill Country is dry, even semiarid. Creeks lie empty. Newcomers see tranquility, not danger. They build homes, camps, and parks at the water's edge.

Partly, it is human psychology. Warnings lose power if they are repeated too often without disaster. People grow numb. Then, when the storm finally hits their county, it is too late. The July 2025 flood illustrated both. Campers and those in RV parks along the Guadalupe went to bed with a light rain falling. They awoke to a river rising thirty feet. The science was clear, but the human response was not.

Reflection: The Sky's Role in Flash Flood Alley

The land shapes water, but the sky provides it. The Hill Country floods not simply because of thin soils or steep valleys but because the atmosphere repeatedly sets the stage for catastrophe. Tropical moisture, stalled systems, orographic lift, and storm repetition: This is the recipe. It has cooked disasters in 1932, 1978, 1987, 1998, 2002, 2015, and 2025. It will cook more. As Nielsen-Gammon's study concludes, extreme rainfall is not rare in Texas. It is part of the Hill Country's DNA. For Kerr County, perched at the edge of the escarpment, this truth means only one thing: Floods are not a possibility. They are destiny. The sky ensures it.

The Physics of a Wetter Atmosphere

At its core, the link between climate and rainfall is simple: Warm air holds more water vapor. For every 1°C of warming, the atmosphere can carry about seven percent more moisture. This is not theory; it is physics, measurable in the lab and confirmed by satellites.

Texas has already warmed by roughly 1–2°C since the mid-twentieth century. That means storms now have seven to fourteen percent more moisture to work with. When lifted over the Hill Country, that extra vapor condenses into extra rain. In practical terms, a storm that once dropped ten inches may now drop eleven or twelve. It may not sound like much, but when rivers rise vertically by the foot, that margin can be the difference between inconvenience and catastrophe.

Nielsen-Gammon's research documents this shift. He notes that what engineers in 1960 would have called a "one-hundred-year storm" has already grown about seven percent wetter. By the 2030s, Texas climatologists expect extreme storms could be ten percent heavier still. The atmosphere itself is changing the odds.

Numbers That Terrify: The Statistical Backbone

Behind every dramatic flood story lies a quieter, more technical one told not in eyewitness accounts but in numbers and charts. Long before the first thunderhead forms on the horizon, engineers and emergency managers are already asking questions that determine whether a bridge will hold or a town will flood: *How often should we expect ten inches of rain in a single day? Or five inches in just one hour?*

Those questions are the backbone of flood planning. In 2007, US Geological Survey (USGS) scientists William H. Asquith and Meghan C. Roussel published an atlas that set out to answer them with statistical precision. Their work introduced what is known as Depth-Duration-Frequency, or DDF, analysis, a way of quantifying rainfall extremes.

The concept is straightforward but powerful. "Depth" is simply how much rain falls. "Duration" measures how long it takes, whether over minutes, hours, or days. And "frequency" estimates how often such an event might recur: once every ten years, once every hundred years, or, in theory, once every five hundred.

When the numbers are plotted for Kerr County, they leap off the page. In just one hour, four to six inches of rain is statistically possible, with recurrence intervals of only ten to twenty-five years. Stretch that to a full day, and the models show twelve to fifteen inches falling at the so-called hundred-year level, some of the highest values anywhere in Texas.

Of course, statistics are only as neat as the weather allows. The Hill Country's flood history shows how quickly reality outpaces even the grimmest forecasts. The 1935 flood near Comfort produced totals that matched the fifty-year benchmarks for a single day. In 1978, widespread rains of ten to fifteen inches lined up perfectly with the hundred-year curves. And then came October 1998, when twenty to thirty inches fell across parts of Kerr and surrounding counties in less than two days, well beyond anything plotted in the atlas. As hydrologist James Smith later observed, in Central Texas so-called "hundred-year" storms often arrive not once a century but once or twice a generation. Nielsen-Gammon added that rainfall distributions here consistently stray outside expected ranges, making statistical norms less reliable guides than they are in other parts of the country.

This helps explain why Kerr County stands apart from places that, on paper, receive more rain. Houston, for example, logs higher annual totals, but Kerr County is defined by its short, brutal bursts. What might be considered a once-in-five-hundred-year downpour in the Midwest may register here as a fifty-year event. That mismatch between public perception and hydrological reality is one reason flash floods catch communities so off guard. Residents assume totals like fifteen inches in a day are extraordinary, when in fact they fall squarely within the Hill Country's climatological norms.

For planners, the implications are sobering. The USGS atlas is not a matter of academic trivia; it is a blueprint for survival. Bridges and culverts must be designed to withstand rainfall far beyond national averages. Floodplain maps, including those required by FEMA, must reflect updated rainfall frequencies or risk grossly underestimating exposure. Emergency managers cannot prepare for ten-inch storms when the region's history makes twenty-inch totals a genuine possibility.

In Kerr County, the lesson is clear. To ignore the statistics is not simply to gamble with nature, it is to invite disaster to repeat itself, over and over again.

The July 4, 2025, Flood: Science in Real Time

Meteorologists had been watching the sky for days. A surge of Gulf moisture was streaming northward, supercharged by the fading remnants of Tropical Storm Barry drifting from the Pacific over Mexico. The setup was familiar: tropical humidity, a stalled weather system, and the Balcones Escarpment waiting to wring the air dry. Forecasts warned of flash flooding, but the timing and location remained uncertain.

To residents, the warnings sounded routine. Flash flood watches are common in summer. Rain had been scarce in June, and many welcomed the showers. Visitors, arriving for Independence Day, were less aware. Campers pitched tents at the river's edge. Children fell asleep to the sound of distant thunder, thinking little of it.

Predawn Hours: The First Downpour

On the night of July 3 and into July 4, storms erupted over western Kerr County. Johnson Creek's headwaters were among the first to feel the deluge. Within an hour, three to five inches had fallen across the basin. Normally dry channels began to run brown with mud and debris.

By 3 a.m., Turtle Creek was also surging. Ranchers awoke to the sound of water roaring through pastures. As early as 2 a.m., 911 calls were beginning to come in with reports of roads underwater. Records later noted the intensity: Ten to fifteen inches fell across uplands in less than twelve hours. This was not rain showers; it was a wall of water from the sky.

4 to 6 a.m.: The Waters Converge

The Guadalupe River at Hunt, where the South Fork and North Fork converge, and downstream Johnson Creek, which also flows into the Guadalupe River, swelled rapidly. Gauges leapt by feet each hour. Residents who had seen floods before sensed what was coming. Some moved vehicles uphill; others slept through the warnings. At Ingram, the tight river loop began to flood low-lying homes and businesses. By sunrise, water was chest deep in some streets. The river had become unrecognizable, a torrent filling the entire valley.

By 6 a.m., Kerrville faced the surge. The Guadalupe River, which had stood barely above a foot two days earlier, screamed toward thirty feet. The rise was so fast that many compared it to a dam break. Between 2 a.m. and 7 a.m., the river climbed more than thirty feet, a vertical wall of water sweeping downstream.

The Gauges Tell the Story

Science records the flood in numbers as stark as any human account.

- **Rainfall totals:** ten to fifteen inches countywide; localized peaks even higher.
- **River rise:** thirty feet in Kerrville in four hours. As high as forty feet in and near Hunt.
- **Flow rates:** Estimates exceed 300,000 cubic feet per second at peak, comparable to Niagara Falls, in a riverbed designed for a fraction of that volume.

For hydrologists, these numbers confirmed what they had long warned: Kerr County behaves like a hard surface. Once soils are saturated, rainfall becomes runoff almost instantly. Tributaries funnel it into the main stem, stacking vertically within canyon walls. The result is a system that reacts faster than people can.

Not a "One Hundred-Year Flood"

One of the report's most sobering insights is actuarial. The July 2025 flood was not a once-in-a-century freak. Kerr County experiences major floods every decade or two. The actuarial tables are clear: This is not anomaly but pattern. For insurers, this means recalibrating risk. For communities, it means abandoning the illusion that floods are rare. The science demands a different mindset: Floods are normal, expected, and recurring.

Reflection: The Flood as Destiny

In the end, the July 4 flood was not random. It was the inevitable outcome of a recipe written by land and sky. The atmosphere supplied Gulf moisture, a stalled system, and orographic lift. The land converted rainfall into runoff with ruthless efficiency. The river rose as it always does, as it always will.

What was extraordinary was not the flood itself but our failure to treat it as ordinary. The science had long predicted it. The history had long recorded it. The actuarial tables had long priced it. Yet people still lived, camped, and played in the floodplain, surprised when the water came. The July 4 flood was science in real time; that is, the natural consequence of living in Flash Flood Alley. The question is not whether it will happen again, but whether Kerr County will remember when it does.

Cary Burgess on July 4: Radar Gaps and Respect

Scientific literature explains the structure of extreme rainfall in Texas. DDF curves quantify it. Climatologists describe the moisture transport. Hydrologists model runoff efficiency. But occasionally the most illuminating perspective comes from someone who has lived inside the system his entire life.

Cary Burgess (no relation to the Burgess family taken by the flood) grew up in Kerrville. He is not only a certified broadcast meteorologist with more than twenty-five years of experience; he is also a Hill Country native who has watched the Guadalupe River rise in 1978, 1987, 2002, and now 2025. His professional training allows him to interpret atmospheric mechanics. His local memory allows him to recognize pattern.

When asked what the river meant to him growing up, Burgess described it as serene, clear, spring fed, and constant. But he used one word repeatedly: "respect." That word bridges science and survival.

The Setup: A Saturated Atmosphere

From a meteorological standpoint, Burgess described the July 4 flood not as a surprise, but as a culmination. The Hill Country entered early summer in drought. By late May and June, rainfall began returning in frequent showers. Totals of three to four inches fell across Kerr County in the weeks leading up to July 4. The soil profile, shallow and limestone bound, was no longer desiccated. It was primed. Then came the deeper atmospheric ingredients.

The remnants of Tropical Storm Barry, having crossed Mexico, became entangled with a broader low-pressure impulse in Texas. At the surface, Gulf moisture flowed northward on southeasterly winds. Aloft, Pacific-origin moisture transported from western Mexico was caught in the jet stream and drawn over Central Texas, specifically the Texas Hill Country. The result was unusually high precipitable water values. In Burgess's words, when those values climb above two inches, "you can end up with rain showers or storms that produce up to three to five inches per hour."

The atmosphere over Kerr County was not simply humid. It was loaded. The official flash flood watch issued the afternoon on the afternoon of July 3 reflected this. Models suggested that somewhere in the fifty-county watch area, five to seven inches could fall within 24 hours. That forecast was correct in principle—but incomplete in *where* the rain would fall.

The Dual-Core Catastrophe

The defining feature of July 4 was not simply heavy rain. It was *where* the heaviest rain fell. Two intense rainfall cores, estimated at ten to twelve inches in less than two hours, developed directly over the headwaters of the North Fork and South Fork of the Guadalupe River. They occurred simultaneously. This was not a broad basin saturation event like 2002. It was a headwaters strike. In Burgess's assessment, that coincidence explains the devastation at Hunt and the catastrophic force experienced downstream.

When both forks carry equal and extreme volumes at the same moment, there is no staggered surge. There is no delay. There is no absorption. The waters converge with compounded energy. He had never seen both forks take equal, torrential rainfall at the same time. The result was not merely flooding. It was hydraulic stacking.

At Camp Mystic, where Cypress Creek drains into the Guadalupe River, it surged at extraordinary velocity through its confined canyon—so much so that Cypress Creek could not discharge normally. The larger river blocked the smaller system's outflow. Water backed up. The canyon walls limited lateral escape. Drainage was physically obstructed until river levels equalized.

This was not a failure of a single creek. It was the dominance of the main stem: The largest basin wins.

Model Limits and Radar Geometry

One of the most sobering elements of Burgess's explanation concerns forecasting limitations. Weather models predicted heavy rain. They did not pinpoint Kerr County. More critically, they could not resolve the dual-core structure over the two forks. Several structural constraints explain this.

First, once tropical systems lose official hurricane designation, they are no longer tracked by the National Hurricane Center. Oversight transitions to the Weather Prediction Center and NWS. There are no reconnaissance aircraft sampling the core. Mexico provides limited upper-air balloon data. Until the system crosses into the United States and is sampled at sites such as Del Rio, atmospheric inputs remain partially inferred by satellite.

Second, Kerr County sits in a radar-geometry gap. The primary radar sampling the region is located in New Braunfels, approximately sixty miles away as the crow flies. Secondary coverage comes from Del Rio (approximately one hundred ten miles from Kerr County) and San Angelo (approximately one hundred twenty-five miles from Kerr County). The Hill Country terrain, with elevation changes and canyon interference, distorts radar beams traveling more than seventy-five to one hundred miles. Burgess described it plainly: Kerr County lies in a relative dead zone between radar sites. Rainfall intensity is inferred from distance. Precision decreases with range.

In this event, the most violent rainfall occurred in precisely the area where sampling was least optimal. Models are powerful tools. They are not omniscient. The July 4 flood demonstrated that atmospheric setup can be recognized days in advance while exact geographic targeting remains uncertain until real-time radar detection. By the time radar confirmed extreme reflectivity, the warning window had narrowed to minutes.

WARNING CULTURE
"Treat the Watch as Seriously as the Warning"

The flash flood watch was issued in advance. The flash flood warning was issued at approximately 1:14 a.m. The distinction is procedural. It is also cultural. Burgess is unequivocal, "Treat the watch as seriously as the warning."

A watch signals atmospheric capability. A warning signals immediate hazard. The watch is the planning stage. The warning is action stage. The difficulty on July 4 was temporal. The most extreme rainfall began in the early morning hours. Pitch black, no stars, no moon, no light with nothing but pounding water. When the warning sounded, many were asleep. Some saw phone alerts and dismissed them. Others lacked reliable cell coverage in western Kerr County.

Flash floods do not respect circadian rhythms. In Burgess's assessment, the lesson is not technological alone. It is behavioral. The watch must trigger preparation: relocation to higher ground, contingency planning, heightened alertness. Waiting for a warning in canyon terrain is often too late. This is not alarmism. It is pattern recognition. The Guadalupe River has demonstrated repeatedly that once headwaters receive extreme rainfall, downstream response is swift and unforgiving.

Reform: Radar, Mesonet, and Real-Time Integration

Tragedy often produces reform. After 1987, river gauges and warning systems were expanded. After 2025, further upgrades are underway. Burgess described several structural improvements already in motion:

- Additional rainfall Mesonet stations positioned in critical headwater locations;
- Generator-backed real-time data transmission to integrate rainfall totals into forecasting models within an hour;

- Enhanced atmospheric sampling towers measuring temperature and moisture at multiple heights; and
- Proposed installation of an additional radar site, likely in Gillespie County near Harper (about twenty-two miles from Kerrville), to close the sampling gap between New Braunfels, Del Rio, and San Angelo.

A Mesonet is a network of automated weather stations spaced closely together, typically every ten to twenty miles, that measure atmospheric conditions in real time. Designed to monitor "mesoscale" weather phenomena, such as thunderstorms, wind gusts, and boundary-layer changes, these stations fill gaps between sparse federal stations. Mesonet stations are not hobbyist weather monitors. They are calibrated, professionally maintained systems that transmit instantaneous rainfall rates, wind data, humidity, and atmospheric conditions directly into modeling frameworks. The objective is simple: Reduce blind time.

If rainfall totals can be measured precisely in real time, models can adjust subsequent hourly forecasts dynamically. Warnings can escalate more rapidly and more precisely. The additional radar would reduce geometric distortion and terrain shadowing. Sampling storms within twenty-five to fifty miles instead of one hundred significantly improves intensity accuracy. These reforms will not eliminate floods. They will narrow uncertainty.

Respect and Inevitability

Despite technological optimism, Burgess returns to a single word: "respect."

He is firm about development along the river. Beauty does not neutralize hazard. The Guadalupe River's scenic character is a product of the same forces that carve its destructive power. The canyons were formed by violent water. The oversized channel is evidence of historical extremes. In his lifetime alone, he has witnessed catastrophic floods in 1978, 1987, 2002, and now 2025. That cadence is not anomaly. It is rhythm.

"Three or four times a century," he observed, "it is going to do what it does." The bottom line is that:

- The land guarantees rapid runoff.
- The atmosphere periodically delivers tropical-scale moisture.
- Climate physics increase moisture-holding capacity.
- Statistical frequency understates lived recurrence.

Burgess reinforces that conclusion from lived experience. The Guadalupe River is tranquil most days. It is catastrophic some days. Both truths coexist. Neither cancels the other.

The reforms underway—radar expansion, Mesonet integration, warning system upgrades—represent resilience. They represent learning. They represent adaptation. They do not change inevitability. The Hill Country will flood again. The sky will assemble the ingredients again. The forks will converge again. The only variable is preparedness. In the end, Burgess's words bridge science and culture: *Respect the river*.

In Flash Flood Alley, that is not poetry. It is survival.

Remember and Respect

Floods are written twice: once in water, once in memory. The water recedes, leaving debris tangled in cypress roots, mud lines on walls, and boulders rearranged in creek beds. The memory endures, or at least, it should. Yet one of the strangest truths about Kerr County is how quickly floods fade from human memory, even as the river remembers them perfectly.

Flatten warns of this danger. The Guadalupe River, he writes, is a one with a long memory. Its channels, oversized for normal flows, are shaped by centuries of catastrophic floods. Every generation experiences them. Yet every generation seems surprised. People build, flood, rebuild, and flood again. It is not that the river hides its tendencies; it is that people forget.

Flatten's Call for Institutional Memory

Flatten argues counties like Kerr County must institutionalize memory. Oral stories fade. Individual recollections die. Without permanent reminders, each generation repeats mistakes.

He proposes:

- **educational initiatives** in schools about flood history
- **public signage** marking historic high-water levels in towns and parks
- **oral history projects** to capture survivor accounts before they are lost
- **community drills and anniversaries** to keep the risk alive in public consciousness

Such measures may seem mundane compared to levees or dams. Yet they may be more powerful. Remembering is prevention. Forgetting is risk.

Scientists also emphasize the importance of memory. Hydrologists rely on long rainfall and streamflow records to model risk. Without data, predictions are blind. Communities are no different. Without memory, they cannot prepare. The river keeps its own record, in scars and sediment. Our challenge is to match it with human memory. Where we forget, the Guadalupe River will remind us, often brutally. These are not luxuries. They are survival strategies.

The Science of "Loaded Dice"

Climatologists often use the metaphor of dice to explain climate change. Imagine a die with six sides: one side for extreme rainfall, five sides for ordinary weather. In the past, rolling an extreme storm might happen once every six tries.

Now climate change is repainting the die. One side becomes two, then three. Extreme events occur not once a century but once or twice a generation. The dice are loaded, not by chance but by physics. In the Hill Country, this means the next Amelia or 2025 flood is not only possible, it is likely—and soon.

What the Science Demands

Flatten, Nielsen-Gammon, and others' reports converge on the same conclusion: Kerr County cannot treat recent floods as anomalies. They are signals of a future where "historic" floods are the norm.

This demands new strategies:

- **Updated maps:** Floodplain boundaries must reflect current and future climate, not just past averages. The last update to the official FEMA Flood Plain Map was in 2011. Although they are required to be updated every five years, this has not been done.
- **Stricter zoning:** Development in vulnerable areas must be limited or prohibited.
- **Buyouts:** Repeatedly flooded properties should be acquired and cleared.
- **Public education:** Residents must understand that climate is changing the odds.

These are not merely policy choices; like Flatten's proposed measures, they are survival strategies.

Science as Survival

Floods in Kerr County are never just stories of tragedy; they are also stories of science. Every disaster on the Guadalupe River is an equation solved in real time: geology plus meteorology plus hydrology plus human choice. The July 4 flood was no exception. It was science acting itself out in the most brutal way possible. To live in Flash Flood Alley is to live inside a laboratory where the experiments are relentless and the stakes are measured in lives.

What, then, is the role of science? Not to prevent floods—they are inevitable—but to teach survival. The rivers will rise again. The atmosphere will unleash more torrential rains. The land will funnel water into narrow valleys. Climate change will load the dice further. The only real question is whether people will use the science we already know to prepare, or whether they will repeat the cycle of surprise and forgetting.

We have seen how three distinct but complementary perspectives illuminate Kerr County's floods. Taken together, the science provides a hard truth: Floods here are not random. They are designed.

The Five Scientific Lessons

From geology to actuarial tables, from climate physics to cultural psychology, the science of Kerr County floods delivers five enduring lessons.

- **The land guarantees floods:** The Guadalupe River basin is a machine for flash floods. Thin soils saturate instantly. Limestone offers no buffer. Narrow canyons stack water vertically. Creeks like Johnson and Turtle can rise from trickles to torrents in an hour. Nothing in engineering can change these fundamentals.
- **The atmosphere conspires:** Texas sits at the collision point of dry northern air and Gulf moisture. When systems stall, when remnants of tropical storms linger, when the Balcones Escarpment lifts humid air, the results are predictable: torrential rainfall. The Hill Country is not unlucky; it is targeted by geography.
- **The past is prologue:** The Guadalupe has flooded in every decade of the past century: 1932, 1978, 1987, 1998, 2002, 2015, 2025. Each was called "historic." Each was followed by vows to remember. Each was eventually forgotten. Science tells us the next flood will come. Memory is the challenge.

- **Climate raises the stakes:** Warmer air now holds more moisture. What were hundred-year storms may now be fifty-year storms. By the 2030s, Texas climatologists predict another ten percent increase in extreme rainfall. In the Hill Country, where even six inches in an hour can trigger catastrophe, that extra margin is explosive.
- **Preparedness must be local:** While upstream dams have been proposed, no reservoir or downstream dam can save Kerrville. Canyon Lake helps New Braunfels, not Kerrville. Here, survival depends on local action: warning systems, zoning, education, and cultural remembering. The science is not abstract; it must be embedded in every family's choice.

Memory and Forgetting

Perhaps the most sobering scientific insight is not about water but about people. We forget. Hydrologists call it the problem of "collective amnesia." Psychologists call it "recency bias." Flatten calls it the cycle of forgetting.

After each flood, the pattern repeats:

- Disaster strikes.
- Memories are vivid.
- Communities vow: Never again.
- Years pass. Memories fade.
- Development returns to floodplains.
- The river rises, and tragedy repeats.

The Guadalupe River remembers. Its scars, gravel bars, and oversized channels bear witness. Our task is to remember as well. Science can give us rainfall statistics and recurrence intervals. But only culture can turn those into durable memory.

Climate as the New Context

Science also tells us that the future will not look like the past. Climate change has shifted the background conditions. The dice are loaded. Kerr County cannot expect the same frequencies or magnitudes of floods it once knew. The 2025 flood is not a ceiling. It is a preview. For planners, this means floodplain maps must be redrawn. For insurers, actuarial models must be recalibrated. For families, choices about where to live, where to camp, and where to build must be reconsidered. Science is the messenger of this new reality. Whether we listen will determine the cost of the next storm.

The River of Two Faces

The Guadalupe River is both lifeblood and destroyer. In drought, it sustains wells and springs. In summer, it cools campers and kayakers. Its cypress-lined banks are among the most beloved landscapes in Texas. Yet in flood, it kills. It has done so for centuries and will continue to do so. Science does not ask us to hate the river. It asks us to respect it. To treat its floodplain as sacred ground, not real estate. To see its beauty and its menace as inseparable. To understand that to live with the Guadalupe River is to live with floods.

Toward a Science of Resilience

What does resilience mean in Flash Flood Alley? It means translating science into practice.

- **Hydrology into zoning:** Respect the floodplain. Do not build where floodwaters will inevitably return.
- **Meteorology into warnings:** Use below-water radar, above-ground rain and water gauges, and alert sirens to buy precious minutes for evacuation.
- **Climatology into planning:** Assume heavier storms. Design infrastructure for the future, not the past.
- **Psychology into education:** Teach children the stories of past floods so memory does not fade.

Resilience is not resistance. We cannot stop the floods. But we can stop them from killing as many, from destroying as much. That is the promise of science: not to erase disaster, but to blunt its edge.

Closing Thoughts

While scientists dissect patterns, residents live through consequences. Floods in Kerr County have killed more Texans than tornadoes and hurricanes combined. The NWS 2019 fact sheet drives this point home. The phrase "Flash Flood Alley" was popularized not just to describe geography but to educate. The NWS wanted the phrase to stick in public memory. Central Texas residents, they argued, must never underestimate the skies above.

Kerr County is riddled with low-water crossings, more than a hundred in total. These crossings may be dry most of the year but become deadly traps during storms. The NWS stresses that most fatalities occur when drivers attempt to cross flooded roads. The campaign slogan "Turn Around, Don't Drown" emerged from this reality. Despite decades of awareness efforts, dozens of deaths have been recorded. Some victims were swept from cars, others from homes near creeks that rose in minutes.

Flash floods differ from river floods precisely because of their speed. Eyewitnesses in Kerrville saw water rise several feet in minutes. That same speed was reported by survivors of the July 4 flood. Walls of water up to thirty-five feet with speeds estimated at up to fifteen miles per hour were reported. For emergency responders, that speed means little time to react; for families, campers, visitors, and anyone else, it means evacuations often fail. This is why the NWS emphasizes preparedness: Residents must know their risk before the skies darken. Warnings are useful only if people believe them and act immediately.

One of the most insidious challenges is generational forgetting. After 1978, residents swore never to underestimate the Guadalupe River again. But by the 1990s, new arrivals and fading memories dulled the lessons. The 1998 flood became another painful teacher. The same for the 2002 flood. When I moved to

Kerrville in 2021, people still talked about the 2002 flood. But for those in western Kerr County for the first time, such as boys and girls at the summer camps or visitors at the RV campsites, there was no such knowledge and, more importantly, no such warnings. The NWS insisted in its 2019 publication that public education is never finished. Each generation must be taught the dangers anew. Otherwise, complacency guarantees tragedy.

The science shows inevitability. The history proves recurrence. But it is the human equation that makes Kerr County's story so urgent. Flash floods will happen again; whether lives are lost depends on decisions at crossings, on zoning boards, and in living rooms. For the people of Kerr County, survival in Flash Flood Alley is not about mastering the weather; rather, it is about respecting Mother Nature and learning to live within the risks that clearly can become events at any time.

To live in Kerr County is to live with paradox. The Guadalupe River offers beauty, recreation, and sustenance, yet it also brings sudden destruction. The limestone hills draw visitors for their rugged charm, but their valleys channel waters that rise faster than anywhere else in the nation. Locals know this truth instinctively, and science confirms it: Kerr County is the beating heart of Flash Flood Alley.

Kerr County's floods are not anomalies, nor punishments, nor acts of chance. They are the predictable result of atmospheric conditions that converge here more often than almost anywhere else in the United States. Geography may amplify runoff, but the skies are the true architects of disaster.

The implication is sobering. Each generation in Kerr County will face its own flood, as certain as spring follows winter. The only variables are preparedness, awareness, and resilience. Will communities remember the past, or be forced to relearn it? Will infrastructure be built for extremes, or for averages? Will residents heed warnings, or risk the crossings once more?

The Hill Country's skies embody paradox. The same Gulf-fed storms that replenish aquifers and keep rivers flowing are the ones that unleash sudden death. The same dramatic weather that paints the land green can strip it bare in hours. For Kerr County, this paradox is permanent. It is the price of living in Flash Flood Alley. To stay is to accept the bargain: beauty and bounty, shadowed by the inevitability of deluge.

And so, the conclusion is both scientific and poetic: In Kerr County, the extremes are not the exceptions, they are the rules.

NINE
UGRA: FROM RIVER STEWARDSHIP TO FLOOD WARNING

The Institution That Was Already Listening

Long before the river rose in the dark hours of July 4, before meteorologists issued warnings that no one could yet translate into lived consequence, before the camps and crossings and quiet backroads that tie Kerr County together came into view beneath a sheet of rain, one institution had already been listening to the water. In a landscape where creeks vanish into limestone, where the river makes promises and breaks them in equal measure, the Upper Guadalupe River Authority, known across the county simply as UGRA, has grown into something unusual: a civic memory keeper.

The flood did not create UGRA's purpose. It revealed UGRA's boundaries. It also revealed, with painful clarity, the space between two different kinds of public expectation. One expectation is long-term stewardship: the daily, patient work of knowing a river, protecting it, and keeping it healthy for the people who live along it. The other expectation is immediate warning: a system that sees danger moving through the watershed and turns that danger into time, so that families, camps and first responders can act.

Kerr County learned on July 4 that the second expectation

cannot be met by good intentions or a single agency acting alone. The prediction and projection system also required a shared effort, built on the kind of credibility that only years of stewardship can produce. That is why UGRA's story matters in this book. This chapter is not a debate about what should have happened. It is a narrative about what exists, what UGRA was built to do, what it is now building with partners, and why sober confidence is earned through structure, not slogans.

The arc runs from statute to stewardship, from governance to operations, from operations to construction. It runs through three voices: Dr. William "Bill" Rector, chairman of the UGRA Board; Tara Bushnoe, the UGRA general manager; and Tom Moser, a retired NASA engineer who has taken on the role of systems architect and phase-driven project manager for the flood prediction and warning effort.

Their perspectives differ in texture, but they align in direction. Rector speaks in terms of mandate, public trust, and accountability to the people UGRA serves. Bushnoe speaks in intervals and decision points: data streams, lag times, thresholds, and how human beings actually process information under stress. Moser speaks in phases: what must be built first, what must be integrated next, and what must work reliably when everything else is moving too fast.

Together, they tell a story that ends in reassurance, resolve, and sober confidence. Not because Kerr County can eliminate flash flooding. It cannot. The confidence comes from the fact that the county can build a system that respects reality: a watershed where, in the headwaters, the difference between safe and swept away can be measured in minutes.

Beginnings and Statutory Authority: A Local Mandate With State Backing

UGRA's roots go back to a time when Texas was formalizing how communities would protect and manage water. In 1939, the state created UGRA through enabling legislation designed to give Kerr County a durable home for watershed stewardship. The statute, paraphrased plainly, authorized UGRA to conserve, manage, reclaim, and protect the waters of the Upper Guadalupe River Basin, specifically confined to Kerr County. It provided that the authority do the work required to make stewardship real: to enter into contracts, acquire property, build or operate river-related works, and carry out projects connected to the river's health and management.

That legal foundation matters for two reasons. First, it established UGRA as a public institution with continuity. Rivers are long stories. The public institutions that protect them must be able to outlast election cycles, budget moods, and shifting attention spans.

Second, it set boundaries. The statute defined UGRA as a river authority, not an emergency management office. Its core purpose was and remains watershed stewardship in Kerr County. Over time, the scope expanded in specific ways. In 1971, the Legislature amended UGRA's enabling authority to explicitly authorize the construction and operation of sewage and wastewater facilities. That expansion reflected a practical truth: Water quality is not protected by words. It is protected by infrastructure.

In Kerr County, this statutory framework is not academic. The Guadalupe River is not merely a scenic feature. It is the backbone of community life. It shapes recreation, tourism, local identity, and daily routines. People do not experience the river as a utility line. They experience it as a place. The statute formalized the idea that stewardship needed a permanent home, and that home needed authority to act.

The other structural feature is governance. UGRA is overseen by a nine-member board. Directors are appointed by the governor of Texas, serve four-year terms, and must reside within the district. That is not merely a legal detail. It is the mechanism through which public trust is anchored: local residency paired with statewide appointment; continuity paired with accountability.

That structure matters in a post-flood environment, when the public naturally asks who is responsible, what are they responsible for, and what happens next?

Dr. William Rector: Stewardship as Public Trust and Governance Accountability

Dr. Rector's role in this story is not technical. It is institutional. When you speak with a board chair, you are speaking with a steward responsible for an organization's purpose, boundaries, and integrity.

Rector's lens begins with stewardship as a form of public trust. UGRA exists because the state recognized that the Guadalupe River watershed in Kerr County needed a durable institution to protect it. Rector speaks from that foundation: A statute creates authority, but trust is earned through consistent performance over time. In practice, that means UGRA's work is defined by continuity, reliability, and credibility with the people who live along the river.

Rector also emphasizes governance accountability, which is a different kind of accountability than the one demanded in the immediate aftermath of disaster. Governance accountability asks:

- What was UGRA built to do?
- What does UGRA do well today?
- Where does UGRA's responsibility end, and where does partnership begin?
- What must UGRA do now to help Kerr County reduce harm in the future?

This is where Rector's candor matters. Kerr County is living with the mismatch between midcentury statutory design and twenty-first-century hydrologic reality. The statute that created UGRA was not written with modern flash flood intensification, rapid land-use pressures, or the speed of real-time information systems in mind. Yet UGRA has been operating in that reality for years, often without the public explicitly noticing. When the river behaves within expected ranges, stewardship is quiet. The flood changed that.

Rector's big-picture overview begins by clarifying a key distinction: UGRA has long been charged with watershed stewardship and river management in Kerr County, but it has not historically been designed as a standalone flood-warning-system provider. That does not mean UGRA is irrelevant to flood warning. It means the solution must be integrated into UGRA's stewardship mission and delivered through partnerships because warning requires multiple lanes: engineering, operations, communications, and community adoption.

In other words, Rector frames the post-flood work of UGRA as an evolution: using UGRA's credibility, relationships, and data culture to help build an early warning capacity that fits Kerr County's geography and human reality. That is governance accountability in action: a board chair looking at the statutory mandate, acknowledging what has changed, and committing the institution to a course that strengthens public safety while remaining faithful to the authority's legal and operational boundaries.

Rector is also clear about what the public often assumes incorrectly after a disaster: One institution does not "own" the river, and no institution can promise zero harm. The responsible promise is different. It is a promise to reduce uncertainty where possible, shorten the time between detection and warning, and increase the community's ability to act. That promise is not inspirational. It is operational. It is built with systems.

UGRA Today and the Shift Toward Warning: From Mandate to Modern Risk

UGRA's long-term work has always been rooted in measuring and understanding the watershed. Years of water-quality monitoring and river stewardship create a baseline that is easy to underestimate until something breaks the frame.

In the days following the flood, many residents described the river's transformation in sensory terms: the way clarity vanished, the way debris lines climbed higher than memory, the way the river rose with an almost unreal speed. Those observations were not "data" in the formal sense, but they were the human translation of what UGRA's decades of work makes possible: a community that has a baseline for what "normal" looks like and how dramatically July 4 departed from it.

That is one reason UGRA is central to the post-flood warning effort. A warning system is not only hardware and software. It is a culture of measurement and interpretation. It is the discipline of building trust in the numbers.

As the county moved from shock toward rebuilding, UGRA's board and leadership began aligning that culture with a new strategic priority: flood warning in the Guadalupe River watershed within Kerr County. That shift did not appear out of nowhere. It emerged from the same logic that created UGRA in the first place: The Guadalupe River is central to life here, and stewardship must adapt to reality. What does it mean for UGRA to "move toward warning" without abandoning its core mission?

It means that UGRA uses its strengths to help build a system that can do four things reliably:

- detect conditions in the watershed in near real time
- interpret those conditions through modeling and thresholds
- decide when the conditions cross from information to action
- disseminate a warning through channels that people actually receive and trust

Those steps sound straightforward until you apply them to a county where the headwaters can deliver catastrophe in fifteen to twenty minutes. In that environment, warning is not only about accuracy. It is about speed, redundancy, and human usability. That is where Tara Bushnoe and Tom Moser enter the story, carrying the arc from mandate into execution.

Tara Bushnoe: The Operational Center of Gravity

If Dr. Rector represents the institutional memory and governance lens of UGRA, Tara Bushnoe represents its operational center of gravity. Where Rector speaks in statutes and stewardship, Bushnoe speaks in intervals, gauges, data streams, and decision points. Rector's lens is stewardship across time. Hers is stewardship in motion.

Bushnoe is the General Manager of UGRA. When asked to state the mission of UGRA, General Manager Tara Bushnoe does not improvise. She quotes it precisely: "To protect the health of the Guadalupe River watershed in Kerr County by managing water quality, water quantity, promoting stewardship, and providing services to the community."

That mission statement matters because, in the days following the flood, confusion emerged about what UGRA was designed to do and what it was not. Bushnoe does not treat that confusion as a public relations problem. She treats it as a systems problem. People cannot partner effectively when they do not understand roles. From Bushnoe's perspective, the post-flood effort requires that the community hold two truths at the same time:

- Mitigation is the long-term work of reducing risk through planning, infrastructure, land and water management, and projects that lower vulnerability over time.
- Warning is the real-time work of detecting imminent danger and communicating actionable information fast enough for people to respond.

Bushnoe does not collapse these into one concept because they behave differently. Mitigation is measured in months and years, sometimes decades. Warning is measured in minutes. Confusing them leads to unrealistic expectations and misaligned solutions. Bushnoe's operational story begins with an unglamorous but decisive challenge: data fragmentation.

Before the current push, an emergency manager seeking a full picture of river conditions had to consult multiple websites and platforms. Streamflow gauges might live on one portal. Rain gauges on another. Mesonet data on yet another. Each system reported at different intervals. No unified dashboard existed.

In a flash flood environment, minutes matter. Bushnoe's point is not that separate data systems are bad. Her point is that, in a crisis, forcing a human being to navigate multiple portals is not a strategy. It is a delay. And in Kerr County's headwaters, delay costs time that the watershed does not give back.

Bushnoe's description of lag time makes the issue visceral. In the upper reaches near Hunt and along the South Fork, lag times can be as short as fifteen to twenty minutes. Those sub-basins are steep, narrow, and comparatively small. When intense rainfall concentrates over that terrain, water accelerates rapidly. There is little time between runoff and consequence. Downstream near Center Point, lag times may extend to two to four hours because the watershed widens and slope decreases. That difference is not abstract. It defines what a warning system must be designed to do.

A county cannot build one warning workflow and assume it fits every mile of river. A workable system must respect that, in some places, warning means seconds and immediate action. In other places, warning means time to move, time to call, time to close crossings, time to mobilize. Bushnoe also ties this to a practical insight: The most sophisticated prediction model is useless if the information does not reach people in a format they trust and can act on. A warning system is not only about producing a number. It is about producing a decision.

This is where Bushnoe's "into the weeds" perspective becomes a form of leadership. She is not seduced by technology. She is focused on the operational chain, how information flows, where it slows, and what must be built so that the chain does not break when stress is at its highest.

Bushnoe's narrative also situates the work in time. In January 2023, months before the flood, UGRA's board had already added a strategic goal related to flood warning: evaluate and implement resources for flood warning in the Guadalupe River watershed. At the same time, the Texas State Flood Plan process was underway through the Texas Water Development Board, and Bushnoe served on that planning group. The strategy was clear: Position a project within the State Flood Plan so that local funds could be matched with state support.

When the state offered funding at only a minimal match, UGRA made a practical decision. Rather than stall, it used surplus funds to begin a phased approach. In November 2024, it moved toward developing a scope of work to enhance and improve access to existing real-time data and develop recommendations for additional instrumentation. That detail matters because it shows how institutional capability is built: through steps that begin before the public sees the urgency.

Bushnoe's focus remains on what the public can do—because a warning system that no one uses is not a system. She wants the public to sign up for alerts, learn crossings, understand the geography of lag time, demand clarity, and build a culture of flood literacy. This is not a compliance checklist. It is a resilience practice.

How a Warning Triggers: Turning River Conditions Into Actionable Time

A warning system fails in one of two ways. It fails because it does not detect conditions fast enough. Or it fails because it detects conditions but does not convert them into an action that humans can take. In Kerr County, the second failure can be as lethal as the first.

To understand why, consider what "warning" actually requires in a flash flood basin. It requires a chain that begins in the field and ends in a human decision:

1. Sensors measure conditions. Rain gauges register intensity and accumulation. Stream gauges register rising stage and flow. Additional sensors may track soil saturation or other indicators, depending on the design. The goal is not only measurement. It is measurement at a cadence fast enough to match the watershed's speed.
2. Telemetry transmits data quickly and redundantly. Sensors that record data but cannot transmit it reliably in heavy weather are a false comfort. A true early warning architecture assumes bad conditions: power disruption, communication instability, noise in the

data, intermittent outages. Redundancy is not luxury. It is survival.

3. A unified data view reduces human friction. Bushnoe's point about fragmentation is the first operational hinge. If an emergency manager must open five portals to build a picture of river conditions, the system has inserted delay. A unified dashboard does not "predict" flooding by itself, but it removes one of the most common bottlenecks: human navigation time.
4. Models and thresholds convert data into meaning. This is where the work becomes both scientific and practical. Modeling uses rainfall, basin characteristics, and stream response to estimate what conditions will look like downstream. Thresholds define decision points: what amount of rainfall over what period triggers an escalation, what stage rise rate indicates imminent danger, what combination of upstream conditions and basin response suggests that downstream crossings will become unsafe.
5. Automation reduces delay. Human beings are vital, but human beings are also slow under stress. In the headwaters, "slow" can mean the entire warning window is gone. A system that relies exclusively on manual interpretation and phone trees introduces delay. Automation can trigger predefined alerts when thresholds are crossed, while still allowing human judgment to refine messaging.
6. Dissemination must reach people where they actually are. The warning must reach camps, residents, travelers, and first responders through channels that are reliable in bad weather. That may include sirens, phone alerts, push notifications, radio, web dashboards, and integration with existing emergency communication platforms. The channel mix must be designed for reality: spotty service, nighttime storms, and human attention under strain.

7. The final step is human action. A warning is successful only if it creates time that people use. Closing a crossing, moving a camp group to higher ground, changing a route, calling a neighbor, or simply staying off the road can be the difference between a near miss and a tragedy. A warning system does not eliminate danger. It gives people a chance to choose.

It is not enough to say, "We will have a warning system." The system has to move faster than the water, and it has to speak in language people will obey. The hard truth is also the reassuring truth. This is buildable. Not easily, not instantly, but buildable. The work is clear. The phases can be managed. The architecture can be designed for time lag. That is where Tom Moser's story becomes the next step in the narrative.

Tom Moser: A Systems Architect in Flash Flood Country

Tom Moser is a retired NASA engineer, and in Kerr County's post-flood effort, that detail matters for the simplest of reasons. NASA engineers build systems that must work when failure is not an option. They think in dependencies, redundancy, interfaces, testing, and phases. They know that a system is only as strong as the weakest link between detection and response.

Moser has become a central figure in the county's effort to design and implement a flood prediction and warning system. He is not presented here as a savior. He is presented as what the moment required, a systems architect and phase-driven project manager who can translate urgency into structure. Moser's core insight aligns with Bushnoe's operational framing. The watershed does not care about good intentions. It responds to physics. The system must respond faster than physics.

His emphasis on automation is deliberate. A system dependent on human interpretation, phone calls, or manual relay introduces delay. In a watershed where lag times in the headwaters can be measured in minutes, delay costs lives. Moser's planning language is phase-based because phases are how complex systems become real without collapsing under their own ambition. In his work, Phase A is about establishing the foundation: what can be deployed quickly, what data sources exist, what must be integrated first. Phase B builds the next layer: additional instrumentation, stronger telemetry, improved dashboarding, clearer thresholds. Phase C moves toward the mature system: expanded coverage, refined modeling, and reliable dissemination channels that can be trusted under stress. This is not glamorous work. It is civil engineering of information.

Moser also describes lag time in plain language, because he knows that community adoption depends on the public understanding what the system can and cannot do. In certain headwater basins near Hunt, lag times from intense rainfall to peak flow can be as short as fifteen to twenty minutes. The basin is steep. The contributing area is comparatively small. When rainfall intensity concentrates over that area, water accelerates rapidly. By contrast, downstream near Center Point, lag times may extend to two to four hours. The basin broadens. Slopes decrease. There is room for warning based on upstream river stage, provided the upstream detection and modeling chain works.

That gap is measured in minutes. In flash flood country, minutes are the difference between panic and preparation. Moser frames the warning effort as an integration project, not a single device project. The system must bring together sensors, telemetry, dashboards, modeling, and dissemination into one operational picture. A siren without data is noise. A model without dissemination is a report. A dashboard without thresholds is a screen. The goal is not to build "a tool." The goal is to build a chain of reliability.

That chain, importantly, is not owned by one person or one institution. The effort is supported by multiple structures: working groups, oversight committees, partner memoranda of understanding, interfaces with the Commissioners Court, and UGRA board updates. That governance scaffolding is not bureaucracy for its own sake. It is how complex work stays aligned with public purpose.

And now the work has moved into a new operational reality:

UGRA has engaged West Consultants as the engineering firm to design and implement the flood warning system, including sirens, sensors, and the flood prediction infrastructure. The decision to bring in an engineering firm is a marker of seriousness. It turns intent into a deliverable. In a county that has learned what minutes mean, deliverables matter.

System Architecture and Time Lag: Designing for the Watershed Kerr County Has

The architecture of a flood warning system in Kerr County is shaped by one overriding constraint: Time behaves differently depending on where you stand in the watershed.

In the headwaters, the system must do two things simultaneously:

- Detect fast enough to matter.
- Communicate in a way that triggers immediate behavior change.

In downstream reaches, the system must do something slightly different:

- Use upstream signals to create longer warning windows.
- Communicate in a way that supports organized, staged response.

A system architecture that respects both realities tends to look like this:

1. **Field Layer (Detection):** Rain gauges and stream gauges are placed in key sub-basins with an understanding of terrain, historical runoff behavior, and the specific spots where rapid rise is most dangerous. Additional instrumentation is used where it improves the predictive chain.

2. **Communications Layer (Telemetry):** Reliable, redundant transmission of sensor data provides that severe weather does not silence the very system meant to speak.
3. **Data Integration Layer (Unified View):** A single operational picture reduces friction and enables decision-making without portal-hopping.
4. **Modeling Layer (Prediction):** Hydrologic and hydraulic modeling translates rainfall and upstream response into downstream expectations. This is where the system begins to "create time," particularly for downstream areas with longer lag.
5. **Decision Layer (Thresholds and Triggers):** Predefined thresholds, when crossed, activate alerts. This is where automation plays a role, reducing the time between detection and warning.
6. **Dissemination Layer (Warnings People Receive):** This is a blend of channels, potentially including sirens in critical locations, digital alerts, and interfaces with existing emergency communication systems. The choice is not either-or. It is redundancy because the conditions that produce a flash flood can also produce communication failure.
7. **Community Layer (Adoption and Behavior):** Training, education, and repeated reinforcement enables people to understand what an alert means and what action it requires. A warning system without community adoption is a technical artifact, not a safety system.

This architecture is not theoretical. It matches the operational realities Bushnoe describes, and the phase-driven build Moser is managing. It also aligns with UGRA's broader role: stewardship that protects the river's health and provides services to the community.

The time-lag dimension is the bridge among all these layers. The system must be designed so that, in places where lag is fifteen to twenty minutes, the detection and dissemination chain moves with minimal human friction. In places where lag is two to four hours, the system must use upstream information to create staged action: closing crossings, rerouting traffic, notifying camps, mobilizing response. The success metric, in plain language, is not perfection. It is time.

Time to move. Time to close. Time to stop driving into water. Time to pull campers from low ground. Time for a dispatcher or emergency manager to act before the river arrives.

That is why this chapter ends where it began: UGRA is an institution that listens, measures, and builds continuity. The post-flood effort is about turning that continuity into a warning capacity that respects Kerr County's geography and the watershed's speed.

From Principle to Process to Construction: The Arc from Rector to Bushnoe to Moser and Beyond

By the time one reaches this point in the narrative, the arc is clear. Rector framed stewardship as public trust and governance accountability, and he spoke candidly about the need to adapt a midcentury mandate to a modern hydrologic reality. He clarified what UGRA is responsible for and what it cannot do alone, setting the stage for partnership rather than confusion.

Bushnoe described how that mandate translates into real-time operational reality. She explained why mitigation and warning must be understood as different disciplines, and why data integration is not a convenience but a life-saving requirement. She made lag time visible, showing how the watershed's speed shapes every design choice. She also emphasized what the public must do for the system to work: adopt it, learn it, and act on it.

Moser carried the work into construction logic. He framed the system as a chain of reliability, built in phases, with automation used not to replace human judgment but to remove delay where delay destroys the warning window. He translated urgency into structure, and structure into deliverables. The engagement of West

Consultants marks the move from planning into implementation of sirens, sensors, and flood prediction infrastructure.

The movement from Rector to Bushnoe has been from principle to process. The movement from Bushnoe to Moser has been from process to construction. This is how communities rebuild capability: not with a single speech, not with a single purchase, not with a single agency acting in isolation, but with a coherent narrative of responsibility and a disciplined architecture that turns risk into time. While UGRA has led the way, other local institutions, state agencies and private enterprises were involved.

Louis Amestoy, editor and publisher of *The Kerr County Lead*, wrote, "In the span of three days, Kerr County's flood warning system went from concept to construction. On Wednesday, the Upper Guadalupe River Authority unanimously hired West Consultants to engineer the sirens, sensors, gauges, and flood prediction technology that will one day give residents, camp operators, and emergency managers the advance notice they need when the river rises. On Friday, the Kerrville Public Utility Board (KPUB) was awarded $14.7 million in state broadband funding to build the communications network that will carry all of that data in real time." He went on to state, "This level of interagency collaboration is unprecedented. KPUB, LCRA [Lower Colorado River Authority], UGRA, two cities, the county, a telephone cooperative, and a state agency all aligned around a single project. That is extraordinary. It should not be taken for granted."

One additional point belongs here. Bushnoe drew an important distinction between warning and mitigation. Warning is about minutes. Mitigation is about years. UGRA's post-flood work has necessarily focused on building a warning system that can turn upstream conditions into time to act. But former UGRA board member Mike Hughes has pressed a related and longer-range question: whether Kerr County should also study flood control infrastructure on the upper forks of the Guadalupe as a complementary form of protection, not as a substitute for warning. That distinction matters. A warning system helps people respond. A mitigation structure, if feasible, might reduce the physical force of the flood itself. Bushnoe's distinction between mitigation and warning runs throughout this chapter, and Hughes's proposal belongs squarely on the mitigation side of that ledger.

Hughes's idea is not a call for massive reservoirs or a Tennessee Valley Authority-style chain of permanent impoundments (retention dams). Rather, he argues for studying a series of smaller *detention* dams on the upper tributaries, particularly the North Fork, South Fork, and Johnson Creek. He explained that these would be designed to remain mostly empty, with an opening at the base sized to pass ordinary stream flow while holding back part of a flood surge when runoff exceeds that capacity. In his words, the structures would be "purposely designed to not remain full."

The concept is straightforward. As floodwater builds, the opening can pass only so much. The excess begins to back up behind the dam, temporarily storing part of the surge and releasing it more slowly. Hughes described the process as a kind of metering system that "prevents the peak flood," adding, "that's that peak that does all the damage." He emphasized that this is not speculative engineering. "There are over two thousand of these kinds of dams in the country," he said, and noted that San Antonio is protected by detention-type dams as well.

He also stressed their relative simplicity. Unlike larger retention structures, detention dams do not depend on constant active management. Hughes called them "basically dumb structures. You build them, and you walk away." That phrase should not be read as casualness. His point is that their function is mechanical rather than heavily supervised: They are built to slow and meter water, not to maintain a permanent pool or rely on frequent operational decisions.

Hughes does not overstate the case. He recognizes that the upper watershed is complex and that no single intervention can eliminate flood risk. Even so, he believes the idea is serious enough to deserve study because the goal is not perfection. It is reduction of the peak. In practical terms, he argues that detention dams might narrow the floodplain footprint and reduce downstream destruction enough to help protect camps, cabins, crossings, and lives. That makes his proposal an important final reminder that Kerr County needs warning systems now, but it may also need to think just as seriously about long-term mitigation. The path is long, but the idea deserves a place in the county's future-facing conversation.

Reassurance, Resolve, and Sober Confidence

Kerr County will never be able to promise that the Guadalupe River will not flood again. The watershed's terrain, the speed of runoff, and the volatility of storms make that promise impossible. The only honest promise is a different one: that the community will build systems that reduce uncertainty and expand the time available to act. UGRA's story is a story of that honest promise. Amestoy stated, "Kerr County took meaningful steps toward making sure that the next time the Guadalupe rises, the people in its path have a fighting chance."

The statutory foundation gave Kerr County a durable institution for watershed stewardship. Decades of measurement and public service built credibility. The flood revealed the difference between stewardship and warning, and it forced the community to confront what "minutes" actually mean in flash flood country. The response has not been a search for a single hero. It has been the construction of a system: governance scaffolding, operational clarity, engineering phases, and a growing commitment to turning data into decisions.

That is where reassurance comes from: The work is structured, roles are clarifying, and the community is building capability rather than chasing comfort. That is where resolve comes from: The flood was a catalyst, not a conclusion. It forced a new chapter of stewardship that includes warning, built through partnership.

And that is where sober confidence comes from: not from optimism, but from architecture. A system that respects lag time, that reduces human friction, that builds redundancy into communications, and that speaks in language people can act on is the kind of system that can save lives. In Kerr County, the river will always be part of the story. UGRA's work, and the work now underway with partners, is to ensure that when the river rises again, the community has more than memory. It has time.

TEN
LOCAL PRESS AS INFRASTRUCTURE

The Press That Stayed: Local Journalism as Rural Infrastructure After the Flood

In the first hours after a small-town catastrophe, people do not need cleverness. They need clarity. They need to know what is true, what is not yet known, what to do next, and where to go for updates that will not change every time a new rumor blows through. In Kerr County after the flood, the national press arrived, worked hard, and then moved on. That is the nature of national news: It is episodic, and it is built to chase the next large story.

Local journalism is built differently. It lives inside the community it covers. It knows the roads, the landmarks, the names, and the unspoken history that explains why a particular camp matters, why a bend in the river is more than a bend in the river, and why a county exhibit hall can become, overnight, the nerve center of information and misunderstanding all at once. Most importantly, local journalism stays. It is there in the immediate aftermath, and it is still there deep into recovery, when the story becomes less dramatic, more complicated, and far more consequential for the people who will live with the outcome.

For this chapter, I interviewed Louis Amestoy, editor and publisher of *The Kerr County Lead* (*The Lead*); John Wells, publisher of *The Kerrville Daily Times*; and Irene Van Winkle, *West Kerr Current* journalist. Their voices are different in cadence and vantage point, but they point to the same truth: In rural America, local press is not merely a commentator on community life. It is part of the community's infrastructure. When everything works, people barely notice it. When a disaster hits, they suddenly realize how much they depend on it.

Two refrains are apparent because they ran through the lived experience of the flood's information environment. First, what people needed to know. Second, what was rumor. Those two forces collided, repeatedly, in the days and weeks after the flood. The local press did not eliminate that collision. No one could. But it helped the community navigate it.

What People Needed to Know: Service Information as Public Safety

The first obligation of local journalism in a catastrophe is not to deliver a grand narrative. It is to deliver service. That word can sound small, even quaint. It is not. Service information is public safety. Amestoy described the early posture as disciplined repetition: frequent updates, consistent delivery, and a clear distinction between what is confirmed and what is still being checked. The key is not speed for its own sake. The key is a steady, reliable cadence that the community can trust. In a crisis, time does not merely pass. It compresses. The decision window shrinks. People make choices with partial information because they must. The most valuable newsroom product in those hours is not the perfectly crafted story. It is the dependable update that reduces uncertainty, even by a little.

Van Winkle captured the same need from the perspective of West Kerr, where distance, darkness and the practical reality of rural geography compounded the early uncertainty. In her telling, communication was "sketchy at first." The flood hit in the middle of the night. Many people were asleep. Roads were compromised.

Emergency responders were operating in conditions in which even they could not immediately assess the full scope. In that environment, the local press becomes a translator and a stabilizer. It helps residents understand what is happening without amplifying panic.

This is also where a critical distinction emerges between the kinds of outlets that make up a local press ecosystem. A digital outlet can update in near real time. A weekly paper cannot. A weekly paper has a different strength: It can synthesize, contextualize, and document in a way that becomes part of the historical record. Van Winkle was direct about this: A newspaper is different, and a weekly is different still. The difference is not a weakness. It serves as a reminder that "local press" is not one thing. It is a set of complementary tools serving the same community, under constraints that are rarely visible to readers.

That is the first lesson of "what people needed to know." It is not only the content. It is the reliability of the channel.

Press Conferences: When Volume Is Not Clarity

Press conferences are often designed for institutional convenience, not community clarity. They are built to show coordination, to demonstrate visibility, and to establish an official narrative. In a catastrophe, they can also become a place where the public hears fragments: partial numbers, cautious language, agency boundaries, and competing priorities. When the room is full, the microphones multiply and the stakes are high, the output can sound like information while functioning as noise.

Van Winkle described the news conferences as crowded with agencies and many outlets. In a rural county, that sudden concentration of officials and media can look like decisive action. Yet to the family trying to find a missing loved one or the resident trying to understand whether a particular road is passable, it can feel remote. News conferences can provide the "official frame," but the local press still must do the most important work: Translate what was said into what it means for Kerr County people right then.

Amestoy's emphasis on hour-by-hour confirmation reflects that translation. A news conference might tell you that "assessments are ongoing." A local update tells you what is confirmed, what is still uncertain, and where to go for the next verified piece. In short, a news conference can create volume. The local press creates clarity.

Rumor: The Information Hazard No One Can Ignore

If you want to understand rumor in a catastrophe, start with compassion, not condemnation. Rumor is what human beings produce when uncertainty becomes unbearable. It is a coping mechanism that turns into an information hazard.

Rural geography intensifies the hazard. Van Winkle pointed to distances between camps, houses, and towns, and the difficulty of getting eyes on what was happening. When people cannot see for themselves, they fill in the gaps. In the early hours, when official communication is inconsistent and firsthand reporting is constrained, rumor can move faster than fact. It also "feels" true because it carries emotion, urgency, and often a moral storyline.

This is where local journalism earns its keep. Local journalism does not merely state facts. Local journalism understands its community, and it holds government authorities accountable on behalf of its readers. It tells readers: Do not chase every claim. Come back here. We will update what we can confirm. We will say plainly what we cannot confirm. We will not launder speculation into certainty.

That discipline is hard because it runs against the emotional momentum of a community in shock. It is also hard because rumor pressures the newsroom from multiple directions. Some people beg the press to publish something because they want it to be true. Others insist the press is hiding information when it is simply refusing to publish what cannot be verified. In a small town, those pressures feel personal. The journalist is not an abstract brand. The journalist is a neighbor.

And this is where the national-versus-local distinction matters again. National outlets can publish, leave, and never face the grocery-store conversation. Local outlets cannot. They must live with the consequences of what they amplify. That reality does not guarantee perfection. But it creates accountability as a daily condition of work.

Verification Under Uncertainty: Publish, Hold, Correct

A reader might assume verification is a simple binary: Either you confirm something or you do not. In a catastrophe, verification is a set of choices made under time pressure, uncertainty, and deep human need. It is a discipline, not a slogan.

Van Winkle described her method in the simplest possible terms: Seek firsthand knowledge. When she could not see something herself, she sought witnesses and victims, people with direct experience, and she worked to separate what they personally observed from what they heard. This is not glamorous work. It is careful, patient, and often emotionally heavy. But it is the only path to reporting that does not become rumor.

Amestoy emphasized the same principle from a digital, high-frequency posture: comprehensive, competent, real-time reporting, measured and vetted. Those words matter. "Real time" without "measured" becomes chaos. "Comprehensive" without "vetted" becomes rumor at scale. The point is not to publish first. The point is to publish responsibly and to keep returning to the community with updates that do not whiplash.

In practice, verification during the flood followed three core actions that readers can understand, even if they never see the machinery behind it:

- Publish what is confirmed, and label it as confirmed.
- Hold what is not confirmed, even when the community demands it.
- Correct quickly and clearly when you get it wrong—because you will get something wrong in a disaster of this magnitude.

That third point is not a weakness. It is a mark of institutional integrity.

Trust Is Built in the Open

Amestoy offered a story that captures the hardest truth about crisis reporting: Sometimes the most responsible act is to retract something that people desperately want to believe. He described a story that circulated about two girls that was not true. When *The Lead* corrected it, the reaction was intense. People begged the outlet not to retract. The correction sparked more attention than the original claim.

Here is the part that matters: The correction traveled farther than the error. In Amestoy's telling, the original reached hundreds of thousands; the retraction reached roughly a million. That is not merely a social media curiosity. It is a demonstration of how trust is negotiated in public during a catastrophe. Corrections do two things at once. They acknowledge fallibility, and they demonstrate accountability. The national media can correct too, of course. But the local press corrects with a different kind of stake. It is correcting in front of neighbors, friends, sources, critics, and grieving families, and it is doing so while still covering the story.

If you want to know why local press is critical in rural America, start here. It is not because local outlets never make mistakes. It is because they have to live with their mistakes and address them in the same community they serve. That produces a correction culture that is not performative. It is operational. Van Winkle's ethic of calm accuracy fits naturally alongside this. "Just the facts" is not a slogan. It is a discipline that makes correction possible because it rejects the temptation to publish what *feels* true instead of what can be *shown* to be true.

Internal Community Conflict: The Pressure Cooker Nobody Escapes

The information environment after a catastrophe is always a

pressure cooker. In that pressure cooker, people do not merely seek information. They seek meaning. They seek blame. They seek reassurance. They seek someone to tell them that what happened makes sense. And when official answers are incomplete, the community will generate its own narratives. Some of those narratives are healthy. Some are corrosive. Many are a mix of both.

The local press cannot pretend that conflict does not exist. If it does, it loses credibility. At the same time, the local press cannot become an accelerant. This is where the local outlet's long-term relationship to the community becomes an asset. Local journalists know which claims are recycled from past disputes, which grievances are longstanding, and which rumors are simply the mind trying to resolve chaos with a story.

The discipline is to report what can be confirmed, give voice to the community's pain without turning pain into accusation, and keep the focus on what helps the county move forward.

Amestoy's decision to keep updating hour by hour, and then to continue deep into later hearings, reflects a belief that information is not a one-time delivery. It is a continuing obligation. Van Winkle's emphasis on neutrality and long-term presence reflects the same point: The local press is not visiting. It is home.

The Newsroom Under Strain: Producing Steadiness When You Are Not Steady

One of the easiest mistakes readers make is to imagine a newsroom as a machine that runs the same way under all conditions. It does not. In a catastrophe, the newsroom is made of people. Those people are tired, worried, and sometimes personally affected. They are also working under constraints that are not visible on the page.

Van Winkle described basic but powerful constraints: road conditions, access limitations, and the inability to get to certain areas immediately, especially in West Kerr. This is the reality of rural reporting: You cannot simply hop in a car and appear anywhere in twenty minutes. Even getting to a place can be a logistical challenge, and in a disaster, it becomes a safety question.

At the same time, the demand for information multiplies. Amestoy described the early volume of output, including a striking number of bylined stories in the first week. That is not a brag. It is a clue about the workload required to keep a community informed when the normal channels are stressed or failing.

This strain matters because it shapes the kind of reporting the community receives. A high-frequency outlet can provide continuous updates, but it must guard against exhaustion-induced error. A weekly paper can provide synthesis and documentation, but it must guard against the perception that it is "behind" when, in reality, it is operating in its own cadence.

What you see as a reader is the finished product. What you do not see is the effort to maintain tone and steadiness when the journalist is not steady at all. And this returns us to news conferences. In a strained environment, a news conference can either help or hinder. It helps when it provides clear, consistent, actionable information that the local press can validate and deliver. It hinders when it produces contradictory fragments that the local press must untangle while the public interprets those fragments as certainty.

Local outlets do not merely report the news conference. They translate it. They filter it. They check it. They correct it when needed. That is not ancillary work. It is core community service.

Recovery: From Warning to Memory, From Damage to Meaning

After the first days, the story changes. The immediate danger recedes. The public's questions evolve. The community moves from "What is happening?" to, "What does this mean?" and, "What comes next?" This is where national attention often fades because the story becomes less visual and more complex.

Local press does not have that option. It stays to tell the recovery story, which is where resilience is actually measured. Van Winkle described the recovery phase with a reporter's eye and a neighbor's heart: memorials, crosses, flowers, gatherings, the continued mourning and healing, and a deliberate focus on responders and "unsung heroes." This is not "soft" coverage. It is community documentation. It preserves memory. It honors loss without exploiting it. It records the small acts that, in hindsight, define a county's resilience.

Amestoy described staying with the story as it moved into longer civic processes, including a major hearing before the Texas Legislature that ran for nearly twelve hours. He also referenced that the story continued into courts. It continued into legal processes, policy debates, and community arguments about what should change. Those are the kinds of issues that do not fit neatly into a two-week national cycle. They are the kinds of issues local press must cover because local residents must live with the outcome.

This is why the "local press ecosystem" matters. The county needs fast updates during the emergency. It needs careful synthesis and documentation during recovery. It needs a continuing civic record as the story moves into hearings, rebuilding, and yes, into courts.

Our Duty is Simple: Remember

Daily journalism runs on velocity. In a flood, that is not a criticism; it is a public service. People need "where," "what," and "now." They need to know road closures, shelter locations, fatality confirmations, and the next official update. That is the kind of information that keeps a community from being crushed a second time by rumor.

But velocity has a limit. A fast update cannot carry the full weight of loss. It cannot hold names long enough for them to become more than a number. It cannot explain, in a way that is both accessible and accurate, how multiple systems failed to meet one another at the moment they were most needed. And it cannot, by itself, create the kind of durable public record that a rural community can return to when the national spotlight turns elsewhere.

That is why *The Lead*'s magazine, entitled *Our Duty is Simple: Remember*, matters. It is not a replacement for the rapid-fire digital coverage that *The Lead* and other outlets provided during the crisis.

It is part of the spectrum of media releases that followed the flood: the immediate posts, the rolling web updates, the print products that marked time, and finally the long-form piece that tried to do what breaking news cannot. It is the capstone because it was designed to outlast the day-to-day churn. It was meant to sit on a table, not disappear into a feed.

Amestoy told me plainly that he wanted to gather "our best journalism in a single place." He did not believe he could accomplish that digitally. He wanted "to try it in a magazine." He also acknowledged the cost of that choice, saying, "Honestly, it was probably one of the hardest projects I have ever done because I did it by myself with, of course, Jennifer's help." Even that line tells you something important about rural press after catastrophe; the work is often heroic, and it is often done with fewer hands than the public assumes.

The reason behind the project was duty, and duty in this context meant community care. Amestoy described the magazine as "literally almost a book as far as the size of it goes." Then he drew the line that defines the entire product: "The editorial purpose of the magazine was to remember all those who lost their lives." It was to win an argument, settle a score, or prove a point. It was to remember.

That emphasis matters because remembrance is not only emotional. It is civic. A community that forgets its dead also forgets the obligations it owes the living: to learn, to improve, and to reduce the chances that the same failures repeat. Memory is a kind of governance. It is the long tail of accountability. All of this is a part of the infrastructure that local press brings to a community.

Amestoy's own path to that conclusion ran through the very human question many communities wrestle with after tragedy: How many memorials are enough? He described being "on the fence" and struggling with the idea of how many physical memorials Kerr County would need. Then he attended a service where names were read aloud, and he found himself moved by the act of public naming. Afterward, he sent a text to a family member who had lost a child at Camp Mystic: "Your kid, your child will not be forgotten."

That is not a reporter soliciting a comment. That is a neighbor, a friend, making a promise.

And then he connected that promise directly to the magazine: "I think that is kind of why I did the magazine too, that it is very easy for us to forget about this, or *want* to forget about it. And I wanted to have it as a sort of a physical reminder of what happened that day and the importance of remembering those who were lost." In one paragraph he gave the three pillars that define this capstone: memory—do not forget; accountability—this happened for reasons that can be examined; and explanation—the public deserves the story in its full, unvarnished form.

Print s Not Nostalgia. It Is Retention

A key decision in *Our Duty is Simple: Remember* is that it is print-first in an era that expects everything to live online. Amestoy is not sentimental about that choice. He is tactical. He said, "I believe this very firmly, that print in its form still matters. It still resonates with the audience. The audience remembers it more clearly." He described the difference in recall that comes with physical reading: "When you read something physically ... you have a tendency to kind of recall things more." He admitted he did not know if there was "scientific evidence," but he had seen it play out in how communities remember what they read and where they read it.

That observation is not quaint. It is a direct response to a modern weakness: the way platform algorithms decide what people see and what they miss. During the flood, *The Lead* pushed information constantly. Amestoy described the digital work as "exhaustive," grounded in hard-earned lessons from other disasters: "You give as much information as you possibly can repeatedly throughout the day." He recalled the sheer volume: "There were 11 stories that day and 55 updates on the web, on the Facebook page." That is what it looks like when local press tries to be an information utility.

But he also described the structural problem: "Unbelievable traffic," yet "only a small percentage of people probably saw our content on a regular basis." Someone told him they saw "three stories" that day, and his response was blunt: "Oh, no, that was nothing." The point is not that the reader didn't fail; The point is that the distribution system is broken. A flood is not the time to discover that your community's information supply chain is governed by friction, feed design, and attention collapse.

Print pushes back against that. A magazine does not solve every distribution problem, but it does create a stable artifact. It gives the community a shared reference point. It is a way of saying: This story is not a series of posts; it is a record.

How the Magazine Handled the "Alert Gap" Narrative

Shortly after the flood, one storyline began to harden: Someone must be at fault because people did not receive the alerts they expected. In a disaster, that kind of narrative is understandable. When the unimaginable happens, human beings reach for a cause that fits in a sentence. What failed? Who failed? Why was I not warned?

Amestoy did not deny the legitimacy of these questions. In fact, he framed it as central to his own reporting: "My big question in my reporting early on was always...why did we not get alerts where I live?" Yet he also saw how quickly the question became a simplified accusation. He described that narrative getting "pretty bad pretty quickly."

This is where *Our Duty is Simple: Remember* becomes more than remembrance. It becomes a correction to oversimplification. Not by exonerating anyone nor by inflaming tensions, but by insisting on a more accurate frame: the alert gap as an expectation mismatch in a system that was not designed to meet the public's assumptions.

Amestoy pointed to confusion around CodeRED, the county text system that some outside observers treated as if it were a universal public warning tool. He was clear: "That is an opt-in service as a text message service, essentially." In other words, it is not FEMA. It is not the WEA system. It is not a mandatory broadcast that reaches every phone. It is a subscription tool, and like any opt-in tool, it will always miss a large share of the population in a sleeping county at 4 a.m. if uptake is low.

But even with the opt-in, *The Texas Tribune* reported that the alerts only reached 1,113 users in Kerr County. Under 2,000 recipients in a county-wide emergency, with over 55,000 residents is not a workable reliance point. It is a helpful supplement for those who sign up, not the backbone of public warning. When the public expects opt-in to function like universal broadcast, disappointment becomes anger, and anger becomes a demand for blame.

Our Duty is Simple: Remember's contribution, as I read it and as Amestoy described it, was to restore proportion. It put the alert question in context, not to dismiss it but to make it actionable. That is how local accountability is supposed to work. A community cannot fix what it refuses to name, nor what it describes inaccurately.

In the immediate aftermath, news conferences and partial explanations can become gasoline. Amestoy noted that the first news conference "kind of got sideways" and "made it look like Kerr County was not prepared for this event." He said the reality was "far different," and that public records already pointed toward that. The magazine, by design, creates the space to show what "far different" means without turning the work into an indictment or a defense brief. It is an explanation product, and explanation is a form of de-escalation.

Explanation That Goes Deeper Than "Weather Happened"

A second major contribution of *Our Duty is Simple: Remember* is that it refuses to let the flood be explained away as a one-off act of nature. Again, this is not a move toward blame. It is a move toward understanding. Amestoy told me that one of the most important pieces in *Our Duty is Simple: Remember* was "explaining the science of the storm," and he credited Jennifer Dean as a key part of that effort: "She really dug into that deeply."

That kind of long horizon is not what most crisis coverage can carry. But it is exactly what communities need if they are serious about prevention. It connects the present tragedy to choices made over decades. It reframes "unpredictable" into "patterned." And it gives public officials, landowners, and civic institutions something more useful than grief: a map of contributing factors that can be acted upon. This is another reason *Our Duty is Simple: Remember* belongs in the spectrum of releases. Digital coverage is the oxygen mask. The magazine is the rehab plan. They do different work, but both matter.

The Capstone Function: Memory as a Public Service

The capstone role of *Our Duty is Simple: Remember* is not only what it contains. It is what it signals: that the dead are not an accounting line. They are names. It signals that remembrance is not passive. It is an act of care for families still living with a wound that does not resolve on the timeline of a news cycle. It signals that the community's story will not be surrendered to outsiders who arrive late, ask the loudest questions, and then depart when the answers get complicated.

It also signals something structural about local journalism itself. Amestoy described local outlets as "extremely vulnerable institutions," "underfunded and understaffed," and he spoke from experience when he said, "I am a one-man show." He also noted there were other similarly situated print media in Kerr County. He reminded us what a one-person show still managed to do: get the need-to-know information out quickly, provide local context, and then build a durable record.

This is where *Our Duty is Simple: Remember* quietly became an accountability mechanism for the community as a whole. When a story is captured in long form, with care and with names and with context, it becomes harder for leaders, institutions, and even neighbors to hide behind amnesia. It also becomes harder for the community to outsource its responsibility to a single villain or a single failure. The record insists on complexity. Complexity, handled responsibly, is not an excuse. It is the beginning of improvement.

For me, *Our Duty is Simple: Remember* is the final proof point that local press stays. Not only in presence but in commitment. It stays through the grind of updates. It stays through the backlash and the rumor storms. It stays into recovery, when attention drops and fatigue rises. And then, if it has the capacity, it stays long enough to do the hardest thing journalism can do in a wounded community: tell the story in a way that preserves dignity.

Amestoy's words about the "physical reminder" is the simplest statement of why *Our Duty is Simple: Remember* belongs. In the wake of catastrophe, communities do not only need information. They need a way to hold the truth without being crushed by it. They need a shared artifact that honors the dead and steadies the living. They need a record that can be read by those who were here, and by those who were not, years from now, when the river looks calm and the temptation to forget grows stronger.

Our Duty is Simple: Remember the title stays. In practice, it is not simple at all. But it demonstrates what that duty looks like when a local outlet decides the job is not finished when the headlines stop.

John Wells and the First Hours: The Text That Changed the Morning

John Wells woke on the morning of July 4 to what still felt, at first, like a bad Hill Country storm and little more. During the night, lightning had cracked so loudly that it frightened his four-year-old out of bed and into his parents' room. The family had holiday plans. His first thought was not catastrophe but of inconvenience: Perhaps the weather would wash out the town's Fourth of July celebrations. In retrospect, that ordinary parental frame captures how disasters begin for many people, not with a clear alarm but with a half-understood interruption to normal life. Wells was not waiting for a mass casualty event. He was listening to thunder, comforting a child, and assuming the day ahead might simply be wet and disappointing.

Then came the text at 6:45 a.m. *The Kerrville Daily Times*

Managing Editor Jeanette Nash messaged him that Tom Holden, a former photographer, had reported flooding in the park and that she was going to get photographs. Wells immediately told her not to worry about it because he lived closer and would go himself. He put on his boots and headed out about 7:10 a.m., still believing he was going to photograph a flood, not document a countywide trauma. As he drove, Facebook began filling with images and videos. He passed the dam and saw roads being blocked off. He stopped, filmed, and kept moving, then reached the library area where the water had already swallowed much of the path. Even there, standing near places he knew well, he still did not yet understand that lives had been lost. He only knew that this was "more than we thought."

This sequence is revealing for what it says about local journalism. Wells did not enter the story through an assignment desk hundreds of miles away. He entered it by driving familiar roads and recognizing that landmarks he knew well no longer looked right. Local catastrophe reporting begins in that act of recognition. It begins when someone who knows the place understands that the place has suddenly become unrecognizable. He was not waiting for officials to organize the narrative. He was beginning the work of seeing, confirming, and trying to understand in real time.

Even before he reached the office, Wells's role shifted from observer to organizer. While downtown, recording video, he realized he needed to check on his people. Some staff members lived near the river or close enough to creeks and low areas that they might be in danger. He texted them to ask if they were all right. At the same time, townspeople began reaching out to ask whether he could confirm reports they were hearing, especially those about the camps upriver. The pattern was already set: The community was desperate for facts, while the facts themselves were still scattered, incomplete, and buried under rumor. Wells told those asking that he had not yet heard anything he could confirm, but that the paper would investigate. That was the first duty line of the day, and in many ways the duty line for the whole section: Hear everything, believe little, confirm what you can.

What People Needed to Know

By the time Wells pulled up to the office, the *Kerrville Daily Times*'s phones were "ringing off the hook." The callers were not only residents. Fox News, CNN, NBC, CBS, and others were already asking the paper to confirm what they were hearing. At almost the same moment, Wells was learning that some of his own people had been directly hit. One employee had lost everything when floodwaters swallowed his house and had to swim out, even going underwater to reach the roof and get his family to safety. Another staff member's family also lost everything. More than half of the paper's staff were out of town on vacation. Others were stranded or managing children and family emergencies. The *Daily Times* was being asked to function as an information hub at precisely the moment it was least equipped, on paper, to do so.

Yet what emerged from Wells's account was not paralysis but prioritization. The first obligation, as he described it, was to get out "timely coverage, but accurate coverage." That was not rhetorical polish. It was an operating discipline. The paper's mission in those first hours was practical: Determine where people needed to meet, what roads were closed, which names on missing lists had been confirmed, what could responsibly be said about the camps, and what updates were solid enough to publish without making a desperate situation worse. When the decision window collapses in a crisis, service information is public safety. Wells understood that instinctively. The paper could not rescue anyone from floodwater. It could help rescue the community from informational chaos.

Wells's job was not to produce a grand narrative in the first hours, it was to reduce uncertainty. Every update that clarified a road closure, a confirmed fatality count, or the status of a public location had direct community value. It is easy to underestimate that function because it can sound mundane. Yet in rural disaster, the practical update may be more important than the elegant story; the local paper is not merely describing events; it is helping the county navigate them.

Verification Under Uncertainty: Hold, Check, Confirm

If there is a core ethic running through Wells's telling, it is verification under stress. He said flatly that if the paper could not confirm that someone was missing or dead, it was not going to publish that claim. The staff would not put out a name or status "until we have cold hard facts" from a family member or another source they trusted. In a small town, that kind of restraint is not easy. The emotional pressure runs in the opposite direction. Families want answers. Friends want hope. Rumor arrives carrying urgency, grief, and a demand to act now. Wells and his staff chose to slow that emotional momentum just enough to check it.

That restraint became even more disciplined after one painful lesson. Wells recalled that the paper did publish one report that turned out not to be true, involving a little girl supposedly being found. The story was not printed carelessly. Three reporters had called, and two local sources had told them the information was true. Yet it was not. Wells described that as a "wakeup call." From then on, the standard tightened further: Before anything went out, reporters were going to make every effort to confirm that it was right.

This is the sort of detail that matters as it demonstrates that verification is not a slogan. It is a series of hard choices made under time pressure, emotional strain, and imperfect evidence. It shows that correction culture begins before the correction. It begins in the decision to hold what cannot be confirmed, even when others are already circulating it. In a disaster, rumor often feels compassionate because people want to share anything that might help. But unverified hope can wound people as deeply as bad news. The discipline Wells and his team showed is the refusal to turn possibility into fact.

The Kerrville Daily Times also had to improvise a publishing cadence that matched the crisis. Because the July 4 holiday edition had already gone to press the day before, that printed paper was instantly obsolete. Wells said the team knew the community would see it and think, in effect, this is not what happened today. He decided to build a complete e-edition reflecting the actual events of July 4, and the staff worked around the clock to make that happen. During the first days, while the normal print schedule could not keep pace, the newsroom updated online stories continuously and then carried those developments into later print editions. This was local journalism adjusting its form without changing its mission.

The Newsroom Under Strain: Producing Steadiness When You Are Not Steady

Wells said his first priority was his staff because "we are a family." He told them that if they needed fifteen minutes, they could step outside. But when they came back in, there was work to do. That statement does not sound dramatic, but it contains the emotional architecture of crisis reporting. There was no fantasy that the newsroom could somehow be untouched by grief. They knew people who had lost everything. Some knew people who had lost their lives. The choice was not between feeling and functioning. The choice was how to keep functioning while feeling all of it.

Wells also emphasized how small the staff was relative to the national attention pouring onto Kerrville. Kerrville is a small town of about 25,000 people, with a modest newsroom, but "all the eyes of the whole country" were suddenly on it. That imbalance meant every *Kerrville Daily Times* story published carried a disproportionate burden. Local people were reading it. National outlets were reading it. Families outside Texas were reading it. Wells said the first day alone produced more than 18 million or 20 million page views, numbers that would never be normal for a small-town paper. That exposure made accuracy even more essential because every error would travel at scale.

At the same time, Wells noted that support came from the wider Texas newspaper community. The Southern Newspapers company and other affiliated papers sent lunches, care baskets, snacks, teas, and simple reminders to the *Kerrville Daily Times* staff that others had been through hurricanes and would stand with them now. A rural paper is local, but it is not entirely alone. It can be sustained by a professional ecosystem that understands both the practical and emotional weight of disaster coverage.

Serving Kerr County First: Why Wells Refused the National Media

Wells made a deliberate and consequential choice in the first hours: He denied interview requests from national television outlets. He said he told his staffers that their normal goal was to support their community, not to tell the story to national news. Taking half an hour or forty-five minutes to sit for outside interviews would have taken time away from the local mission. He also made clear that he did not trust where some of those interviews would go. He was not interested in spending the earliest hours answering blame-oriented questions about what should have been done differently when the county was still in the middle of grief and confusion.

This refusal was not parochial defensiveness. It was a statement about journalistic purpose. Wells later explained that the national media was there for views and would be gone in a week, while the local paper had to remain with the community. The *Kerrville Daily Times* was not going to "play the blame game" in those first days. It was going to focus on what the community needed to know and on the good work still happening around them. Whatever one thinks about the timing of accountability reporting, Wells's position during the immediate aftermath was clear: The local press should not allow the logic of national spectacle to displace the logic of local service.

Information as a Public Good: The Paywall Comes Down

Wells made a decision to take down the *Kerrville Daily Times*'s website paywall for the first couple of weeks. That choice was made within the first few hours because, as he put it, "this information belongs to the public for free." Money did not matter in that moment. As for the first flood print edition, the paper printed and gave away extra quantities, and dozens upon dozens of nonsubscribers came to pick up copies. The point was larger than reader acquisition. The paper wanted family members of missing persons and people outside the county to be able to follow what was happening without obstacle or delay.

This is one of the clearest examples of journalism functioning as civic service rather than simply a product. Wells even described families calling the paper directly asking whether the staff knew anything about missing relatives. In some cases, the *Kerrville Daily Times* took down names and promised to call back if they learned more. That is not a typical function of a commercial news outlet in ordinary times. In extraordinary times, it becomes part of the social infrastructure of a county in distress. The paper becomes not merely a broadcaster of information but a node in the community's search for orientation.

Trust Built in Real Time

Wells had been in Kerrville only eight months when the flood hit. That detail makes what followed more striking. He said the *Kerrville Daily Times* experienced the largest month of subscription growth in its history. Former subscribers returned. New readers joined. Many stayed. To Wells, that surge was not just a business metric. It was proof that the community recognized, in a moment of need, why a local paper mattered. It was also evidence that trust had been built in real time, through repeated acts of timeliness, restraint, and accuracy.

He framed that trust in simple language. The goal was that if someone read the paper, they would believe it was fact. The paper did not care about being first, but it did care about being timely. That is a subtle but important distinction. Timeliness serves the public. Being first often serves ego or competition. Wells's formulation captures the ethic of a local paper that understood its burden and accepted that burden as part of its civic role.

From Warning to Memory: Guadalupe Rising

By the Sunday after the flood, Wells had already concluded that ordinary newspaper coverage would not be enough. What had happened was too large, too painful, and too historically significant to be contained in routine editions. The result was *Guadalupe Rising*, conceived both as a fundraiser and as a keepsake for generations. Wells said plainly that no one from the national media should be able to come to Kerrville, profit from the story, and leave the community without its own durable record. *The Kerrville Daily Times* felt entrusted to preserve what happened because it had the staff, the relationships, and the rootedness to do so.

The title itself reflected Wells's reading of the county's response. It referred not only to the river but to the rising of the community, the way people rallied, volunteered, searched, gave, and stood together. The magazine became more than a commemorative product; it became a vessel for memory, mourning, and civic identity.

Wells stressed how hard the magazine was to produce. It became a second job layered on top of the paper's daily obligations. Interviews lasted hours, not minutes. People broke down in the middle of them. Reporters became, at times, shoulders to cry on. The emotional labor of building the magazine was itself part of the story. When it finally appeared, Wells said, many readers told him it helped them cope. Some broke down when they opened it. Yet the magazine also raised nearly $35,000 for the Community Foundation, making it at once an act of remembrance and an act of material support.

Why Rural and Small-Town Journalism Matters

To understand why rural and small-town journalism matters, one must begin with a simple fact: Local news is about more than proximity. It is about embeddedness. It is about who is still in the room when the story stops being dramatic, when the cameras leave, when the official statements thin out, and when the community is left with the harder work of understanding, mourning, arguing, rebuilding, and remembering. That is the case Wells made most plainly when he described the newspaper as "a reflection of our community," an outlet whose editorial meetings are not driven by clickbait or by what will draw the most views, but by "what is the most important thing today for our community."

That distinction is the heart of the matter. In a rural county or a small-town news ecosystem, journalism is not merely content production. It is civic translation. It tells residents what is happening, what it means, and why it matters here, in this place, among these roads, rivers, churches, schools, camps, businesses, and families. The local paper or digital outlet knows which bridge matters, which stretch of Highway 39 is vulnerable, which camp name will carry emotional weight, and which official statement needs to be translated into practical consequences for ordinary people. That is why a robust local press is not a luxury in rural America. It is part of the civic infrastructure, as necessary in its own way as emergency communications, roads, and public meeting spaces.

What made Kerr County's press ecosystem especially instructive after the flood was that it was not one outlet doing one kind of work. It was three different local institutions, each with a distinct cadence, audience, and strength. *The Kerrville Daily Times* functioned as the county's broadest and most traditional local news institution. *The Lead* provided high-frequency digital reporting, live coverage, repeated updates, and relentless follow-through. The *West Kerr Current* brought the perspective of place-specific proximity in the river-corridor communities that were hit first and hardest. Together, they demonstrated that rural journalism is not strongest when it is uniform. It is strongest when it is layered.

The *Kerrville Daily Times* fulfilled one of the most basic needs of a disaster-struck community: a trusted central source. Wells was explicit that the paper's value begins with being local. Outsiders from San Antonio or Austin are not going to cover city council meetings, local sports, nonprofits, and the daily civic life that gives a town its identity. The local newspaper does that because it lives there. More importantly, Wells said that the paper's number one goal is to serve the community, trusting that if it does that well, the community will in turn sustain the paper. That is not nostalgia; it is an operating model of community reciprocity. And during the flood, the *Kerrville Daily Times* proved it. Wells tied trust directly to the paper's insistence on being timely and accurate, not merely first. If readers saw it in the paper, he wanted them to understand it as fact. The resulting subscription growth told him that the community recognized the value of a dependable local source when the stakes were highest.

If the *Kerrville Daily Times* represented institutional trust, *The Lead* represented the importance of digital presence, repetition, and real-time coverage. Amestoy explained that one of the founding ideas behind *The Lead* was that a local outlet has to be present in "as many places as you possibly can be" so people know you are available. That word, *presence*, is crucial. In rural journalism, especially in crisis, people do not simply need a publication to exist. They need to feel that it is there, active, reachable, updating, and paying attention. Amestoy's description of his journalistic method rested on older newspaper values adapted to a digital environment: frequency, consistency, delivery, and coverage that is measured and vetted rather than reckless or performative.

Amestoy was also candid about why this matters in a rural county. In his formulation, a rural community needs an experienced journalist just as it needs a good doctor or a good lawyer, yet the economic model for sustaining such journalism remains fragile. The flood underscored both sides of that truth. *The Lead* was able to provide comprehensive, competent, real-time coverage, but Amestoy also emphasized how vulnerable local outlets remain: underfunded, understaffed, and often left to fend for themselves even when they are performing a public service of the highest order. Local journalism matters, in other words, not because it is sentimental but because without it a rural county loses one of its few institutions capable of delivering fast, contextualized, and continuing coverage when official communications are partial or strained.

The *West Kerr Current* fulfilled a third need that neither a countywide daily nor a digital-first outlet could supply in the same way: hyperlocal rootedness in the western part of the county, near the nexus of the North and South Forks of the Guadalupe River. Van Winkle described "local" as all three: geography, relationships, and trust. That may be the most concise definition of rural journalism. In a place like West Kerr, local knowledge is not abstract. It is built over years of knowing residents, organizations, fire departments, and the rhythms of small communities. When the flood hit and access was difficult, Van Winkle turned to the people she knew in the area and sought first-hand knowledge from witnesses and victims to understand what was happening and what people were suffering.

Van Winkle also captured something that is easy to miss in a media ecosystem dominated by immediacy: A weekly paper still matters because its strength is different. She noted that a newspaper is different from television or radio and a weekly is different still. A weekly cannot win a speed contest with a live digital feed. That is not its role. Its role is steadiness, synthesis, and documentary care. Van Winkle described trying to be calm and accurate, refusing to spread rumors, and later helping the community stay connected by telling personal stories, both happy and sad, so people could understand how the flood affected them as a community. She also put the enduring value of small-town journalism in particularly plain terms: "We are always taking notes," even after more distant outlets have left to chase the next big story.

That may be the best way to understand the combined work of *The Kerrville Daily Times*, *The Lead*, and the *West Kerr Current*. They each took their stories and their work in a different direction. But together, they reduced rumor, translated official information, documented suffering, preserved memory, and stayed for recovery. That is why rural and small-town journalism matters. It does not merely observe a community in crisis. It helps a community know itself while it is living through one.

In a catastrophe, the community's infrastructure is tested: roads, power, water, emergency response, hospitals, schools, and aid. The flood also tested an infrastructure that is easier to overlook: that of trustworthy information. In Kerr County, that infrastructure had local names and local voices. It had different cadences and different constraints. It was imperfect, because all human systems are. Yet it did what a rural community needs most in its worst hours: It stayed, it verified, it corrected, and it kept telling the story long after the spotlight moved on. That is journalism. It is also community resilience in action.

Why Local Journalism Matters Most When Disaster Strikes

Local journalism in rural America provides five things that no visiting outlet, no matter how talented, can sustainably provide.

First, it provides service information when the decision window collapses. In the first hours, people needed to know what was happening and what to do next. The local press delivered updates with discipline: what is confirmed, what is not, and when to check back.

Second, it reduces harm by managing the two dangers of catastrophe: silence and noise. Silence leaves people isolated and guessing. Noise turns rumor into a second disaster. Local press does not eliminate either danger, but it reduces both by creating a reliable means for truth.

Third, it makes public life legible. News conferences, agency statements, and official updates can be necessary, but they are rarely sufficient. Local press translates them into meaning for the community: what this means for this road, this school, this camp, this river bend, this family.

Fourth, it builds trust through visible correction. Correction culture is not a public relations move. It is a public promise. When local outlets correct errors in front of their neighbors, they demonstrate accountability in the most concrete way.

Fifth, it stays to tell the recovery story. Recovery is where resilience lives. It is where the community learns, rebuilds, argues, mourns, and eventually moves forward. The national media often cannot stay. The local press does—because it is not visiting. It is home.

ELEVEN

GOING FORWARD: LEARNING, PREVENTION, AND PUBLIC SAFETY

When daylight came, it did not bring relief so much as revelation. As roads, crossings, and riverbanks became visible, the scope of damage came into view. Response capacity expanded with visibility, and coordination became easier to sustain. But the night's defining feature remained: The flood had compressed time so violently that the difference between warning and rescue was often measured in minutes that no one could manufacture on demand.

Daylight made the damage visible, but it did not change what had already been true in the dark: The night moved faster than human systems were designed to move. The chronology can tell us when warnings were issued, when calls surged, when roads failed, and when rescue resources mobilized. It cannot, by itself, explain why so many decisions across so many places landed inside the same narrowing window. To understand that, it helps to step back from individual moments and look at the night as a set of compounding conditions: familiar mental models applied to an unfamiliar flood, warning that did not translate into comprehension and movement, situational awareness that arrived in fragments, protocols built for a slower event, and a last mile that collapsed before most safety, escape and rescue protocols could do their work.

None of those conditions is a verdict. Together, they are the environment in which accountability becomes learning and prevention becomes possible.

The bottom line is there is one organizing risk that should anchor every decision going forward. That risk is public safety. Jonathan Marks, a noted risk management expert, believes that high-stakes readiness work starts with a single organizing principle: public safety. When that is the north star, the after-action review becomes a design exercise, aligning warnings, protocols, authority, and communication around manufacturing time. Marks has a framework for assessing risks beyond possibility: Impact, Likelihood, Speed of Onset, Warning Signs, Interdependency. He believes "a useful way to evaluate these areas is not only impact and likelihood, but speed of onset, early warning signs and interdependency." The flood was not simply severe. It was fast, it reduced options quickly, and it cascaded across systems that normally operate independently.

Here, I step back from the chronology to look hard at what lessons July 4 requires us to learn. I have identified ten areas that should be considered in any serious after-action review, not as a scorecard, but as a practical map from experience to prevention. Each area is designed to be a point in time going forward where decisions can be simplified and coordination can begin earlier. The goal is straightforward: to use what we now know and learn from July 4 to strengthen the responses, improve readiness and reduce the odds that a similar event produces the same scale of harm.

Lesson 1: Unprecedented Flood, Familiar Mental Models

In western Kerr County, flood experience is not theoretical. People know low-water crossings. They know the sound of rain on roofs and the way the Guadalupe River can turn from calm to serious in a single night. Most of the time, that lived knowledge is a form of resilience, a practical literacy that keeps people safe. The compounding condition in this flood was that the mind reached for what it knew at the exact moment the river demanded something new. The early hours still carried the cues of prior flood nights: a warning issued, a few calls, scattered reports, roads that went under. This is the core reason that after-action learning cannot be a checklist alone. The night behaved like an interconnected system where small delays and fragmented signals amplified one another.

But the defining facts of this event were different in kind, not merely in degree. The rainfall volume, the speed of the water, and the height it reached compressed time so aggressively that familiar reference points became unreliable. The result was not indifference. It was a mismatch between what people had learned from the past and what the river delivered in the present. All of this demonstrates that risk behaves like a system, not a list. This means that risk compounds through interactions; planning must treat it as a connected system.

Lesson 2: Warning Without Comprehension

The record is clear on one point that matters because it is so easy to misunderstand in hindsight: A warning can exist and still fail to create protective time for those who receive it to respond. The NWS warning at 1:14 a.m. was a formal message with formal language. It carried the kind of phrasing people learn to associate with urgency. Yet the river corridor did not shift, all at once, into an evacuation and protective movement. The reason is not that people did not care. But warnings are not safety by themselves. They convey information, and information only becomes protection only when it is comprehended quickly enough to trigger action. But as Burgess said, "a warning indicates that some type of danger may be imminent, and you need to implement your response to the warning into an action."

In the early hours of July 4, comprehension had to fight through a familiar set of barriers that are rarely visible until a disaster exposes them. The first barrier was time. The 1:14 a.m. alert assumes awake eyes and ready judgment. It assumes that recipients will read or hear it promptly, interpret it correctly and translate it into movement in the dark. But sleep is not a moral choice, and nighttime is not a neutral setting. Darkness narrows what people can see, which narrows what they believe. It also slows what people can or are willing to do, particularly when the action required is disruptive: waking others, moving children, leaving shelter, driving unfamiliar roads, crossing bridges, or walking into a storm with only partial knowledge of what is beyond the porch light.

The second barrier was the gap between abstract language and lived reality. A warning can say "life-threatening." A warning can say "considerable." Those words are meaningful to the meteorological system and to experienced emergency managers. They are not always meaningful to a family in a quiet cabin, hearing rain, seeing nothing yet, and relying on experience from prior storms. The mind tries to locate the warning inside a familiar category. Your mind might ask: Is this like the last flood night*? Is this a river or creek jumping its banks? Is this something that will pass by morning?* That is not denial. It is the ordinary human process of making sense, and it is precisely where time is lost when the event is not ordinary.

The third barrier was fragmented situational awareness. In those pre-dawn hours, information did not arrive as a single coherent picture. It arrived in fragments: a question about road conditions; a report of water over a road; a family on a roof; multiple calls with incomplete addresses; crossings failing; neighborhoods flooding; then, eventually, calls from camps. Each fragment was real, but fragments do not automatically scale in the mind into a countywide emergency, particularly for people who are seeing only their own small slice of the night.

That is why the hours between 1:14 a.m. and 3:30 a.m. matter so much. The record shows limited call traffic early. The threat was not forming, but most people still did not have cues that matched the warning. They did not yet see water, hear the roar, feel the ground shift from routine to danger. In that window, the warning existed, but comprehension and action did not move at the same speed. The Guadalupe River had already begun to take away the core resource that warnings require: time.

By 3:34 a.m., the county crossed into the phase where comprehension was no longer primarily cognitive. It became physical. Phones rang more insistently. Dispatchers translated fear into locations, names, and priorities, doing the essential work of building order. But even here, the compounding condition remained. The information that reached the system was urgent yet still incomplete. Addresses were partial. Reports arrived without the context that daylight provides. The same darkness that slowed household decisions also constrained responders. The response apparatus was moving, but movement is not the same as reach, and reach is not the same as arrival.

The pivot point for this condition is not the existence of channels. It is the translation problem: how a warning becomes something a person acts on in the middle of the night, and how that action becomes protective before conditions overtake the place that warning is meant to protect. In this flood, the translation problem was intensified by a mismatch between what people could reasonably know and what the river was already doing. Translation improves when escalation points are set ahead of time. A warning turns into action when it comes with clear triggers that tell a household, a camp, or a command desk what to do next, and when the next step is no longer optional. Triggers do not replace judgment. They buy time by eliminating hesitation.

People did not know the full amount of rain that would fall. They did not know the speed and height the water would reach in the next hours. They did not know which crossings would fail first, which roads would become impassable, or how quickly the last viable routes would disappear. Like the leadership at Camp Mystic, they may have known that an NWS warning had been issued. And just like at Camp Mystic, many did not yet know what the warning truly meant for their exact location and their exact timeline. Unfortunately, there were many on the Guadalupe River who did not receive the warning.

This is where the last mile enters—because comprehension is local. It must land inside a specific place with enough lead time to move. Word of mouth, knocking on doors, and neighbor-to-neighbor warnings are the oldest and sometimes the fastest systems humans have. But they are still bounded by distance, darkness and time. They are also bounded by the same interpretive challenge: A neighbor can say the river is rising, and the listener still has to decide whether that means "watch it" or "move now." In an unprecedented event, those distinctions are not instinctive. They have to be trained, practiced, and supported by systems that convert meteorological urgency into individual operational clarity.

By 3:57 a.m., a call from Camp Mystic captured the harshest form of warning without comprehension: the moment when the event has already outrun the protective value of messaging. This was the first known 911 call from the camp, made by a counselor or other nonmanagerial staff member. The caller reported that water was rising and that many cabins were flooded. The call itself was information, but it was information arriving at the edge of options. It highlighted that a warning can be technically correct and still arrive too late to be converted into safe movement, particularly when children are involved and evacuation requires coordination, routes, and minutes that have not been preserved.

The lesson of this compounding condition is not that warnings are pointless. It is that warnings are incomplete without translation, and translation is a system responsibility as much as an individual one. A warning must be matched to shared situational awareness, current protocols that reflect the true profile of risk and an operational picture that moves faster than rumor and faster than the water. When those supporting elements are missing or delayed, a warning becomes what it was that night: a message that existed, a message that mattered, and a message that could not, by itself, manufacture time.

In the sections that follow, the story continues to widen from the warning itself to the environment around it: how awareness arrived in fragments, how protocols built for a slower flood met an event that removed optionality, and how the last mile collapsed in places where the river did not allow a second chance.

Lesson 3: Situational Awareness Collapsed at the Edges

Situational awareness sounds like a technical phrase, but in the early hours of a flood it is brutally simple: What do you know, what do you believe, and what do you think you can still do? The compounding condition in western Kerr County was that situational awareness did not arrive as a shared picture. It arrived as fragments, to different people at different times, with darkness and terrain ensuring that no one could see very far beyond their own slice of the river corridor. In that environment, it was possible for a warning to exist, for the river to be accelerating, and for many people to still be living inside a mental model that had not yet caught up.

The first limitation was visibility. At Camp Stewart, on the North Folk of the Guadalupe River, Jeeper Ragsdale said that it was raining so hard and it was so dark that he could not see the hand in front of his face at some time after 1:30 a.m. It only got worse from there. At night, people do not see a river the way they see it in daylight. They hear rain, they hear wind, they hear the distant texture of moving water, but they do not see what is cresting around the bend upstream. They do not see the debris field that telegraphs velocity. They do not see the crossing that has already become a chute. They see what the porch light reveals and what the headlights can reach. That is why a flood can be both present and not yet comprehended. Darkness does not merely slow action. It compresses knowledge.

The second limitation was geography. The Guadalupe River is not a single point. It consists of two forks and Johnson Creek, all of which converge downriver from Hunt. There are 12 watersheds that flow into the Guadalupe River before it gets to Kerrville. Finally, it is a corridor of camps, cabins, crossings, narrow riverbeds, and narrow roads, with pockets of vulnerability scattered along bends and low ground. When situational awareness is local, it can be accurate and still incomplete. A person can look outside and see only heavy rain and assume the river is still within its normal boundaries. Another person, a few miles away, can already be watching water come over a road. Both experiences are true. Neither experience, by itself, tells the full story that is moving through the system.

That is why the call log matters as more than a list of incidents. It tells you how awareness was constructed that night. It did not arrive as a clean, centralized briefing. It arrived as a family on a roof. It arrived as water over the only road out along the South Fork. It arrived as a road that was suddenly not passable. It arrived as cabins flooding. It arrived as the first reports from camps. Dispatchers and responders did what they could with each fragment. They converted fragments into tasks. They requested barricades. They asked for boats. They asked for swift water rescue. They began the difficult work of assembling a picture from the edges inward.

But a picture assembled from the edges is always late compared to a river assembled from the sky. But at the time, there was no one person looking at this bigger picture. There was no one person in formal charge of the county's emergency operations who could have put it all together and tried to marshal and allocate resources accordingly.

There is another dimension to situational awareness that is easy to miss: It is not only about knowing that water is rising. It is about knowing how fast it is rising and what that speed does to options. In many disasters, the central question is, "How bad is it?" In this flood, the central question became, "How much time is left?" The first question invites observation. The second demands movement. When people do not appreciate the speed and height that are coming, they can remain in observation mode long after movement should have begun. They can interpret early cues as something that will be managed the way it has been managed before: watch, wait, reassess. That habit is rational in common storms. It is lethal in an unprecedented one.

Beginning around 3:30 a.m., the calls began to shift in category, from road questions to rescue requests. By 3:34 a.m., phones were ringing in rapid succession. That transition tells you what it felt like in the moment: Awareness did not gradually build. It snapped into place in pockets, one roof at a time, one crossing at a time, one frightened call at a time.

For families caught in those pockets, situational awareness often arrived at the worst possible moment: when the water made it unavoidable but also made it too late to move safely. In one survivor account, the line is simple and devastating. They gathered, they climbed, they looked out, and what surrounded them was not a nuisance rise but dark, fast-moving water. A 911 call did not produce certainty, because certainty was not available. The dispatcher could not promise help or estimate when help might come. That is not a failure of compassion. It is the honest boundary of a system that is being asked to respond to too many simultaneous emergencies while access routes are collapsing. It is situational awareness colliding with physical constraint.

The same dynamic shaped organizational decisions. People cannot act on what they cannot see, and in the early hours they could not see the scale. Meteorologist Alan Gerard told Amestoy that the the leaders at Camp Mystic "were looking at their apps, trying to see when rain was going to quit, and they were looking at their rain gauge. That's really not helpful. They were trying to be meteorologists and hydrologists and what was going to happen rather than reacting to what was happening."

That shared picture did not exist early enough to become protective time across the river corridor. Instead, awareness remained fractured. It lived in individual experiences, individual calls, and individual observations. It moved unevenly, sometimes faster through word of mouth than through formal channels, sometimes slower because the person receiving the message still had to interpret it through a familiar reference point. The compounding condition was not that people ignored reality. It was that reality arrived in pieces, and the river moved faster than those pieces could be assembled into a single, urgent truth.

This is also why the later heroics, as real as they were, could not fix the early awareness problem. Once the flood has turned roads into barriers and crossings into hazards, awareness becomes something you can possess without being able to act. Knowing the risk is not the same as being able to reach safety. The system can be moving, and still be late, because the environment has taken away the key resource that every response requires: minutes.

Lesson 4: Protocol Mismatch and Outdated Guidance

When the night stopped making sense, people reached for the thing that is supposed to make emergencies manageable: the plan. At Camp Mystic, as in most places, the dominant guidance for many hazards has long been some form of shelter in place. Amestoy produced a picture of the camp's emergency instructions. They read, "*in case of flooding, all campers on Senior Hill must stay in their cabins*." It is familiar. It is simple. It is often correct. In fires, under tornado warnings, in severe storms that bring lightning and debris, staying put can be the safest available option. The compounding condition in this flood was that a familiar protocol met an unfamiliar hydrologic reality. What was meant to be protective in common scenarios became mismatched to an event defined by the water's extraordinary speed and height.

Protocol mismatch is not protocol negligence. It is what happens when guidance is built on assumptions that remain invisible until an extreme event exposes them. "Shelter in place" assumes that the shelter will remain a shelter. It assumes that water, if it rises, will rise slowly enough to allow reassessment. It assumes that access routes will remain viable for responders. It assumes that people will have a durable margin for decision-making. Those assumptions are not irrational. They are the background logic of many emergency plans, and they align with most floods people have experienced. The problem in this flood was not that people relied on a plan. The problem was that the plan was built for a slower flood.

Speed changes everything. In a slow-rising flood, shelter in place can buy time. It allows families to stay off roads, avoid panic travel, and wait for clearer guidance. In a fast-rising flood, shelter in place can become entrapment. The same walls that keep wind out can keep water in. But here the water was moving at up to seventeen miles per hour. This means the same place that felt safe at 3 a.m. could be uninhabitable at 3:15 a.m. A plan that depends on reassessment is only as good as the time available for reassessment. In this event, time was not an available resource. The flood did not negotiate with protocols.

In the early window, the night still looked and sounded like storms that had come before. There were warnings, but local cues were uneven. Reports arrived in fragments. People in some locations had not yet seen high water. In that environment, following established guidance feels prudent. It feels calm. It feels like the opposite of panic. But by the time calls shifted from questions about roads to requests for rescue, the protocol environment had already started to break down. Roads and crossings that plans assumed would remain routes became barriers. Access that responders depend on began to disappear.

Outmoded or ineffective protocols fail in two ways. The first is obvious: They give the wrong instruction for the conditions. The second is subtler: They delay escalation. They keep people in an observation posture because the protocol implies that observation is still safe. That is what Gerard meant when he said that the leadership at Camp Mystic did not react to the events as they were unfolding. "Wait and see" is not written on most emergency checklists. Yet it can become the practical effect of outdated guidance because sheltering feels like compliance with safety. When water arrives with the force and velocity of the July 4 flood, waiting is not neutral. It is a choice made by default, and defaults are the most dangerous decisions in a compressed-time event.

When children are involved, the margin for protocol mismatch is thin. Children cannot self-evacuate. They cannot assess risk. They cannot drive. They cannot decide that the warning tone on a phone means "move now." Their safety depends on adults translating uncertainty into action early enough that movement can still be controlled and orderly. The compounding condition here is not that adults lacked concern. It is that adult concern operated inside guidance and assumptions that did not match the event profile. Shelter in place is a stabilizing instruction. In this flood, that same stability was an illusion that could dissolve in minutes.

In mature emergency management, protocols are living documents. They are supposed to be revised after close calls, after new data changes the understanding of local risk. The flood revealed that the working protocols did not reflect the true worst-case speed and height. They did not encode the hard lesson that "unprecedented" is a category that requires different triggers, different thresholds, and different language.

Consider the mechanics of action at night. Even if someone decides at 1:30 a.m. that they should move, they still must answer practical questions that protocols are supposed to simplify. Move where? Move by what route? Move with what transportation? Move with which children? Move through what weather? Move past which crossings? A protocol that simply says "shelter in place" avoids those questions because, in most events, those questions are dangerous. In this event, avoiding them meant surrendering time to the river. That is why protocol mismatch is so consequential: It does not just give an instruction. It determines what questions get asked soon enough to matter.

This condition also helps explain why the response system, despite professionalism and courage, could not create safety at scale once the event crossed certain thresholds. Emergency systems are built to respond. They are not built to outrun water moving at highway speed. When protocols keep people in place until the flood has already turned roads into barriers and neighborhoods into islands, the system inherits a rescue problem rather than an evacuation problem. Rescue is always harder. It is slower. It is more dangerous. It also depends on access routes that are exactly what the flood removes first.

Lesson 5: The Last Mile Failed Repeatedly

It is tempting, after any catastrophe, to argue about warning channels: which system sent which alert, which platform was used, whether a siren should have sounded, whether a message should have been worded differently. Those debates can matter, but they can also miss the point. The compounding condition in this flood was not the absence of warning channels. It was the collapse of the last mile, the short and decisive stretch between information and protection. A message can exist. It can even be accurate. Yet if it does not arrive in the right place, at the right time, in a form that triggers movement before conditions overtake the route, then the last mile has failed. In western Kerr County that night, it failed repeatedly, in different ways, across different locations, because the flood moved faster than the environment could support delivery. Here Marks said, "In fast-moving incidents, the decisive phase is recognition and escalation, not impact. When recognition is late, stabilization becomes rescue, and rescue is always constrained by physics and minutes you cannot recover."

The last mile is where warnings stop being general and become personal. It is where "life-threatening flash flood" has to become, "You, move to a higher elevation now!" It is where a family has to decide whether to wake children, whether to step into the dark, whether to move vehicles, whether to risk a crossing, whether the road they used yesterday will still exist in ten minutes. It is where an organization has to decide whether to move a group, not just a person, through terrain that is already beginning to change. The last mile is not just communications. It is translation into action under very challenging constraints.

That night had multiple channels of warnings. There was the NWS warning heard at Camp Mystic. There were informal communications, including door knocks and word of mouth heard by Valerie and her husband. There were calls to 911 and professional responses. There were requests for broader alerting, including a request that a CodeRED be issued for Hunt. Each channel had value. Each channel also had limits, and the flood exploited every limit at once. A warning assumes the recipient receives the message and correctly interprets it, putting a pre-planned response into action. A text alert assumes cell phone service, devices near a bed, awake recipients, and immediate comprehension. A door knock assumes neighbors are close enough, willing to move, able to move, and can reach the door before the water reaches the threshold. Word of mouth assumes the person hearing it trusts the messenger and trusts the urgency. Every channel assumes time. The flood's defining feature was that time could not be assumed.

One disruption immediately affects other domains; cascades are predictable. This is why fragments are so dangerous: They hide cascading failure pathways. Once again, Marks believes, fragmented awareness masks interdependency. This is the set of cascading effects. When roads fail, communication routes fail. When communication fails, coordination fails. When coordination fails, the last mile collapses faster than any single channel can compensate.

You can see the last mile beginning to collapse in the chronology. The early hours were still, in many places, a warning environment rather than a rescue environment. Then the calls shifted: water over roads, families on roofs, crossings no longer passable. By the time dispatchers were processing dozens of rescue-related calls and hundreds of radio transmissions, the event had moved beyond the phase where a message alone could protect. At that point, information did not merely need to be delivered. It needed to arrive faster than the river, and in many locations it could not.

The sharpest illustration of last-mile collapse is not a debate about which alert went out when. It is the physical sequence described in survivor accounts: the moment when the environment changes so quickly that action becomes reactive rather than preventive. In one account, what happened next took only seconds. In less than fifteen seconds, a cabin came apart and dissolved into the river. That is not a communications problem in the narrow sense. It is a last-mile impossibility. No channel, however well designed, can create safe evacuation when structures fail in seconds and water behaves like a moving wall.

The same dynamic played out along the camp corridor. The call at 3:57 a.m. from Camp Mystic did not introduce the first danger. It documented that danger had already reached a place where children were separated from normal options. The last mile for a camp is not a single decision by a single person. It is a coordinated movement of many, in the dark, under stress, with duty-of-care responsibilities that do not allow improvisation. Even if a warning is heard, the last mile demands routes, vehicles, supervision, and time. In this flood, the camps and affected individuals were overwhelmed before most channels ever had the chance to work as designed. The last mile did not fail because people did not care. It failed because the flood removed the normal conditions under which the last mile can succeed.

It is also important to recognize that last-mile collapse is not uniform. It happens in pockets and that unevenness can create false confidence. One household may receive a door knock and have enough time to move to higher ground. Another, a mile away, may never hear a knock because the neighbor cannot reach them. One person may receive an alert and interpret it as immediate. Another may interpret that same alert as advisory because their local cues still look ordinary. One road may remain passable long enough to exit. Another may become a water channel. It may become a channel for destruction while you are driving on it. This unevenness is a cruel feature of flash floods: They produce stories of survival that can sound like proof that the system worked, and stories of loss that can sound like proof that it did not. In reality, both can be true at the same time because the last mile is local and the flood is not.

That is why the CodeRED request and the CodeRED issuance must be considered with restraint. The timestamp can be recorded. The intent can certainly be assumed to be protective. The operational reality can be stated plainly: Between a request for mass alerting and a message landing on a device, time continues to pass. The question is not whether a message was sent. The question is whether it arrived early and widely enough to trigger movement before routes and structures were overtaken. In the most impacted pockets, the chronology strongly suggests the answer is that the event had already advanced beyond what messaging could correct. That is not an indictment of alerting. It is an acknowledgment of physics.

The last mile also includes the moment when messaging gives way to rescue—once people are trapped, on roofs, on hills, in cabins with water rising. By then, the last mile becomes no longer about warning. It is about reach. It becomes boats, high-water vehicles, helicopters, and responders trying to do an extraordinary job inside collapsing access. The night's call logs and radio traffic show the system attempting to widen reach: requests for swift water rescue, requests for barricades, escalations to air evacuation. Those are the tools of the rescue phase. They are essential. They are also slower than the flood's arrival in the most violent pockets along the river.

This compounding condition matters because it points toward prevention. If last-mile collapse is a recurring risk in flash floods, then preparedness cannot depend solely on receiving an alert. It depends on what the alert triggers: protocols that assume less time, triggers that push action earlier, shared situational awareness that reduces hesitation, and systems designed to translate meteorological warnings into local, actionable directives. Most of all, it depends on building and practicing for the truth that "wait and see" is not a neutral posture when children are involved. In a compressed-time flash flood, waiting is often the decision that the river makes for you.

Lesson 6: The Pre-Dawn Command Gap

By the time the last mile collapsed in the most exposed pockets, the night had already turned into what emergency managers call a multi-incident event: not one problem, but many problems arriving at once, each urgent, each local, and each competing for the same scarce resource. In that setting, the most important commodity is not equipment. It is not even staffing. It is a shared operational picture, the ability to see, early enough, what is happening across the corridor and to treat it as one unfolding emergency rather than a series of disconnected calls. The compounding condition in this flood was that a unified picture, held by a senior coordinator with authority to drive priorities, did not fully form in the pre-dawn window when minutes were disappearing fastest.

This is a difficult condition to write about because it is easy to confuse structure with character. The point here is not to measure anyone's dedication. It is to describe the reality of coverage and coordination in the hours when the event moved from warning to saturation. In Kerr County government, the three top officials were not available until roughly 5 to 5:30 a.m. The county judge (in Texas, a top administrator akin to a city's mayor) was out of the county, at his house on Lake Travis. The county sheriff was at home asleep. The head of the county's emergency services office was at home, asleep, on an approved medical leave.

Before that half-hour period, the response system was not absent. It was active. Dispatchers were taking calls, calling for swift water rescue, requesting barricades and trying to keep a coherent record in a night that was producing chaos faster than any one person could absorb it. But activity is not the same as unified command. Movement is not the same as a shared picture.

The record of the night shows a response apparatus that came alive in increments. First came the warning. Then came the early, scattered reports. Then came the surge, the moment the phones began ringing in rapid succession and the call log filled with roofs, crossings, flooded cabins, and stranded families. The response expanded geographically as volunteer fire departments were called out and special operations were activated. The river corridor began to close down in real time, turning roads into not simply obstacles but even death traps. All of that can and did occur, without a single senior figure holding the whole map, defining priorities for the corridor as a corridor, and signaling to every operational lane that this flood was outside the range of normal experience.

That is what a pre-dawn command gap looks like in practice. People are doing their jobs inside their lanes; in this case, those lanes did not converge into one coordinated picture. Dispatchers were triaging calls. Patrol deputies were confirming crossings and closing roads. Volunteer departments were mobilizing. City and county functions were moving on separate tracks. Meanwhile, residents and the camps were experiencing the event as immediate and personal, with no ability to see whether their emergency was one of ten or one of a hundred. It happened at Camp Mystic; it happened to Jane Ragsdale at Heart O' the Hills, and it happened at Camp La Junta. In that environment, the system can be fully engaged and still be late in recognizing the scale—because scale is what you see when you can connect individual incidents.

The most consequential effect of this gap is not paperwork or optics. It is time and prioritization. In a multi-incident flood, the system must answer questions that do not have comfortable answers: *Where is the highest duty of care? Which calls signal imminent loss of life? Which evacuation or even escape routes are still viable? Which assets can reach which pockets before access disappears? What is the threshold for declaring that shelter-in-place guidance no longer applies? What message is consistent across the corridor?* Those are not questions for any one dispatcher or any one person in the field. Those are questions that require someone, early, to be assigned to the overall picture and empowered to drive a unified operational posture.

July 4 also demonstrates another structural truth: The earlier the unified picture forms, the more preventive the posture can be. When the picture forms late, the posture becomes rescue-heavy by default and then recovery. Rescue is always more dangerous and more limited than early movement. It depends on boats and trained responders. It depends on access. It depends on time that the river is actively destroying. A late-forming unified picture does not cause the flood. It does not cause the rainfall. It does not create the speed and height. But it can increase the likelihood that the system will spend the most critical hours responding to emergencies one at a time rather than shaping the corridorwide response with consistent priorities.

This is also why the chronology's markers matter. According to ABC News, a CodeRED was requested by a firefighter in Ingram, just upstream from Kerrville, who asked the Kerr County Sheriff's Office to alert nearby residents to the unfolding situation. Recordings show he asked, "Is there any way we can send a CodeRED out to our Hunt residents, asking them to find higher ground or stay home?"; a CodeRED was issued at 5:01 a.m. While some reports indicate a 5:01 a.m. issuance, others confirm residents did not receive the alert until 5:34 a.m. Whichever time it was issued, the county judge told *The Lead*'s magazine, "the alert came too late due to the speed and magnitude of the event."

A command center was formally established by 5:56 a.m. The sequence suggests an organization reaching for broader coordination as the event escalated. Yet it also suggests that, in the deepest part of the night, coordination was being built while the event was still accelerating. Those are two different tempos, and the faster tempo won. But because there was no one person in command, there was still confusion on rally points for first responders.

By the time the command center was stood up, the system had already been moving for more than two hours. Dispatchers had been working through saturation, turning panic into locations and tasks. Responders had been dealing with roads that vanished, crossings that failed, and neighborhoods that became unreachable. A unified command structure is essential in disasters, but it is not a time machine. It cannot restore the minutes that were lost earlier to fragmented situational awareness, protocol mismatch, and last-mile collapse. It can only organize what remains, and it can only do so within constraints that have already hardened.

A pre-dawn command gap is not unique to this flood or to Kerr County. It is a predictable vulnerability in any community that relies heavily on part-time, volunteer, or distributed response capacity, particularly in rural corridors and in overnight hours. It is a structural problem that must be designed for, not hoped away. Leadership coverage is not a question of goodwill. It is a question of planning, staffing and authority lines. The flood revealed that, in the hours when the river left no room for improvisation, no single senior coordinator owned the full operational picture early enough to drive corridorwide urgency.

But it is a fair question to ask: During the pre-dawn hours in Kerr County, who was in charge?

The next compounding condition follows naturally from here. When the command picture forms late, the system leans heavily on the people who are always there first: the dispatchers, the first responders, the volunteers. Their professionalism becomes the scaffolding that holds the response together. In this flood, that professionalism saved lives. It also ran into a hard limit that no amount of courage can repeal; rescue capacity cannot outrun the water's will.

Lesson 7: Professionalism Could Not Outrun the Water's Will

If you read the call logs and radio traffic from the early hours, one truth is abundantly clear: The system did not freeze. People did not simply stand by. The 911 operators and first responders moved into action as the night accelerated, doing what trained professionals do when uncertainty multiplies: They created order, they asked the next best question, they assigned resources, they documented what could be documented, and they kept going. In any honest accounting of accountability as learning, that professionalism has to be named. It is part of the story's integrity. It is also, by itself, not enough to prevent tragedy when the event erases time.

The question here is not about effort. It is about limits. A flash flood with extraordinary speed, depth and height changes the relationship between response and outcome. In most emergencies, response time is a meaningful variable. Faster response can change results. In an extreme flood, response time can become a cruel illusion. You can mobilize quickly and still arrive too late because roads vanish, crossings fail, and water moves through the corridor faster than vehicles can safely travel. You can have courage, skill, and discipline and still be constrained by physics.

This is why the dispatch narrative matters so much. Dispatchers are the first line of coordination. They do not control the weather. They do not control the river. They control the conversion of chaos into process, the act of turning frantic calls into locations, priorities, and tasks that can be handed to responders.

But the same record that shows professionalism also shows saturation. According to *The Lead*, Kerr County's 911 system received 172 emergency calls between 3 a.m. and 5 a.m. Those numbers are not statistics for their own sake. They are a measure of concurrency. There were too many urgent situations arriving at once for any system to solve sequentially. In a multi-incident flood, the system is confronting dozens of emergencies at a time, and each one competes for the same boats, the same trained teams, the same passable routes, and the same minutes.

First responders and volunteers also faced the most demoralizing constraint of all: access. The record shows crossings becoming impassable, roads barricaded by debris and responders becoming landlocked. A sergeant abandoned a cruiser because the vehicle could not move is not merely a dramatic detail. One of the first swift boat response teams to arrive came from San Antonio. They lost their boat and escaped with their lives because they went all the way to the strip center parking lot across from Ingram Dam. There was no one person to tell them the raging floodwaters had reached Ingram Dam and they were about to be overcome.

All of these stories are signs that the response environment was being shaped by the flood, not by the plan. When a responder cannot reach the call, the call remains urgent but becomes unserviceable in the moment. That is not a failure of compassion. It is the boundary of what a responder can physically do.

In many communities, people expect leaders to be the ones who appear in the first hours. In this flood, the most visible leadership in the pre-dawn hours was operational leadership: the dispatcher who kept asking the next question; the volunteer department officer who requested swift water resources; the deputy who confirmed a crossing was no longer passable; the sergeant who made the call to abandon his vehicle but went to help others; the responders who kept moving toward danger because people were calling from roofs, from cabins, from hills. That kind of leadership does not come with a microphone. It comes from the heart but with a radio, a flashlight, and the discipline to function when clarity is scarce.

Yet the flood also teaches the hardest lesson for prevention: You cannot rely on professionalism to compensate for missing systems. Professionalism does not create a warning network. It does not manufacture real-time situational awareness. It does not modernize protocols. It does not fix the last mile. It responds to what arrives. In this flood, what arrived was an unprecedented volume of rain and an unprecedented speed and height of water. The response system, even at its best, could not outrun a river behaving like a moving wall.

That truth is not meant to diminish the people who responded. It is meant to protect their response from being turned into a substitute for prevention. Communities sometimes tell themselves that they are safe because they have good people. Western Kerr County did and does have good people. The flood proved it. The flood also proved that good people need systems that match the hazard profile. When the hazard removes time, the only way to save lives at scale is to preserve time before the event reaches homes, camps, and crossings.

The next compounding condition moves from response limits to prevention design. Prevention has to be built so that warning becomes lead time, lead time becomes movement, and movement happens early enough to stay orderly. In Kerr County, that path runs through the governance history of warning-system efforts and through the post-flood work led by UGRA and championed by Moser: a prediction and projection system designed to move faster than the water.

Lesson 8: Prevention Delayed, Then Built

The flood's most painful lesson is not simply that the river rose quickly. It is that once the first rescue calls began, the night turned into a narrowing corridor with more water coming down than goes over Niagara Falls on a daily basis. Decisions that might have been deliberate at 3 a.m. became compressed by 3:30 a.m. By the time the emergency phones lit up in earnest, the range of safe options collapsed. In the chronology, that is the missing margin of time: the window that exists before the situation becomes a rescue problem or even a recovery operation. The night shows that when action starts late, even extraordinary effort is forced to operate inside physics, darkness, and imperfect information.

Prevention is not a slogan or a poster on a wall. It is the intentional act of moving the action point earlier in the timeline so that fewer decisions have to be made under duress. It is the discipline of manufacturing time. And to manufacture time at scale, you need more than a warning. You need a shared picture and actionable triggers that translate a forecast into coordinated movement. Warning without translation becomes noise. Translation without shared situational awareness becomes fragmentation. Fragmentation becomes delay, and delay becomes a rescue call.

That is why the prevention conversation cannot start with heroics. It has to start with systems. A system that changes outcomes does two things at once: It speaks early enough to matter, and it speaks clearly enough to produce action across different organizations and different levels of experience. It does not merely tell you that something might happen. It tells you what to do and when the moment arrives, it tells multiple decision-makers the same thing, at the same time, in the same language. In the flood's chronology, prevention is the difference between a late-night scramble and an earlier, calmer series of choices that reduce exposure before the river makes choices for you.

Prevention is operationalized through capabilities such as inspection, real-time monitoring, clear communication, trained staffing, defined decision authority. Marks believes that systems-based prevention are not abstract. Moreover, prevention is built from a small set of capabilities: inspection to find vulnerabilities early, real-time monitoring to see deterioration as it begins, communication that is clear and trusted, staffing that is trained for surge conditions, and decision authority that is defined before the night arrives. These capabilities do not guarantee a perfect outcome, but they do manufacture time. And time can be the difference in such an event.

The governance reality is that prevention work inside public institutions is not instantaneous, even when the need is obvious. It moves through approvals, budgets, procurement rules, technical validation, and authority lines. It can stall. It can be delayed. It can also be accelerated. None of this requires blame to be true. It is simply how public safety infrastructure is built when it is built the right way: transparently, lawfully, and with controls that protect the public trust. The challenge is that governance timelines can move slower than the river's timelines, and the flood exposed that mismatch with brutal clarity.

That is why the work of Moser and the UGRA has been so critical. Moser had been thinking about a prediction and projection system for years, as far back as 2015. He said, "I looked at this flood as a catalyst—for a flood warning system that would be using high technology, using current technology that existed. I, as a county commissioner in 2016, recognized the flood that happened in 2015 on the Blanco River, where families died down there, several people died. So, I looked at what they had done and brought it back to this community. Had a meeting with Commissioners Court, the City Council, UGRA, every public entity that could exist and said, 'Let's do something about enhancing our flood warning system.'"

After July 4 he was ready with a sketched-out preliminary diagram of what he called a "Flood Warning System." Bushnoe explained that UGRA added a strategic plan goal in January 2023 to "evaluate and implement resources for flood warning in the Guadalupe River watershed." The UGRA explored the State Flood Plan funding route, then decided to use UGRA surplus funds to "get the ball rolling" and define a phased approach. She noted it began developing the scope in November 2024, aimed at improving access to existing data and planning additional monitoring instrumentation. The authority was moving toward implementation of Phase 1 in 2025. After July 4, UGRA and Moser worked to put those plans into action.

Better safety stewardship and clear accountability are the correct manner to think through this issue. They point to a duty of care without calling anyone negligent. They recognize that prevention is not just a technical problem but a governance obligation: who owns the risk, who has authority to act, who has funding responsibility, and who is accountable for deadlines when the work is about public safety rather than convenience.

When prevention is treated as discretionary, it competes with every other discretionary project. It is always important but rarely urgent. The flood taught what happens when "important but not urgent" meets "unprecedented but real." The only responsible response is to elevate a prediction and projection system to a top-tier public safety obligation. That shift does not magically eliminate process. Moser and UGRA showed us that. The catalyst of the July 4 flood changed the priority inside the process. It changed the energy behind approvals. It changes how quickly questions are answered. It changed whether delays are accepted as normal friction or treated as risks that must be managed and reduced. Governance still exists, but it moves with intent.

The natural question, after absorbing these compounding conditions, is simple: *What changes now?*

The answer is not a promise that tragedy is impossible. The answer is the rebuild, made concrete. The prediction and projection system is the most direct response, not as a guarantee against future loss, such as the dam system advocated by Hughes. Rather, it should be seen as a mechanism to manufacture time. It reduces the dependency on fragmented situational awareness. It replaces a patchwork of reports, calls, and guesses with a shared picture that updates in real time. It allows protocols to be updated using projections rather than assumptions. It improves the last mile by giving organizations, camps, and families clearer triggers earlier. It does not eliminate difficult decisions, but it makes difficult decisions possible earlier, when the margin is wider and movement is safer.

If awareness arrives in fragments, prevention must create a shared picture sooner. A shared picture is not just data. It is a common operating language. It is the difference between multiple parties seeing the same river through different windows and multiple parties seeing the same projection on the same screen. When awareness is unified earlier, coordination starts earlier. This is one of the critical elements of the UGRA proposal, the coordination of incoming data with the analysis and then projection of that analysis out to those along the Guadalupe River.

If protocols mismatch, prevention must update guidance for speed and height realities. The flood made clear that prior assumptions about timing, passibility, and safe routes can fail under extreme rainfall and rapid rise. Prevention means rewriting the playbook to reflect what the Guadalupe River can do now, not what it used to do. It means building protocols around the speed of onset, not merely the peak height.

If the last mile collapses, prevention must preserve time and simplify decisions. The last mile fails when communications are unclear, routes are cut, or decision thresholds are ambiguous. Prevention preserves time by making triggers simpler and earlier. It reduces the number of decisions that must be made at the worst possible moment.

If command converges late, prevention must plan leadership coverage and authority early. Coordination cannot depend on improvisation. It requires pre-defined authority lines, backup coverage, and clear leadership handoffs so that early action is possible even when the incident is evolving and personnel are rotating. Prevention is governance made operational.

If heroics cannot outrun nature, prevention must reduce the need for heroics. This is not a critique of those who acted. It is an honoring of them. The most respectful response to extraordinary effort is to build a system that demands less of it. When the system moves faster than the water, fewer people have to gamble their lives against it.

That is what the prediction and projection system represents. It is not a single device or a single dashboard. It is an engineered commitment to earlier clarity. It is a community choosing to treat time as a resource that can be designed, not merely hoped for. It is better safety stewardship and clear accountability made visible in technology, protocols, and training.

No one person, entity or governmental authority can promise perfection because perfection is not how public safety works. However, you can promise seriousness. You can promise engineering. You can promise the discipline of learning. The flood taught a truth that is both simple and demanding: It is not enough to say you will have a warning system. The system must move faster than the water. That is buildable. That is the point of learning. And that is how prevention becomes the most constructive form of accountability.

Lesson 9: Paper Readiness, Field Reality

In the months and years before the flood, the county's posture in the categories that matter most—detection, alerting, response coordination, after-action learning—could be described as good to high on paper. Plans existed. Roles existed. The vocabulary of emergency management was present: warnings, protocols, mutual aid, command structure, communications pathways. None of that is trivial. On ordinary storm nights, it can be enough. The compounding condition revealed by the July 4 flood was the gap between documented readiness and operational performance under a truly extreme event. What was described as capable did not consistently translate into capability at the speed the river demanded.

This is not an argument that anyone was careless. It is a description of a very common vulnerability in complex systems: the difference between knowing a process and living it at 3:30 a.m. in the dark, when information arrives in fragments, when roads fail, when calls surge, and when the same tools that functioned well in common scenarios are suddenly required to function at a tempo they were never tested against. Plans often assume a certain sequence: warning, assessment, escalation, coordinated action. This flood collapsed the sequence. It forced steps to occur simultaneously or not at all. A system that looks mature in a binder can struggle when it has to operate in parallel at scale.

This readiness gap shows up in the pattern of the night itself. Early, the hazard was present but not yet comprehended widely. Then the event accelerated, and the system shifted abruptly from routine to saturation. Dispatchers and responders worked with discipline, but discipline has limits when the environment is removing access and time. Protocols existed, but they were mismatched to the event profile. Warning channels existed, but the last mile collapsed in the hardest-hit pockets. Coordination existed, but a unified operational picture formed late relative to the river's pace. Each of those is a "performance under stress" problem, not a "policy exists" problem.

This condition also clarifies why the public can experience a disaster as "the system failed" while the inside view is "the system worked as hard as it could." Both perceptions can be true at the same time because the measure of performance changes when concurrency explodes. When one house floods, a response can be dispatched. When an entire river corridor becomes a set of simultaneous emergencies, the system is no longer deciding whether to respond. It is deciding where response can physically reach, which calls can be served first, which routes still exist and which tasks must shift from rescue to prevention even as prevention time is evaporating. Those choices are not moral choices. They are triage choices forced by capacity, access and hydrology.

The readiness gap becomes sharper when you place children at the center of the duty-of-care framework. Children do not benefit from "paper readiness" unless it becomes muscle-memory readiness. They do not benefit from a plan unless the plan can be executed quickly, at night, under uncertainty, with a clear threshold for action that does not rely on "wait and see." When the event is unprecedented, readiness is measured by how quickly it can move from normal assumptions to extreme triggers. That shift is not automatic. It is practiced. It is taught. It is embedded in protocols and rehearsals and decision thresholds that assume less time than the mind wants to believe it has.

This is why you can discuss "after-action learning" as part of this discussion without drifting into blame or politics. In other words, it is not, in the words of Governor Greg Abbott, "for losers." It is a learning tool, to hopefully prevent it from happening again. The flood revealed that improvement came after the event. That is a hard sentence to write. The type of improvement needed, like real-time prediction and projection, updated protocols calibrated to speed and height, clearer escalation triggers, better translation of warnings into action, and earlier convergence of a shared operational picture—all were not fully in place before the night demanded it. The event forced modernization by the most painful route possible.

Human beings tend to trust the existence of systems they cannot see. If there is an alert system, people assume it will alert them. If there is a response system, people assume it will reach them. If there is a plan, people assume it will be executed. Those assumptions are not irrational. They are how modern life works. In this flood, the assumptions collided with the limits of speed, darkness, geography, and access. The tragedy was not that the system did nothing. The tragedy was that the system could not do enough, fast enough, everywhere at once.

The bottom line is that you must align what exists on paper with what can be executed in the field at the worst time and in the worst conditions. That includes the prediction and projection system, but it also includes the quieter work that one rarely sees or hears about. Such things as updated protocols that assume less time, rehearsals that treat "unprecedented" as an actionable category, leadership coverage that converges early, communications that translate warnings into local triggers, and a culture that understands that in certain hazards, waiting is not neutrality.

It also involves training and testing. Redundancy and readiness can be illusory if not tested against real tempo, real demand, and real failure modes. The existence of a system is not the same as its performance under stress. System readiness has to be load-tested against the tempo of the real incident: nighttime, surge call volume, partial addresses, failing roads, and fast-rising water. Otherwise, the community inherits false security, and false security steals time.

The bottom line is that these conditions existed at every level, and learning must exist at every level as well. Individuals can learn how to interpret warnings as immediate when the hazard profile demands it. Organizations, especially those responsible for children, can and indeed must learn how to set earlier thresholds for movement. Institutions can learn how to build systems that create time and clarity before the first rescue-request call ever reaches dispatch. The government at both the state and local level must operate more efficiently in prevention, detection and recovery. None of that erases the night. But it does honor it by making prevention measurable rather than aspirational.

Lesson 10: What Every Level Can Learn

A flood like this one tempts a reader toward a single explanation: one failure, one missed moment, one person who should have known. The record does not support that simplicity. The night unfolded as compounding conditions, which do not belong to one level of a community. They belong to every level, from governments to institutions to organizations to families to individuals. That is not an argument for shared guilt. It is an argument for shared learning. If the most defensible facts of the event are rainfall volume and the speed and height of the floodwaters, then the most constructive response is to build habits, protocols, and systems that create time and clarity before the river arrives.

Institutional lessons: Stewardship is measurable

The institutional lesson begins with ownership. In a river corridor with recurring flood exposure and a concentration of children at camps, prevention is not only an engineering problem or an emergency management problem. It is a stewardship obligation. Stewardship is measurable in three ways: who owns the prevention outcome, how quickly the operational picture converges when the event begins, and whether protocols and warning translation reflect the hazard profile that actually exists.

Institutions can learn to treat leadership coverage and unified situational awareness as capabilities that must be designed for, not assumed. A distributed response system can be active and still be missing a corridorwide picture early enough to be protective. The lesson is to reduce the time it takes for a shared operational picture to form and for authority to be clear about priorities when concurrency explodes. This does not require blaming any individual for being unavailable. It requires designing a structure that does not depend on any one person being awake, reachable or perfectly informed at 3:30 a.m.

Institutions can also learn to professionalize prevention in ways that the public can see and trust. The post-flood work led by UGRA and championed by Moser points toward a measurable standard: a prediction and projection system that can move faster than the water. That is what stewardship looks like in a flash flood corridor. It turns warning into lead time, lead time into earlier protective movement, and earlier movement into fewer rescue demands inside collapsing access.

Operational lessons: Protocols must assume less time than people want to believe they have

Operational learning is where the night becomes practical. The flood exposed protocol mismatch, not because guidance is inherently wrong, but because guidance is only as protective as the assumptions beneath it. Shelter in place is stabilizing advice in many hazards. In a fast-rising flood with extraordinary speed and height, stabilization can become entrapment. The operational lesson is to recalibrate protocols, so they are anchored to the event profile, not to the most common scenario.

That recalibration includes escalation triggers that do not require perfect certainty. In the pre-dawn hours, uncertainty is not a defect. It is the normal state of knowledge. The question is whether uncertainty produces earlier protective action or delayed observation. A mature protocol for extreme flash flood risk builds decision thresholds that assume uncertainty and still move early enough to preserve options. It also builds language that clarifies what "life-threatening" means operationally for people who are reading a message in the dark or hearing sirens go off.

Operations can also learn to treat the first hours as a period of concurrent demands rather than a sequence of incidents. When the system moves from routine to saturation, dispatchers and responders are forced into triage. That triage becomes safer when it is supported by shared situational awareness, real-time projections, and updated road and access intelligence. The more complete the picture, the less the system has to learn it one roof call at a time.

Organizational lessons: Duty of care requires earlier triggers, especially where children are present

Organizations, especially camps and any entity responsible for children, face the most demanding duty-of-care standard. Children cannot self-evacuate and cannot interpret warnings with adult judgment. They rely on adults to translate uncertainty into action early enough that movement can be orderly rather than improvised.

The organizational lesson is that the threshold for "move now" must be earlier when children are involved because the cost of delay is so high and the logistics of movement are so complex. A camp does not evacuate like a household. It evacuates like an operation: accounting for every child, maintaining supervision, navigating routes, coordinating transportation, and doing it at night in weather that may already be degrading access. That requires triggers that fire before the flood is visible at the doorstep.

Organizations can also learn to reduce dependence on informal last-mile communications. Door knocks and word of mouth can save lives, but they are bounded by distance, darkness and time. Organizational safety cannot be built on the hope that a warning will arrive early enough through informal channels. It must be built on rehearsed action, updated protocols, and connection to a shared situational awareness system that provides earlier clarity. The point is not to replace community. The point is to avoid placing community in the position of being the only safety net.

Individual and family lessons: Early action is not panic when the hazard removes time

For families and individuals, the most difficult learning is psychological. People tend to treat warnings as advisory until local cues confirm them. In ordinary storms, that habit is rational. Burgess's admonitions on weather alerts is still haunting. A watch means you should have a plan in place. A warning means you need to be ready to execute on that plan. In an unprecedented flash flood, that habit can consume the only resource that matters: minutes. For the Parsleys, for Valerie Tucker, for Karen Johnson, for Cindy Collier, for Lorena Guillen, it was literally minutes before the Guadalupe River nearly took them all.

The family and individual lesson is not to live in fear. It is to adopt a different posture toward certain signals, especially at night. An alert that communicates life-threatening flash flooding is not a suggestion to keep watching the rain. It is a prompt to move into readiness immediately: waking others, gathering essentials quickly, checking escape routes, and preparing for rapid movement to higher ground if conditions begin to change. In a compressed-time flood, readiness is not anxiety. Readiness respect for physics.

A second individual lesson is that "wait and see" is not a neutral strategy where children are concerned. Waiting feels calm, but waiting is a decision made by default, and defaults are dangerous when the river is accelerating. The correct posture is not reckless movement. It is earlier movement when safe routes still exist and earlier decision-making before water turns roads into channels.

Finally, individuals can learn to treat preparedness as a shared responsibility rather than an outsourced service. Modern life encourages the belief that systems will warn, systems will respond, and systems will arrive. Those systems matter, and they should be strengthened. The flood also revealed their limits in the most violent pockets. Preparedness, at the household level, is the ability to act before the call becomes a rescue call.

Institutions can build time through prediction and projection. Operations can align protocols to speed and height realities. Organizations can adopt earlier triggers and rehearsals where children are present. Individuals can treat certain warnings as immediate and readiness as rational. No single lesson undoes the night. Taken together, these lessons reduce the chance that a future warning becomes only a record of what was said, rather than the first step in what was done.

TWELVE
THE GUADALUPE RIVER AND THE COUNTY IT SHAPED

The central feature of Kerr County is, both literally and figuratively, the Guadalupe River. Joe Herring Jr., current mayor of Kerrville, has called it "the spine of Kerr County." It flows the length of the county, shaping roughly thirty miles of land and life before it moves on, carrying with it the memory of everything it has touched. Its origins lie in far western Kerr County, where two forks and a creek rise quietly from limestone and spring. Just past Hunt, the North and South Forks merge and, shortly thereafter, Johnson Creek joins the Guadalupe River, becoming a single river that flows through Ingram, through Kerrville, past Center Point, and onward into Blanco County and beyond. Long before there were towns to name or boundaries to defend, there was the river, moving steadily through the Hill Country, indifferent to ownership, patient beyond human measure.

But the Guadalupe River has never been merely water. Herring wrote, in an article entitled *The Spine of Kerr County*, "To understand Kerr County, you must first understand the Guadalupe River. Not as a line on a map, or a recreational amenity, or even as a hydrologic system, but as the living spine around which everything here has grown. Long before there were towns, roads, bridges, or names, there was the river."

It is sound and movement and presence. It is the low, constant murmur that fills the space between limestone hills. It is the mirror that catches early light and holds it, bending gold into green. It is the feature that gives coherence to a rugged land of thin soil and exposed stone. Long before names were carved into maps, the river was the first road through the wilderness, the first promise that survival was possible here. And long after the lights of Kerrville began to glow against the bluffs at night, it remained what it had always been: a pulse, a rhythm, a way of being.

To live in Kerr County is to live by that rhythm. Hunt, Ingram, and Kerrville all curve along the river as if drawn toward it, streets and neighborhoods tracing its slow turns. Direction is still measured in relation to water: upstream or down-, toward Hunt or toward Comfort. The Guadalupe River defines geography here, but it also defines memory. It is the reference point for childhood, for loss, for belonging.

Long before permanent settlement, long before fences or deeds or towns, the river was already known and understood. Archaeological evidence tells us that people have lived beside the Guadalupe River for at least ten thousand years. These earliest inhabitants, while nomadic hunter-gatherers, were not casual visitors. They were river people. They understood its rhythms, its generosity, and its danger. Campsites were placed deliberately, often on the second rise above the water, high enough to survive floods that came with regularity. These people did not build where the river had been merely yesterday. They built where the river had been for generations.

Seasonal movement followed the water. During dry months, families clustered closer to reliable pools and springs. During wetter seasons, they moved back, giving the river room to swell and rearrange itself. The Guadalupe River was not something to be controlled. It was something to be accommodated. Floods were not surprises; they were events anticipated, woven into lived knowledge and oral tradition. The river's power was respected not because it was feared, but because it was understood.

Spiritual understanding flowed from this intimacy. Water was life, but it was also boundary and passage. The river marked transitions: between seasons, between hunting grounds, between safety and danger. Flint quarried from nearby limestone ledges became tools shaped beside the river. Fish were taken from its pools. Game followed its course. Even now, arrowheads still turn up in unexpected places in downtown Kerrville, quiet reminders that we were not the first ones here, only the latest.

The river itself begins modestly. The North Fork surges from a limestone ledge above Hunt, cold and clear when the springs are flowing, emerging from rock with a force that feels almost deliberate. The South Fork begins farther west, near what is now State Highway 41. The two forks join just east of Hunt, and from that confluence the Guadalupe River begins its long journey southeast, more than 230 miles to San Antonio Bay on the Gulf Coast. We live at the source, and that fact has shaped everything about this place, from settlement patterns to industry to culture.

When European names finally arrived, the river had already been known for centuries. Spanish explorers applied several names to different stretches, but in 1689 Alonso de León gave the lower river the name Nuestra Señora de Guadalupe. The earliest written reference to the upper reaches, including what is now Kerr County, dates to 1727. But names did not create the river's importance. The river created the names.

When settlers began arriving in the mid-1840s, they followed the same logic as those who came before them. They came to water. In *The Spine of Kerr County,* Herring wrote, "Early maps of Kerr County tell the same story in ink and survey lines. Tracts along the river were carefully measured and claimed. Land away from the river was often left blank, unsurveyed, as if it had little meaning without access to water." The land surveying logic reflected this reality. Early plats show careful measurement along the Guadalupe River.

Pioneer Joshua Brown, a solitary rider on horseback traveling through an unnamed valley in 1846, did not see a town; he saw opportunity. Cypress trees lined the river, valuable for shingles that would not rot. There was water for men and animals, higher ground for defense, and the sense that this bend in the river could support life. Brown was not alone in thinking this way. Early settlement economics in Kerr County were river economics.

Shingle camps were among the first enterprises. Cypress shingles were durable and in high demand. Trees were felled near the water because the river made transport possible. Logs could be floated, tools washed, camps supplied. These were not permanent communities at first, but they laid the groundwork for permanence.

Mills followed. Water-powered mills transformed the Guadalupe River from a resource into an engine. Grain could be ground. Lumber could be cut. Cotton could be ginned. Later, electricity could be generated. The Starkey-Saner mill above Kerrville, Christian Dietert's mill in town, and others up and down the river were not incidental structures. They anchored local economies. Farmers and ranchers oriented their operations around them. Commerce followed the river's course. Land surveying logic reflected this reality. Early plats show careful measurement along the river and vagueness elsewhere. Land away from water was often left unsurveyed, its value uncertain. Ownership clustered where water guaranteed productivity. The river was not adjacent to development. It *was* development.

But from the beginning, the river was both resource and risk. Floods have always been a part of the Guadalupe River's story. Small dams built of wood and stone attempted to tame it, but they failed repeatedly. Floods washed them away. Mill races silted in. Roads shifted. Bridges disappeared. The Guadalupe River has always resisted permanence. It rearranges the landscape on its own schedule, reminding each generation that control is provisional.

Floods have also always been part of Kerr County's story. In July 1932, the river rose with terrifying speed. Rain fell upstream, unseen by those watching the water in town. By the time the danger was understood, it was already upon them. Herring wrote, in an article entitled *In A Tree*, "On July 2, 1932, the skies opened as they'd never opened before, and the Guadalupe River threw off its mask of green calm and became a charging, swirling bull of mud and debris. When a big event happens in a community, it's noted in stories, photographs, and occasionally song, and while the facts of the stories don't always exactly coordinate, the theme, the stronger message, comes through loud and clear."

Howell Priour, seventeen years old, was swept into the current and survived by clinging to a cypress tree for nearly a full day. Two men drowned trying to rescue him. The town watched, prayed, and waited. Herring continued the story, "this was a fearful time as people in town gathered on the bank back of the Blue Bonnet Hotel and watched and prayed all through the night. The fire department came and kept lights on Howell in the tree. People called and sang and prayed and watched the young man they feared might fall asleep and drown in the raging waters below." Priour was eventually rescued. When the river finally receded, the story did not fade. It entered local memory as a warning carried forward in fragments and retellings. That was not the last time.

The floods of 1978 and 1987 arrived with their own lessons. Older residents remember 1978 as the flood that rewrote the riverbanks, when water rose faster than expected and left behind debris lines that marked just how high it had reached. In 1987, the river surged again, catching some by surprise and reminding others of stories they had heard but not fully believed. Each flood became a marker in time, referenced not by date but by memory: where the water reached, what was lost, who helped whom.

If floods represent the river's danger, memory represents its intimacy. For many who grew up here, the Guadalupe River is inseparable from childhood. It is swimming holes behind downtown shops. It is canoe trips above old bridges that sit at low water crossings. It is islands of rounded river stone placed there by decades of floodwater. It is water moccasins dropping from sun-warmed branches into dark pools. It is the peculiar quiet that exists even when the river runs through the heart of town. The river has been playground, classroom, refuge, and companion.

Infrastructure evolved in response, each generation attempting in its own way to solve the river.

Early roads followed the river or crossed it directly, sometimes running through the riverbed itself during dry months. Bridges were low, practical, and temporary. When they washed out, people rebuilt them. The Sidney Baker Street bridge in Kerrville marked a turning point, lifting traffic above most floods and allowing the town to function even when the river rose. Later widenings and replacements improved capacity but lost something of the original intimacy; Herring admitted that every time he sees a photo of that old bridge, he says, "I loved that bridge."

In his piece *The Story of a Kerrville Bridge*, Herring wrote, "The problem with all of these other bridges was that they were low water crossings, and every time the river rose, they became impassable. The Highway 16 bridge extending Sidney Baker Street solved this problem for all except the most severe floods. There is a small plaque on the current Sidney Baker Street bridge which reads 'Dedicated to Captain Charles Schreiner: a pioneer in citizenship, philanthropy and highway building in the hill country.'"

Dams followed. In the mid-twentieth century, local leaders pushed for permanent structures to stabilize water supply, reduce flood damage, and enhance recreation. These dams reshaped the river, creating lakes and parks, submerging mill sites and altering flow. Each was an attempt to impose order, and each carried tradeoffs. The river was quieter in places but never fully subdued. Here you only had to have witnessed the catastrophic flooding at the Ingram Dam on July 4, 2025.

When summer arrived, the river turned social. Children escaped the glare of Main Street for its green shallows. Burgess, who grew up in Kerrville, remembers Schumacher Crossing as a particularly nice swimming hole. In other parts of the Guadalupe River, couples drifted in canoes, paddles echoing between limestone walls. Families from across America, from outside Kerrville and Kerr County, returned year after year to the same bends, the same gravel bars, the same deep pools, as though the river itself were an heirloom. Burgess said, "You don't think about it as much as a kid, maybe because you take it for granted, because it just was always there."

Herring said, in an article titled *Memories of Our Time in the River,* "In my childhood, Tranquility Island was just 'the island' in the middle of the river, a home to rabbits and water moccasins. The island's banks were heavily wooded, mainly with cypress trees, but its center was a field of rounded river stones, placed there by floodwaters over many decades. We swam to the island many times, thinking we were brave explorers." He added, "Mostly, though, I swim behind the shop at Louise Hays Park, usually between the bridge and the dam, floating in the middle of the river, so close to the bustle of the business district, and yet so far away, too. Usually I swim with my son, but occasionally the sweet Ms. Carolyn will join us there. There is something about the light as it finds its way through the cypress trees along the riverbank, falling on the green river below."

That love deepened with the rise of the summer camps. Beginning in the early twentieth century, camps such as Camp Rio Vista, Camp Stewart, Heart O' the Hills, Camp Waldemar and Camp Mystic all took root along the Guadalupe River. These were not only places of recreation. They became economic engines and cultural institutions. Local families found seasonal employment. Generations of counselors returned year after year. Kerr County's reputation as a place of formation and retreat spread far beyond Texas.

The camps shaped identity. Like myself, many children from across the state and the country came to associate the Hill Country with the Guadalupe River. Songs learned there were carried home. Stories were retold. Families planned summers around sessions. Over time, the camps became part of the county's self-understanding, inseparable from the river that sustained them. For more than a century, the Guadalupe River has been the heartbeat of those camps. Each morning begins with its chill. Each night ends with its murmur. The river teaches its own curriculum: courage, humility, stewardship. First friendships, first independence, first prayers under open sky, all framed by water moving through stone.

The camps endured floods and droughts, wars and recessions. They rebuilt when bridges washed out, replaced cabins lost to storms, replanted cypress trees. The river always returned clear, as if to bless persistence. It was impossible to imagine it any other way.

Yet love, when it becomes tradition, can turn to blindness. The paradox of the Hill Country is that beauty and danger are one. Narrow valleys give the river speed. Rain gathers unseen. For most of the year, none of this is visible. What people remember is light through cypress leaves and water against stone. Then came the night when the river spoke again, on July 4, 2025.

The air was heavy. The sky restless. Rain fell upstream. Creeks turned brown and fast. At Hunt and Ingram, the Guadalupe River rose, first gently, then vertically. At Camp Mystic, water climbed thirty-five to forty feet in less than an hour. Roads vanished. Cabins were erased. Trees were uprooted. Rescue boats moved through places that had been safe the day before. Counselors guided children to safety with practiced calm and borrowed strength.

It was not betrayal. It was the Guadalupe River remembering its shape.

In the aftermath, grief mingled with disbelief. But something shifted. People began to speak of the river differently. Love was joined by reverence. Memory returned. Even now, as I write, when the Guadalupe River runs clear and low under winter light, it seems impossible that it could rage. Families picnic on gravel bars. Campers wade into shallows. The river looks innocent again. But those who remember know better. Burgess reminded us of the meteorological perspective "that moisture got caught up in the jet stream from Baja California and into western Mexico, West Texas, if you will, and tracked right into the Hill Country. Our biggest flood events usually occur with a tropical component to it."

Now people see bent cypress trunks and debris lines etched into bark and memory. They speak of the Guadalupe River the way one speaks of an ancestor: respected, unpredictable, essential. It remains what it has always been, the lifeblood of Kerr County. Without it there would be no Kerrville, no Hunt, no camps strung like beads along its course. The people cannot leave it any more than they can leave their own reflection.

Every drought brings longing. Every rain brings fear. Burgess explained this dichotomy, saying that, it might be folklore or not but it felt to him that, "every drought seemed to end with a flood." Both point to the same truth: The people and the river are bound. In that bond lies something sacred.

The Guadalupe River is not a river to be conquered or explained. It is a presence to be lived with. A reminder that life here exists because of its generosity and remains fragile because of its power. The relationship between Kerr County and the Guadalupe River did not end on July 4. It changed because we had forgotten. We had forgotten the respect the Guadalupe River demands. Burgess said, "I was worried about all the development on the river for years because it did it in '87. I just, I guess we had 40-plus years where we got away without a significant fatality event. But this one here, it's kind of a wakeup call to what it can do."

For generations, people here lived beside the river as though it were fixed, familiar, and finally knowable. Even when floods came, they were treated as interruptions rather than instruction. The river would rise, recede, and life would resume along the same banks, often in the same places. What the flood of 2025 made impossible was the idea that the old relationship could simply be resumed.

Going forward, the Guadalupe River should no longer be understood only as scenery or recreation or tradition. It is a living system with memory, limits, and agency of its own. The river has reminded the county that it does not forget where it has been, no matter how long humans choose to look away.

Kerr County will not turn its back on the river. It cannot. The river still cools the air, sustains wildlife, draws visitors, and shapes identity. Camps will continue. Children will still wade into its shallows on hot afternoons. Love for the river has not diminished. If anything, it has deepened. But it has also matured. When evening wind moves through the cypress and the water turns silver under the moon, the river seems to whisper its oldest lesson: *Love me, but do not forget what I am*.

The relationship going forward will be one of listening rather than assuming, of remembering rather than forgetting. Floodplains will no longer be abstract lines on a map. They will be recognized as part of the river itself. Building decisions will carry the weight of history, not just convenience. Where people once asked whether the river could be controlled, they now ask how space can be given back to it.

There is already a change in language. People speak less about "fixing" the river and more about respecting it. Conversations about warning systems, evacuation routes, land use, dams and camp placement are no longer theoretical. They are grounded in our lived experience. The Guadalupe River has provided the data, written in silt, scars, and lives lost.

For the summer camps, the future relationship with the Guadalupe River will involve stewardship as much as celebration. Campers will still be taught to swim and canoe and laugh in its waters, but they will also be taught its history. They will learn why cabins are placed where they are and where they should go and what to do in a flood. They will hear the stories of floods alongside the songs. The river will be presented not only as a gift but as a responsibility.

For the towns along its banks, the river will remain a source of beauty and economic lifeblood, but planning will reflect humility. Infrastructure will acknowledge that permanence is provisional. Roads and bridges will be designed with memory in mind. Parks will be shaped to absorb water rather than resist it. The Guadalupe River's need to move will be treated as a fact, not an inconvenience.

For families who have lived here for generations, the relationship will include grief carried forward. Some places will never feel the same. Some bends of the river will always hold loss. Yet even that grief will become part of the bond. The Guadalupe River has always held the county's stories. Now it holds its sorrow as well. Burgess noted, "So if you live and respect the river, you know that probably three or four times a century, it's going to do what it does."

And for those who come later, children not yet born, newcomers drawn by the same green ribbon that has drawn people here for millennia, the river will still be the first thing they learn to love. But they will be taught earlier, and more honestly, what it means to live beside it. They will inherit not just affection but awareness.

The Guadalupe River will continue to change—because change is its nature. It will carve, deposit, rise, and retreat. It will be gentle most days. It will be dangerous on some. It will remain indifferent to human schedules and deeply intertwined with human lives. Remember Burgess's words to respect the river, which is "beautiful the majority of the time and a tranquil place to be." But heed the warning that "two hundred yards, maybe less, of a waterway can turn into mile wide or larger as we saw this year."

Kerr County's future with the river will not be defined by control, nor by fear, but by relationship, one grounded in memory, respect, and acceptance of limits. The people will still gather along its banks. They will still watch the light turn silver on the water. They will still listen to the sound that fills the hills. But now, woven into that listening, will be understanding.

The Guadalupe River has spoken clearly. The work for all of us going forward is to remember.

IN MEMORY OF THOSE WHO LOST THEIR LIVES

As reported in *The Texas Tribune*:

Carol Andrews, 65, from Athens
Joyce Badon, 21, from Beaumont
Mary Baker, 8, from Beaumont
Linda Bason, 78, from San Antonio
Anna Bellows, 8, from Houston
Lila Bonner, 9, from Austin
Robert Brake, 67, from Abilene
Joni Brake, 66, from Abilene
Elizabeth Bryan, 61, from San Antonio
James Bryan, 62, from San Antonio
John Burgess, 39, from Liberty
Julia Burgess, 39, from Liberty
James Burgess, 1, from Liberty
John Burgess V, 5, from Liberty
Ella Cahill, 21, from Beaumont
Brian Carpenter, 36, from Austin
Blake Carpenter, 3, from Austin
Chloe Childress, 18, from Houston

Martha Crawford, 61, from Houston
Michelle Crossland, 50, from Midland
Cody Crossland, 45, from Midland
Molly Dewitt, 9, from Houston
Lucy Dillon, 8, from Houston
Ronald Duke, 80, from Hunt
Richard Dunlap, 73, from Andrews
Josephine Dunlap, 68, from Andrews
Katheryn Eads, 52, from Cibolo
Richard Eastland, 70, from Austin
Steve Edwards, 72, from San Angelo
Penny Ferguson, 76, from Odessa
William Ferguson III, 82, from Odessa
Katherine Ferruzzo, 19, from Houston
Jayda Floyd, 22, from Odessa
Miriam Frizzell, 72, from Abilene
Ellen Getten, 9, from Houston
Sally Graves, 91, from Ingram
Hadley Hanna, 8, from University Park
Blair Harber, 13, from Dallas
William Harber, 76, from Dallas
Charlene Harber, 74, from Dallas
Brooke Harber, 11, from Dallas
Josephine Hardin, 28, from Weston, Florida
Alyson Hardin, 64, from Weston, Florida
Aidan Heartfield, 22, from Beaumont
Deana Hillock, 57, from San Antonio
Virginia Hollis, 8, from Bellville
Charlotte Huff, 55, from Kerrville
Janie Hunt, 9, from Dallas
William Huston, 61, from Sherman
Al Iorio, 66, from San Antonio
Mary Kate Jacobe, 8, from Houston
Madelyn Jeffrey, 11, from San Antonio
Penelope Jeffrey, 70, from San Antonio
Emlyn Jeffrey, 70, from San Antonio

Robert Kamin, 50, from Humble
Melissa Kamin, 45, from Humble
Dee Ann Knetsch, 66, from Canyon Lake
Gary Knetsch, 60, from Canyon Lake
Lainey Landry, 9, from Houston
Rebecca Lawrence, 8, from Dallas
Hanna Lawrence, 8, from Dallas
Kellyanne Lytal, 8, from San Antonio
Tianna Mabey, 66, from Ovilla
Claire Manchaca, 21, from Conroe
Sarah Marsh, 8, from Birmingham, Alabama
Bailey Martin, 23, from Odessa
Amanda Martin, 44, from Odessa
Robert Martin, 46, from Odessa
Linnie McCown, 8, from Austin
Blakely McCrory, 8, from Bellaire
Clayton Meadows, 29, from Hamilton
Harley Moeller, 6, from New Braunfels
Megan Moeller, 33, from New Braunfels
Jake Moeller, 38, from New Braunfels
Virginia Naylor, 8, from Dallas
Jose Olvera, 70, from Hunt
Alicia Olvera, 67, from Hunt
Richard Pagard, 71, from Kerrville
Clay Parisher, 1, from Austin
Eloise Peck, 8, from Dallas
Bradley Perry, 49, from League City
Abby Pohl, 8, from Austin
Cynthie 'Jane' Ragsdale, 68, from Hunt
Joel Ramos, 43, from Midland
Tasha Ramos, 48, from Midland
Kyndall Ramos, 17, from Midland
Tanya Ramsey, 46, from Lewisville
Jeffrey Ramsey, 63, from Lewisville
Carlos Romero, 1, from Kerrville
Leonardo Romero, 42, from Kerrville

James Rushing, 64, from Sulphur Springs
Cynthia Rushing, 53, from Sulphur Springs
Julian Ryan, 27, from Ingram
Ileana Santana, 66, from Mobile, Alabama
Mila Santana, 5, from Wichita Falls
Camille Santana, 38, from Wichita Falls
Eddie Santana Negron Sr., 69, from Mobile, Alabama
Mollie Schaffer, 76, from Houston
Shon Scott, 53, from Andrews
Margaret Sheedy, 8, from Houston
Alvaro Miranda Sigala, 69, from San Antonio
Renee Smajstrla, 8, from Ingram
Michael Smith, 67, from Dripping Springs
Pamela Smith, 64, from Dripping Springs
Mary Stevens, 8, from Austin
Cecilia 'Cile' Steward, 8, from Austin
Greta Toranzo, 10, from Houston
Natalia Venzor, 24, from Kerrville
Roy Walker, 63, from Hunt
Mark Walker, 51, from Kentfield, California
John Walker, 14, from Kentfield, California
Sara Walker, 50, from Kentfield, California
Jeffrey Wilson, 55, from Coldspring
Amber Wilson, 45, from Coldspring
Shiloh Wilson, 12, from Coldspring
Reece Zunker, 36, from Kerrville
Holland Zunker, 3, from Kerrville
Lyle Zunker, 7, from Kerrville
Paula Zunker, 35, from Kerrville

EDITOR'S NOTE

As this book was going to press in late April 2026, Camp Mystic withdrew its application for a state operating license, meaning that the camp would not reopen for the 2026 summer season as the Eastlands had originally planned.

The decision came after amid lawsuits, state investigations, and a hearing in which Texas lawmakers questioned the decision to reopen less than a year after the disaster. The hearing included testimony from CiCi and Will Steward, who opposed the camp's efforts. Their daughter Cile died in the flood, and her body has not been found.

"No administrative process or summer season should move forward while families continue to grieve, while investigations continue and while so many Texans still carry the pain of last July's tragedy," Camp Mystic said in a statement. "This decision is intended to remove any doubt that Camp Mystic has heard the concerns expressed by grieving families, members of the Texas House and Senate investigating committees and citizens across our state. Respect for those voices requires that we step back now."

As of this writing, a criminal investigation is ongoing.

ACKNOWLEDGMENTS

Books such as this one are never written alone. That is especially true of a book born from tragedy, memory, and a community still living with loss. Although only one name appears on the cover, these pages were made possible by the generosity of many people who gave their time, their trust, their memories, and, in some cases, their grief. I am deeply grateful to each of them.

I want to offer my sincere thanks to Andrew Gay, Zach Green, Gilbert Paiz, Kathy Ragsdale, Jeeper Ragsdale, Clint Morse, Charlie McIlvain, Judy Eychner, George Eychner, Harry Anthony, Louis Amestoy, John Wells, Irene Van Winkle, Austin Dickson, Dr. William Rector, Tara Bushnoe, Lorena Guillen, Bob Canales, Jonathan Marks, Bill Coffin, Matt Kelly, Victoria Myers, Chris Krimitsos, Severin Wirz, Jaja Daradar, Dr. Charlie McCormick, Matt Ellis, Mary Shirley, Lisa Fine, Dr. Hemma Lomax, Joe Herring, Dalton Rice, Tom Moser, Mike Hughes, Dr. Brent Ringo, Kristy Vandenberg, Bailey McEachern, Craig Wolcott, John and Elisabeth Hay, Valerie Tucker, Rick Sralla, Shelby Balser, Don Randall, Elaine Capers, Dr. Eugene Dowdy, Skyler Derrington, Darrell Beauchamp, Cary Burgess, Maggie Snow, Diane McMahon, Weir Labatt III, Jonathan Letz, Blake Smith, Jack Woodville London, Phil Oakley, Paul McGrath, Marika Flatt, Johnnie Bernhard, Allison Van Hooser, Lanza Teague, Tammy Wren, Sage Walters, Dr. Adolfo Mora, Barbara Radnofsky, Teddy Jones, Craig Garnett, and Jeanne Stacy. Each of you helped this book in ways large and small. Each of you contributed to the telling of this story. Each of you trusted me, encouraged me, and I do not take your trust and encouragement lightly.

Some of those named here shared recollections still close to the surface. Some spoke with the steadiness that comes from long experience. Some offered the perspective of public service, some the perspective of witness, some the perspective of friendship, and some the perspective of mourning. Yet what remains with me is not simply the information each person provided but the grace with which it was offered. In the aftermath of the July 4, 2025, flood, when so much in Kerr County was marked by sorrow, exhaustion, and unanswered questions, these conversations were acts of generosity.

I have tried throughout this book to remember that truth. The stories entrusted to me did not come out of abstraction. They came from lives lived here, from memories formed here, and from a shared love of Kerr County that existed long before the flood and that continues long after it. If this book has any value, it is because so many people were willing to help me understand not only what happened, but what it felt like, what it meant, and why it matters.

As I wrote, I was mindful that this book could never be complete in any final sense. I have left the Camp Mystic story of Heaven's 27 for others to write. There are legislative investigations and civil trials to come. No account of a tragedy such as this can ever fully contain the event itself, much less the grief that followed it. There are voices not included in this book, memories still too painful to share, and dimensions of loss that remain beyond language. This is one attempt to honor an unfinished story. It is offered with gratitude to those who helped shape it and with humility for all that cannot be fully captured on the page.

I also want to acknowledge something larger than any single interview or conversation. The people who helped me with this book are part of a much larger story in Kerr County, one that began before 2025. This place has long been shaped by people who understood the demands of Hill Country life, who respected both the beauty and the danger of the river, and who built a culture where resilience was not a slogan but a way of living. The response to the flood drew on habits of service, faith, neighborliness, and endurance that were handed down by those who came before us. That inheritance has mattered greatly in the long recovery, and I have been reminded of it again and again in the course of writing this book.

On a deeply personal note, I want to offer my love and gratitude to my wife, Michele Rudland. She helped me through the entire process, and I could not have done it without her. She put up with me as I got up each day at 4 a.m. to write. Writing a book such as this requires more than research and interviews. It requires patience, steadiness, and the quiet support of someone who understands both the burden of the work and the necessity of seeing it through. Michele gave me that support every step of the way, and this book is better because of her. She is also my primary editor, so much of her is in this book as well.

I also want to thank Loren Steffy, publisher at Stoney Creek Publishing, for believing in me enough to pick up this book for publication. Loren lives in Wimberly, Texas, which suffered a devastating flood in 2015, and he immediately understood the importance of this book when I pitched it to him. A big thanks to Loren and Leslie Barrett for all their assistance and support.

Finally, I want to thank all those who helped in the rescue and recovery, including many whose names will never be fully known to the wider public. Their work was often done quietly, without fanfare, in circumstances of heartbreak and urgency. They carried others when the moment required it. They showed up. They stayed. They helped restore not only lives and property, but also the bonds of community that make recovery possible.

And to the people of Kerr County, my final thanks. This book was written in sorrow but also in admiration. It was written in memory of those who were lost, in gratitude for those who helped, and in recognition of a community that has drawn on deep reserves of faith, courage, and resilience. May this book honor, in some small way, both the pain you have endured and the strength with which you have begun to recover.

ABOUT THE AUTHOR

Thomas R. Fox is a life-long Texas resident and has practiced law for more than 40 years, the last 15 in legal and regulatory compliance. He has written multiple books on risk management, compliance, leadership, podcasting, and business ethics. His work earned him the name *The Compliance Evangelist*. This is his first book of general nonfiction. Tom founded the Compliance Podcast Network and co-founded the Texas Hill Country Podcast Network. He is a Hill Country resident, and he attended Camp Stewart in 1967 and 1968.

www.ingramcontent.com/pod-product-compliance
Lightning Source LLC
Jackson TN
JSHW040716020826
106027JS00003B/3
9781965766750